Learning Without Limit

Learning Without Limit

Dr. G. VISVANATHAN
Professor, Department of Education,
Annamalai University, Tamil Nadu

and

Dr. S.K. PANNEER SELVAM
Assistant Professor, Department of Education
Bharathidasan University, Tiruchirappalli, Tamil Nadu

RANDOM PUBLICATIONS
NEW DELHI (INDIA)

Learning Without Limit

ISBN 978-93-5111-539-7

Published in 2015 in India by

RANDOM PUBLICATIONS

Reprint 2018

4376-A/4B, Gali Murari Lal, Ansari Road
New Delhi-110 002
Phone : +9111-43580356, 011-43142548, 011-23289044
e-mail : sales@randompublications.com
info@randompublications.com
randomexports@gmail.com

Reprint 2021

Type Setting by : Shah Computer Graphics, Delhi-110094
Printed at: Replika Press Pvt. Ltd.

Contents

3

4

5

6

7

8

16

17

18

19

29

30

31

1

Multimedia: New Educational Technology Tool

Introduction

In the present scenario of the Educational System, It is important that teachers use technology to create new learning environment. Educational systems around the world are under increasing pressure to use the new technologies to teach students the knowledge and skills they need in the 21st century. Education is at the confluence of powerful and rapidly shifting educational, technological and political forces that will shape the structure of educational systems across the globe for the remainder of this century. Many countries are engaged in a number of efforts to effect changes in the teaching /learning process to prepare students for information and technology based society. Multimedia provide an array of powerful tools that may help in transforming the present isolated, teacher-centered and text-bound classrooms into rich, student-focused, interactive knowledge environments. The schools must embrace the new technologies and appropriate multimedia approach for learning. They must also move toward the goal of transforming the traditional paradigm of learning.

In the current scenario of educational institutions, multimedia has dug up its own kind of space in some or the other way as a tool of educational technology. Multimedia has overcome the barriers of time and space .It provides evidence to be accepted as an anytime and anywhere tool for educating multi-disciplinary masses. The process of knowledge acquisition becomes more efficient when the learners experience an event through a multimedia simulation. Multimedia technology empowers the educational process by means of increased interaction between teachers and the students. Apart from the fact that multimedia can provide educators and students with endless possibilities of quality teaching and learning, taking vital considerations of the pedagogical strengths and limitations of Multimedia, it can be used to its fullest potency, and reach the eminence of 'New Educational Technology tool' .

Definition

"Multimedia" is a term frequently heard and discussed among educational technologists today. Unless clearly defined, the term can alternately mean "a judicious mix of various mass media such as print, audio and video" or it may mean the development of computer-based hardware and software packages produced on a mass scale and yet allow individualized use and learning. In essence, multimedia merges multiple levels of learning into an educational tool that allows for diversity in curricula presentation.

Today's multimedia is a carefully woven combination of text, graphic art, sound, animation, and video elements. When you allow an end user, i.e. the viewer of a multimedia project, to control 'what' and 'when' and 'how' of the elements that are delivered and presented, it becomes interactive multimedia.

Multimedia as a Teaching and Learning Tool

In the traditional information communication process (ICP), the teacher is the source of the knowledge and presents the knowledge to the students, who are in turn, passive receivers of the information. With multimedia, the communication of the information can be done in a more effective manner and it can be an effective instructional medium for delivering educational information. This is because it enables the teacher to represent the information in various media, i.e., via sound, text, animation, video and images. With multimedia, the teacher is now the director of the knowledge and can use the various combinations of media elements to create interactive educational content. The result is a stimulating environment for learning and retaining the information delivered.

The teacher-centred methods include presentations and demonstrations to process the information. Students are also able to retain and recall the information as well as obtain mastery in the subject matter with drills and practices, and tutorials, which are highly interactive. The multimedia courseware can also be packaged on the CD-ROM and delivered in a networked classroom leading to a teacher-centered mode where the courseware is opened on their PCs and the students follow the teacher's lecture on their PCs.In the student-centered method, the students construct their own knowledge and bring their authentic experiences in to the learning process with the teacher as the facilitator. The multimedia courseware content can also be packaged as a Web file and delivered on the Internet in a Web browser can result in online courses where the students access the courseware from a browser on their PCs. The student is then free to engage in learning on his or her own time and pace, and consequently, the learning mode is student-centered.

This multimedia material can be used to foster team-processing and active learning as with collaborative and cooperative methods. This encourages higher -level learning, increases comprehension and retention rates, and focuses on the total development of the student in Self-accessed and self-directed learning.

In the mixed mode, the teacher has the flexibility to incorporate the two teaching and learning approaches whenever they deem them useful, to increase and enhance their students' learning processes. Here, the same multimedia courseware content can also be packaged and delivered over satellite and broadband technologies for distance learning. Here, the student learns the materials on his or her own time and pace, and interacts with the teacher via video-conferencing in real-time.

New ways of Using Multimedia in class room

"Multimedia can stimulate more than one sense at a time, and in doing so, may be more attention-getting and attention-holding."Multimedia, the term defines using more than one medium of expression or communication. In other words, it is the combination of various digital media types such as text, images, sound and video, into an integrated multi-sensory interactive application or presentation to convey a message or information to an audience.

Using multimedia in classroom helps educators engage students and provide them with valuable learning opportunities. It's easy to remember a picture than a paragraph, an animated video of a concept worth more of a lecture and a video demonstration of a process (or an instrument) by a scientist gives more real time knowledge than a theoretical explanation. There is no doubt educators consider multimedia as a great tool to improve student learning.

Here are a few benefits of using multimedia in classroom

Multimedia empowers students to create and design rather than absorb representations created by others. It improves reflective thinking. It also provides students with suitable learning resources according to their learning styles and abilities.Most of the educators and administrators are adopting latest educational technologies in order to reach the 21stcentury learning standards. Of all those tech approaches, usage of multimedia is one of the great tools to engage students.

Personalized Learning using Multimedia Resources

Multimedia resources help different learners meet their learning needs. As we know, different students have different learning styles, educators can easily provide them with suitable learning resources using multimedia. Educators use YouTube to provide visual learners with online videos, podcasts for auditory learners and interactive games for tactile learners. Multimedia resources make everything easy for students to learn in their comfortable learning style. Unlike traditional approaches, in which only the teachers used to lead the entire classroom delivering long lectures at the same pace, the use of multimedia results in personalization of learning.

Group Learning

Multimedia tools such as blogs, social networks and wikis enable students to work together in learning a particular concept. Students use these to share their works with others, give feedbacks on others' works and discuss among others a particular topic. It can be done through either blogging or micro blogging (Tweets). Using these multimedia tools, educators can engage students in several works and watch them collaborating with each other, peer assessing each other's works and learning as a group.

Improve Presentation skills

Using storyboarding, videos and slideshows is a great way to improve student learning, because it allows them to engage with text in a very visual way aided by multimedia. Multimedia tools enable students to express their ideas and works in concise ways that capture the attention of the audience and they develop an ability to communicate thoughts and concepts through a variety of resources, including text and recorded narrations.

Giving students a wider choice of software and tools to present their work is an effective approach as it allows learners to decide on the style of presentation that best suits their personality. This is also a way to allow the learners to engage in their education in a more personalized way and also improve their creativity, critical thinking and reflective thoughts.

Multimedia Effective in Educational Process

Multimedia can be treated as a supporting tool, which complements theoretical knowledge with practice. Usage of videos can illustrate a real action or behaviour, Internet provides a variety of solutions, information and life-based examples with simultaneous reinforcement of search skills, and sound appeals to different brain areas than in case of read text.

Whenever multimedia is well built in educational process they can accelerate learning, develop participant's activity, support application of knowledge and strengthen problem solving and decision makes skills. However, to make the whole process work for user's benefit, there are four elements which have to be fulfilled:

1. Presentation of information
2. Guidance about how to proceed
3. Practice for fluency and retention
4. Assessment to determine need for remediation and next steps

Even though those four elements can appear in traditional training, multimedia can make them more effective. It happens, because the use of multimedia effectively employs verbal and visual processing channels to help learners integrate content with the knowledge. What is more, the use of single multimedia is less affective and only in combination of various forms

Educational Benefits of Multimedia Tools

I. **(from an Educator's Perspective)**

Provide students with opportunities to represent and express their prior knowledge.

1. "Allow students to function as designers, using tools for analyzing the world, accessing and interpreting information, organizing their personal knowledge, and representing what they know to others."

2. Multimedia applications engage students and provide valuable learning opportunities.
3. Empower students to create and design rather than "absorbing representations created by others."
4. "Encourages deep reflective thinking.
5. Create personally meaningful learning opportunities.

II. **(from the Student's Perspective)**

Giving students an opportunity to produce documents of their own provides several educational advantages.

1. Students that experience the technical steps needed to produce effective multimedia documents become better consumers of multimedia documents produced by others.
2. Students indicate they learn the material included in their presentation at a much greater depth than in traditional writing projects.

Students work with the same information from four perspectives:

1) As researcher, they must locate and select the information needed to understand the chosen topic;
2) As authors, they must consider their intended audience and decide what amount of information is needed to give their readers an understanding of the topic;
3) As designers, they must select the appropriate media to share the concepts selected;
4) As writers, they must find a way to fit the information to the container including the manner of linking the information for others to retrieve (Smith, 1993).

All of these contribute to student learning and help to explain the improved student learning that is often associated with IT-assisted PBL.

There is another aspect to developing multimedia documents that empowers students. Students quickly recognize that their electronic documents can be easily shared. Because of this, students place a greater value on producing a product that is of high standard. An audience of one–the teacher–is less demanding than an audience of many–particularly one's peers. Students quickly recognize that publishing a multimedia document that communicates effectively requires attention to both the content and the design of the document.

Conclusion

The future of Multimedia in education, Educational systems around the world are under increasing pressure to use the new technologies to teach students the knowledge and skills they need in the 21st century. Education is at the confluence of powerful and rapidly shifting educational, technological and political forces that will shape the structure of educational systems across the globe for the remainder of this century.

Its dimensions and capabilities will evolve and expand at the same time as the potential to author becomes more widely accessible. The potential for students of all ages to author as part of a creative educational programme that is based on achievement of goals and competencies rather than time served will assist educators to shift from teacher to facilitator and mentor. Multimedia provide an array of powerful tools that may help in transforming the present isolated, teacher-centred and text-bound classrooms into rich, student-focused, interactive knowledge environments.

Reference

1. hrsbstaff.ednet,ns.ca/engramja/.../multimedia benefits of multimedia.ht...\
2. http://www.iste.org/research/reports/tlcu/multimedia.cfm
3. www.ijiet.org/papers/181-T10039Pdf
4. www.icte.org/to1-103Pdf

2

Revitalization of Science Teacher Education

Introduction

The present educational scenario of the 21st century has become prone to stress more on Quality than on Quantity. The primary aim of every educational institution is to provide a good and quality education to the students. Unless we built a strong base we cannot think over and strength of the premise. Similarly the country which shows keen interest in providing the quality based education will surely empower the knowledge of the students and in turn it will lead to the development of the Nation. Moreover this century is known for the drastic development of Science and Technology. Day by day numbers of innovations are keeping on growing. It is the duty of the teacher to incorporate recent developments to the students that occur across the world. With an increased availability of the knowledge centers and a rapid rise in the enrolment of the students the responsibilities of the teachers also have increased many folds. In case of science teacher, the responsibility becomes more than the others. Meanwhile if the teacher has enough capability to maintain the larger group of students, then he/she becomes the successful teacher. For this, it is mandatory for the Science teacher to equip, empower, and update the knowledge every day. In this connection the author of this paper has planned to discuss the present status of the Science teacher education and tries to give some suggestions that can improve the quality of the science education in India.

A few decades back the science was given a step-motherly treatment and was considered to be a subject meant for less important subject. Science has now established its claim to be placed in a school curriculum. Due to its utilitarian, intellectual, vocational, cultural moral and aesthetic values it has been placed in the curriculum with due prestige. The training, the student receives in science during his study days can be applied to solve other problems in future life. Moreover the results of the science are generalizable and it does not give any room for superstitions and other facts without proofs. Teacher education is the vital for the development of the country and this is the age of science and technology. Proper science education is must for the advancement of the nation. Several committees have forwarded their suggestions for the development of the teacher education in general and science education in particular, but the standard of science education in India is still to come up to international standard. Unfortunately the present day of teaching science is far from being satisfactory. The education of science teachers is the main concern to be geared up, organized, revitalized and improved in order to shape the science education in the light of the present changing scenario of the educational world.

Problems in Science Teacher Education

In the present science teacher education system the following problems have been identified.

(a) Problems in selection of the candidates
(b) Poor knowledge in preparing lesson plans
(c) Lack of knowledge in preparing and handling teaching aids
(d) Problems in supervision during practice teaching

Problems in Selection of the Candidates

In present condition, the selection of the candidates for B.Ed program are being done on the basis of their academic marks scored in the graduation level. It is not actually valid and reliable. In order to select the qualified candidates, the exclusive selection procedures have to be done through entrance examination. For example, the theory examination may be conducted for 50 marks and the other 50 marks can be allotted for the interview. The theory exam can comprise of general mental ability test, aptitude test, attitude test and general awareness. The interview can be of checking the personality of the candidate, interest of the candidate towards science subject and etc., this kind of selection will ensure the quality of science education and prevent the unwanted entry of the incapable or uninterested candidate into the program.

Poor Knowledge in Preparing Lesson Plans

Due to the short period of the B.Ed program, the student teachers gain inadequate knowledge in preparing the lesson plans. This will lead to the poor performance of the candidate during teaching practice. As a good science teacher, it is must to know the procedure of writing the lesson plan in effective manner. To overcome this problem, the special classes can be handled by the subject experts to provide adequate knowledge in preparing good lesson plans. Copying from the previous year's record books has to be avoided. The concerned faculty member has to look into this concern strictly to avoid such malpractices.

Lack of Knowledge in Preparing and Handling Teaching Aids

As we know that audio-visual aids promote the teaching learning process so that every science teacher must possess good capability in preparing and handling the teaching aids wherever necessary. Unfortunately, considerable number of student teachers are interested in buying the readymade teaching aids available in markets or prepared by the third person. This will lead to the financial burden as well as poor knowledge in preparing teaching aids. The subject teacher should not entertain this practices and he can ask the student teachers to prepare such teaching aids by their own. Teaching aids can be effectively prepared with the help of available low cost materials. Moreover the student teachers have to be trained to utilize the teaching aids in effective manner.

Problems in Supervision during Practice Teaching

Every student teacher undergoes for practice teaching for at least 45 days in B.Ed Program. During practice teaching, the subject teacher must supervise the candidate's way of motivating the students, way of delivering the concepts, way of giving necessary examples, way of using teaching aids and etc., Mistakes done by the student teacher can be corrected with the necessary instructions given by the subject teacher. But unfortunately, during practice teaching, the subject teachers could not find enough time to supervise each and every student teacher's teaching. In some institutions, during the practice teaching the subject teachers are assigned some official works or they take leave. This kind of thing should not be entertained. The authorities of institution should make strict measures in this concern.

Suggestions to Improve Science Teacher Education

1. The present one year B.Ed., program should be made of two years
2. Internship should be of six months instead of 45 days in practice teaching.
3. Scientific activities such as science fair, science club, museum, and exhibition can be encouraged.
4. College of education should be equipped with scientific materials and scientific instruments.
5. Seminars, conferences sand workshops related to science education can be organized every year by the institutions /colleges.
6. Job security should be provided to the selected and passed candidates by the government
7. Revision of curriculum should be made at a regular interval of time.
8. Suggestions from school science teacher and science teacher educators should be received in order to improve the system.
9. The teachers have to undergo for orientation programs, refresher courses every year in order to balance their ability with the recent developments.
10. The science teaching can be done with the help of innovative technologies like CAI, Video Packages etc., during the practice teaching.
11. Monitoring and evaluation should be made an integral part of teacher training program to know the strength, weakness, opportunities and Outcomes of the program.
12. All the existing college of educations should be accredited by NAAC.

Conclusion

In order to maintain the quality, the environment of the teacher education institutions should be improved. The science teacher educators should be given freedom to work. If there is any lacuna found in the system of such privately managed college of educations, their affiliations should be cancelled. NCTE is doing lot of commendable developments to improve the quality over nationwide. The relationship between the institution and the workers should be transparent and everyone should work to the betterment of the quality of education. In order to compete with the global knowledge market, the quality of education in our nation needs more betterment. This is becoming crucial for survival. So there is an urgent need to reform and revitalize the present education system for ensuring and creation of the quality of intellectual infrastructure in India.

References

1. Das, R.C. (1992): "Science teaching in Schools". Sterling Publishers private limited, New Delhi.
2. Deka, K.K. and Sharma, J.K. (1992): "Teacher education in the third world countries: India as a case study", The Educational Review, Chennai, pp.201-205.
3. Krishna, D.G. and Rao, K.V.(1992) : "Effective Science Teaching: A trainers Paradigm", Journal of School science, NCERT, pp. 18-20.
4. Nadeen, N.A. (1989): Profile of Effective Teacher, Fulbright publishing company, Srinagar.
5. Panda B.N. & A.D.Tewari (2009): "Teacher Education", APH Publishing House, New Delhi. pp. 397-404.

3

Designing Learning Environment of Tomorrowinnovation in Teaching-Learning Process

Education is the most important invention of mankind. It is more important than his invention of tools, machines, spacecraft, medicine, weapons and even of language, because language too was the product of his education

Information Communication Technology is the most powerful engine to accelerate the growth of developing countries. It is evident to equip the young generation with the skills of ICT so that they will be fit to meet the challenges ahead of them. Today school children are well exposed to T.V. shows, computer programs, video games, e-mail based information exchange, internet browsing and many other forms of educative entertainment. Using the experiences of the children as the base, providing further learning experience is a challenging task

Computers are often a catalyst for student activity. Internet also known as cyberspace or information super highway plays a vital role in education. One of the most powerful and rewarding instructional material at the fingertips of the learner is the internet. Within seconds an entire civilization of the country thousands of miles away is at your desktop. Internet is also an ideal mechanism for encouraging students to assume responsibility for their own learning. As students find different learning resources on the internet, they become active participants in their quest for knowledge. Students are able to define their learning needs, find information, assess its value, build their own knowledge base, and communicate their discoveries.

Traditional classroom techniques will not do justice to the learners of this generation. They require technique that will stimulate them to explore, discover and learn by themselves as much as possible and the role of teacher is to be aneffective facilitator.Teachers should have the freedom to innovate, to devise appropriate methods of communication and activities relevant to the needs and capabilities and the concerns of the community, says National Educational Policy. The quality of education we provide to our children depends in large measure upon the quality of teachers we inject into the educational system other things remaining equal. The quality of teachers in turn depends on the quality of preparation they receive in our teacher training institutions.

Modern Media and Education

We live in the age ofcomputers. There are growing demands on almost everyone, including the learning and teaching community to become technologically literate. Computers are often a catalyst for student activity. Internet also known as cyberspace or information super highway plays a vital role in education. One of the most powerful and rewarding instructional material at the fingertips of the learner is the internet. Within seconds an entire civilization of the country thousands of miles away is at your desktop. Internet is also an ideal mechanism for encouraging students to assume responsibility for their own learning. As students find different learning resources on the internet, they become active participants in their quest for knowledge. Students are able to define their learning needs, find information, assess its value, build their own knowledge base, and communicate their discoveries.

The implementation of different branches of technology in the information and communication processing is called information communication technology. Their application in education includes web based learning, e-tutoring, computer assisted instruction, computer managed instruction, tele-conferencing, interactive video, multimedia learning, satellite instructional television programme, edusat, reach the unreached, virtual classroom, e-book, digital library and electronic community etc.

Web- based learning

Web-based learning environments may be designed for students of distance education as well as conventional classroom students.

Principles of web-based learning

1. The learning experiences designed for web-based teaching must focus specific learning objectives and outcomes.
2. The learner should be actively engaged and made to feel the real-life experiences through simulation.
3. Keeping in mind the various learning styles of students, a variety of media are made use of to develop appropriately learning environment to achieve the desired learning out comes.
4. Learning environment must include both knowledge based as well as problem based learning.
5. Learning experiences must reflect the needs and interests of the community.

E-Learning

E-Learning includes different forms of technology enhanced learning such as online learning. E-learning is used to define a specific mode to attend a course or programmes of study where the students rarely or never meet face to face nor access on campus educational facilities, because they study online.

Advantages of e-learning

1. Improved performance – It has been proved that higher education students in online learning performed better than those in face to face courses.
2. Increased access – Instructors of the highest caliber can share their knowledge across borders, allowing students to attend courses across physical, political, and economic boundaries.
3. Convenience and flexibility to learners.

In many contexts e-learning is self-paced and the learning sessions are available 24x7. Learners are not bound to a specific day or time to physically attend classes. They can also pause learning sessions at their convenience.

E-tutoring

E-tutoring can be defined as teaching, support, management and assessment of students on programmes of study that involves significant use of online technology. Thus at first glance e-tutoring is only different to tutoring in terms of the involvement of technology. Herein, however, are contained vital differences in terms of time, distance and the specific technologies adopted, and these are all the Implications for teaching staff. The capabilities required can be quiet different to face to face teaching both in terms of integrating appropriate forms of technology into learning activities and in managing and supporting students' learning online .

Computer Assisted instruction (CAI)

In Computer Assisted Instruction, the lesson and its continents to be learnt are recorded in the software of the computer. The software in the form a C.D. or cassette is inserted in the computer and when the student presses the keys in the keyboard, lessons appear in the monitor as small texts, each followed by a question. The student has to answer the questions by pressing the keys and the answers to appear in the monitor screen. If answer given by the student matches with the answer provided in the study material booted, it will be acknowledged and he is allowed to proceed further. If the given answer is incorrect, he is given alternate explanations or asked to study the same frame again before answering the question. In this way the computer manages the response of the individual learner.

Merits of Computer Assisted Instruction

1. The learner can receive the content very fast and that too without any error.
2. As the quality of learning material presented is rich, with animation and appropriate background sound, interest for learning is kindled.
3. Since the learner himself operates his computer and learns, learning interest is sustained throughout the session.
4. The computer successfully manages the different responses of the learner by directing him appropriately what to do further.
5. The content of the lesson cold be presented as text, diagrams or in animated forms.
6. Based on the learner's achievement, the computer will decide the nature of his further learning.
7. Computer can act according to the speed of the learner and his learning needs.
8. The computer can help any number of students to learn humpty number of times, without getting tired unlike a teacher. The same learning package can be repeatedly used for any number of times.
9. The quality of the study materials could be upgraded in a short span of time.

10. The cost and labour involved in providing computer assisted instruction though appears to be high in the beginning, it works out to be cheaper when we take into account its repeated use and the present cost of educating a student through teacher –centred methods.

Computer Managed Learning (CML)

Unlike CAI, wherein computer is used in tutorial work CML makes use of the computer in a different role in instruction. In CML the main role of the computer is record keeping and it does not provide any direct instruction to the leaner. It takes over the other responsibilities of the teacher like evaluating the response sheets of students, gathering and sharing information about each learner and updating the same periodically, finding the resource options available for every individual student to learn a topic, monitoring the learning of the student while he is making use of the instructional programme selected to suit his potentials and directing the learners what to do next. This type of instruction, though indirect, helps to assess the learner's present level of knowledge, weakness or gaps in his learning and remedial action possible.

Tele-Conferencing

In Tele-Conferencing, people situated at distant places establish direct contact through tele-communication and converse among themselves. In a tele-conferencing procedure all the three types of tele-conferencing such as audio, video and computer is integrated and supplements each other so that the participants get almost the feeling as if they are present physically in the conference.

Virtual- Education

Virtual education is a term describing online education using the internet. It refers to instruction in a learning environment where teacher and student are separated by time or space, or both, and the teacher provides course content through course management applications, multimedia resources, the internet, videoconferencing, etc. Students receive the content and communicate with the teacher via the same technologies.

Virtual course is similar to online course which is delivered on the internet. "Virtual" is used here to characterize the fact that the course is not taught in a classroom face to face but through some substitute mode that can be associated with classroom teaching that means people do not have to go to the real class to learn.

A virtual programme is a study program in which all courses or at least a significant portion of the courses are virtual courses.

A virtual classroom is a learning environment created in the virtual space. The virtual classrooms improve access to advanced educational experiences by allowing students and instructors to participate in remote learning communities using personal computers; and to improve the quality and effectiveness of education by using the computer to support a collaborative learning process. The explosion of the knowledge age has changed the context of what is learnt and how it is learnt – the concept of virtual classrooms is a manifestation of this knowledge revolution.

Instruction Modes for Virtual Education

1. Video-based courses are like face-to-face classroom courses, with a lecturer speaking and PowerPoint slides or online examples used for illustration. Video-streaming technologies are used. Students watch the video by means of freeware or plug-ins (e.g. windows media player, real player).
2. Audio-based courses are similar but instead of moving pictures only the sound track of the lecturer is provided. Often the course pages are enhanced with a text transcription of the lecture.
3. Animated courses: enriching text-oriented or audio-based course material by animations is generally a good way of making the content and its appearance more interesting.
4. Web-supported textbook courses are based on specific textbooks. Students read and reflect on the chapters by themselves. Review questions, topics for discussion, exercises, case studies, etc. are given chapter wise on a website and discussed with the lecturer.
5. Peer-to-peer courses are courses taught "on-demand" and without a prepared curriculum. a new field of online education has emerged in 2007 through new online education platforms.

Homework assignments are normally submitted electronically, e.g. as an attachment on e-mail or uploaded to the system in a view complete. When help is needed, lecturers, tutors, or fellow students, or a help desk are available, just like in a real university, the difference is that all communication goes via electronic media.

Advantages of virtual education

Cyber School economizes time and cost, as the student does not require traveling to a real classroom to learn. Online learning creates the opportunity for integrating digital media into the curriculum in an interactive format making teaching and learning more students –centered regular full time students,, distance education students, and in fact any one learning through cyber schools need not go in search of libraries to gather needed information. Online learning promotes self-learning, critical thinking and problem solving skills.

Conclusion

In modern days media play a vital role in education. Virtual schools now exist all around the world. Some of these virtual schools have been integrated into public schools, where students sit in computer laboratory and do their work online. In other situations students can be completely home schooled, or they can take any combination of public or private home schooling and online classes. Enlightened, emancipated and empowered teachers lead communities and nations in their march towards better and higher quality of life. They reveal and elaborate the secrets of attaining higher values in life and nurture empathy for the fellow beings. Teachers are the torch bearers in creating social cohesion, national integration and a learning society. They not only disseminate knowledge but also create and generate new knowledge. They are responsible for acculturating role of education. No nation can even marginally slacken its efforts in giving necessary professional inputs to its teachers and along with that due status to their stature and profession.

References

1. Andrews, R. (ed.) (2004), The Impact of ICT on Literacy Education. London, RoutledgeFalmer.
2. Cox, M. (1997), The Effects of Information Technology on Students' Motivation. Coventry, Council for Educational Technology.

4

Flipped Classrooms Learning

Introduction

The "flipped classroom" has been making waves in the educational world for some time now. The concept of the flipped classroom has become one of the hottest debates in the academic world among primary educators, professors, and administrators alike. As education-based technology and online platforms continue to grow and improve, more and more devices, programs, and concepts are entering the educational world and shaking things up. Where at one time the concept of online learning, computer-based assignments, and the virtual classroom were scoffed at, today online education and technology in the classroom are top priorities for schools, teachers, and researchers.

Within our increasingly digital world, most of us agree that education must respond to the changing atmosphere of society. We accept that online learning and certain academic technologies are worthwhile. However, with education and learning, this flipped classroom remains both positives and negatives to the approach.

Flipped classroom education

The reason flipped classrooms are improving education around the world is because the role of the teacher has been flipped from a lecturer to a tutor. The focus of the classroom transforms one-size fits all instruction into individualized coaching.

What Does a Flipped Classroom Look Like?

Flipped Classroom will certainly look very different from a traditional classroom. Instead of students sitting in individual desks facing the front while their teacher lectures, students sit at tables or desks pushed together or are off by themselves doing work. Students are out of their seats, accessing books, computers and others students for information. Although a Flipped Classroom may appear chaotic, loud, or even messy at first glance, the action and collaboration taking place in this non-traditional classroom is a direct result of student learning. Have fun physically setting up your classroom for a flip by providing areas for group and individual learning and don't forget to involve students in the new Flipped Classroom design.

Flipped Classroom Model

The flipped classroom model is revolutionizing teaching methods and strategies around the globe, addressing these concerns by creating time for individualized 1:1 instruction between teachers and students.

Flipped classrooms are a reversed teaching model that "flips" the settings for instruction and homework.

In a flipped class, instruction is provided to students at home through video or Internet based lectures and class time is used to complete homework-like assignments. By moving instruction to the home and homework to the class, students are given more 1:1 time with their teacher to work through their assignments. This 1:1 time helps to ensure that each student fully understands the key concepts presented in each lesson plan before moving on to the next lesson.

Here's how it works

1. Teachers provide students with digital instruction to watch at home (or after school)
2. Students watch the instruction to familiarize themselves with concepts to be covered in class the following day
3. Students spend class time completing assignments, based on the previous night's instruction, with the assistance of teachers
4. Students with a firm grasp of the lesson are encouraged to move on, and students who need assistance have a teacher readily available to help

Benefits of flipped classroom

1. **More efficient for teachers:** While there is an initial up-front investment that teachers have to make to set up a flipped classroom – creating a video can take 15 minutes or two days – they can ultimately save a lot of time using this model. In the future, recorded lesson plans and collected resources can be easily transferred to other classes. Plus, if students miss a class, teachers don't have to spend time going over missed material because it's all online.
2. **Students control their learning:** Research has shown that we all learn in different ways and at different speeds. If students are learning content at home, they can take their time to read through a passage, re-watch a video lecture or even initiate a Google search to better understand an idea. Instructors can also post multiple kinds of materials so that students are more likely to find a source that will help them, whether it's an article, video or interactive tool.
3. **Inexpensive for schools to implement:** Besides investing in a new video cameras or better classroom computers, the only other thing you need is time. This model is much more cost-effective for schools than purchasing hundreds of new classroom gadgets to increase engagement.
4. **Versatile, engaging way to share content:** One of the greatest things about this model is that teachers can share so many different kinds of content. Learning isn't restricted to a whiteboard or textbook. Instead, students can be directed to any website, mobile application or other kind of content. Teachers can create learning modules that allow students to quickly jump from one resource to the next.
5. **Students—including special education students**—having difficulty with concepts can pause and rewind the videos to give themselves extra time to parse out what a teacher means. "That's one of the most powerful things about these videos: that students who process slower, can process slower,"

Administrator role in implementing flipped learning

"Absolutely, they are critical as instructional leaders and lead learners in their schools,"

"They can support innovation, provide collaborative time and professional development, assign resources to innovative teachers, communicate with parents about new teaching strategies, and provide feedback and a view from outside the classroom.

The primary reason administrators balk at flipped learning is a lack of familiarity: "They need more information about how it works the issues that come up like how to evaluate flipped-learning teachers, the problems of rolling it out."

Administrators says that flipped learning can greatly increase a teacher's ability to provide differentiated instruction given that students work at their own pace in the classroom—and teachers can provide more challenging work for those who are breezing through.

Administrators also continue to support the use of video within instruction and believe that it has an important role within classrooms today and tomorrow. Approximately one quarter of school principals indicated that their teachers are using videos they found online or creating their own Videos as part of their flipped learning model implementation. And thinking ahead to the next generation of classroom teachers, some of the principals said that they want pre service teachers to learn how to create and use videos and other digital media within their teacher preparation programs.

Advantage of flipped classroom learning

1. Students are able to approach material and take it in at their own speed. By covering lecture material at home and from a video-based platform, students can privately view the material. This allows them to approach things at their own pace without worry of peers noticing them moving slower or faster. Students can stop, pause, rewind, and fast forward material so that they can examine things in their own way.
2. By taking the lecture portion of the classroom home with them, students are able to utilize their teachers' one-on-one attention more successfully in the classroom. Students sit through lecture, gather questions, and prepare themselves for the day with the teacher to tackle "homework". Because the actual exercises are done in the classroom rather than at home with this model, students have their teacher available for questions with problems when they occur.
3. The flipped classroom also allows teaching to adapt more easily to the different teaching styles that individual students may be most successful with. By putting lectures in a video format, students can listen to the lesson and watch the video illustrate the lesson. Of course, this largely depends on how successful the actual video lecture is. You want a lecture (like the Khan videos) that explains

concepts verbally, but also draws them out in images and pictures. This provides adequate learning opportunities for verbal learners and for visual learners. With in-classroom lecturing, the visual aspect of lecturing can be significantly more difficult to accomplish.

Disadvantage of flipped classroom learning

1. Classroom lecturing works better for some and doesn't work for others; the flipped classroom method is not going to accommodate every individual perfectly. The biggest setback today to the flipped classroom method is that not all students and schools have access to technologies that can really work for this method.
2. Students from lower income areas and lower income families may not have access to the computers and internet technologies that the flipped classroom requires. The structure really hinges on every student having personal access to his or her own personal device. This simply is not the case for every student and every school district. Students who do not have personal home computers or access to the internet would be forced to use public computers at a library or at the school. This, to some degree, eliminates the personal and private experience of taking in the lecture. What makes having lectures as homework so powerful is that students can do it on their own time and in their own way. At a library computer or school computer time limits typically exist and access can be limited if it is busy. This is problematic.
3. Another downside to the idea of the flipped classroom that many people bring up is the fact that students would be spending all of their "homework time" plugged-in in front of a computer screen. Not only do not all students do well with learning from a screen, but this also adds to a student's time in front of a screen and sitting inactively. While this concern isn't singular to the flipped classroom, the teaching concept doesn't help our young students to get up and get away from their computers, televisions, and iPods.

Conclusion

Flipped classroom learning are shifting the way teachers provide Instruction by inverting traditional teaching methods to engage students in the learning process. Using technology, lectures are moved out of the classroom and delivered online as a means to free up class time for interaction and collaboration. In order to effectively implement a flipped classroom, teachers must possess a set of requisite technical skills, conceptual knowledge and pedagogical expertise.

References

1. Bergmann, J., J. Overmyer, and B. Wilie. 2011. "The Flipped Class: Myths Vs. Reality." http://www.thedailyriff.com/articles/the-flipped-class-conversation-689.php.
2. Hertz, M. 2012. "The Flipped Classroom: Pro and Con." *Edutopia.* http://www.edutopia.org/blog/flipped-classroom-pro-and-con-mary-beth-hertz.
3. Makice, K. 2012. "Flipping the Classroom Requires More Than Video GeekDad | Wired.com." *GeekDad.* http://www.wired.com/geekdad/2012/04/flipping-the-classroom/.
4. Strayer. 2007. "The Effects of the Classroom Flip on the Learning Environment: a Comparison of Learning Activity in a Traditional Classroom and a Flip Classroom That Used an Intelligent Tutoring System". Thesis, Ohio State University. http://etd.ohiolink.edu/view.cgi/Strayer%20Jeremy.pdf?osu1189523914.
5. Strayer, J. 2011. "The Flipped Classroom: Turning the Traditional Classroom on Its Head." http://www.knewton.com/flipped-classroom/.

5

Learning Without Limits

As early as 1916 when John Dewey published his seminal work "Democracy and Education", it was acknowledged that learners should become active participants in the educational process. From this proposition it clearly follows that in learning from their own experience, students become, in a sense, their own teachers. The changed role of the learner has, in turn, implications for that of the teacher. Instead of the source of knowledge, teachers become facilitators of the learning process; that is, their role is to create the set of conditions under which students can best learn from their experiences. Moreover, teachers can fulfill this role only by becoming learners themselves, and a primary source of their learning must be their students. Simply put, teachers who learn become better teachers, and learners who teach become better learners. Although this idea seems straightforward enough, educators have been very slow to put it into practice. However, the rapid technological changes of the last few decades may well provide the catalyst food that finally brings about these needed reforms in the field of education.

Good teachers design learning

Recently, when I perused my twitter feed, I came upon a blog post titled Teacher as Learning Designer. Andrew Miller, the author, states: "If you are a teacher and you are trying to explain what you do, say, 'I am a learning designer!' Teachers need to be empowered with a variety of instructional designs to meet the needs of all students. They need to be honored for their expertise to create creative and engaging learning environments. We can re-frame the concept of "teaching" to truly encapsulate all that teachers can and should do!"

The way teachers teach their students has, I believe, a direct correlation to the way in which they learn themselves. We have all read in the latest teaching journals that teachers of today have to be devoted to lifelong learning. But what does that mean, really? What elements affect teacher learning and then in turn affect how that teacher teaches?

Eight influences on teacher learning

Life and career experience. Life experiences do affect the way we learn. I was personally challenged when I had to teach soil characteristics to inner city students. These students hadn't had experience of playing in dirt as I had as a child in the suburbs. My students' life experiences were very different than mine in so many ways. In order to engage them in the process of learning, I had to understand what their life was all about. I did that by listening to their stories and their experience.

Personal Beliefs. What a teacher believes about a learning concept or a new teaching style greatly influences whether or not that teacher implements the idea. How many teachers were tuned out to early implementation of technology because of the belief that "technology integration is a fad", or "the way I've taught this unit has been fine for the last 20 years"? Personal attitudes, I believe, do color the words an instructor uses and the manner by which he/she approaches the topic.

Emotional Well Being. A lot had been written on the importance of emotional intelligences with regards to student learning. But, what about an instructor and his or her well being? Show me a teacher who has enough self confidence to fail in front of the class, and I will show you a teacher who can help his/her students learn to succeed by building on failure. Show me a teacher who is not fearful of fiascos and I will show you an educator who is not hesitant to use new technology.

Knowledge. This is a multifaceted aspect to learning since it relates not only to the specific content of the curriculum but also to teaching strategies, different types of learner intelligences, and even interpersonal and intrapersonal skills. The teacher who is equipped with a wide understanding of these topics can create an environment that truly supports every learner in their quest to discover the truth.

Skills. This is the "tool belt" that is the arsenal for any good teacher. The tools include different modes of engaging students such as, but not limited to, project based learning, cooperative learning, and peer review. Educators should be skillful enough to alter any style of teaching to meet the specific learning needs of the students.

Motivation to learn. "Motivation is the starting point for learning. For a busy and often overworked teacher to devote effort to change and new learning, there has to be a good reason for the change: some sort of catalyst or urgency – a sense that 'what I'm doing doesn't seem to be working.'" We can all look over the history of our teaching practice and recall times when we were motivated to learn something new because the old way just didn't work.

Personal Confidence. Face it, sometimes teaching can be like mud wrestling; it's messy and exhausting! But the educator who believes that the job of teaching is worth the effort shakes off the mud and makes a difference in the lives of those is being taught.

Sense of Interdependence. I used to be the Queen Mother, Judge, Arbitrator and Center of my classroom. Then I began to shift ownership of learning to my students. With the added presence of technology, my classroom became a hub that had spokes in all parts of the world. Collaboration, creativity, team building, and collegial aptitudes are now huge elements in the culture of my students' learning experience.

In a nutshell, today's teacher needs to be able to learn continuously from their students as they present the curriculum. To quote Anna from Mister God, This is Anna, "in the dark you have to describe yourself. In the daylight other people describe you." Educators have to be comfortable about being in the dark and journeying to the light by learning with students.

To learn without limit

More recently, technology has drastically changed how students learn in and out of the classroom. Teachers can no longer pretend to have all of the answers because students have an immense amount of knowledge at their fingertips with the internet; more specifically, Web 2.0 enables students to be not only learners but also teachers. All users not only to post comments, articles, and reports on the internet but also to edit and respond to those articles and reports. Teachers can use wikis in their classrooms and have groups of students work together or individually to research and become experts on a topic and then post their reports on the internet for all to read and learn from. This new area of education is allowing all students to become the teachers to not only the students in their classes but to the world. Any student who is interested and wishes to explore and research a particular topic is able to do so and publish his or her work. This not only increases the motivation to do a good job, but since anyone can go in and edit the work, it helps students to be flexible and open to new ideas and procedures. This technology also enables any topic to be approached from multiple perspectives. Students in the past have grown up learning subjects such as history from only one biased perspective. Now, individuals will be able to help contribute to online textbooks and add sections about topics that have never before been taught in the public schools. This technology will revolutionize our education system as it becomes more widely used and accepted (Alexander, 2006; Standen, 2006).

Conclusion

Largely as a result of technological change, the forces of globalism, multiculturalism, and multimodalism have conspired to transform and ultimately enrich the roles of both teacher and learner. As teachers extend their learning, learners can claim full ownership of their knowledge in the process of teaching it to others. This results in more effective teachers as well as a greater depth of understanding in students. This model of mutual learning can reform the educational system from within and help it to realize maximum benefits for both teachers and learners.

6

Learning Environment of the Speech Disordered

Introduction

Speech disorder is a widespread disabling problem which is associated with very adverse, long term outcome affecting the individual's family, academic and vocational achievements. Many attempts have been made by doctors, speech language pathologist, researchers, educationists etc to identify the causes of speech disorders to intervene it and to assist all who are working with the speech disordered to understand their problem better in all aspects of their everyday living experiences. This article is intended to be guidelines for speech-language pathologists, audiologists, parents, teachers, administrators, school boards, architects, and building contractors. It contains minimum requirements for creating optimal learning environments for students and is designed to be a substantiating reference for use when building a new school, redesigning an already existing structure, and/or advocating for improvement of facility work conditions. The ultimate goal of this article is to be a reference guide for providing the best learning environment which will contribute to the overall success of students.

Adequate working conditions and facilities in schools for teachers, speech-language pathologists and audiologists have always been acknowledged as an essential one for creating an optimal learning environment for the children with speech impediments, but the quality of work settings and equipment varies widely in schools around the country. Implementation of the Individuals with Disabilities Education Act Amendments of 1997 (IDEA '97) increased school administrators' awareness of the importance of providing adequate learning environments for children with disabilities, including those with speech-language-hearing disorders.

Common Practices in School for Learning

Learning environment is commonly designed as listed below for the speech disordered:

1. Teachers will want to reduce un-necessary classroom noise as much as possible. This helps the child focus without contending with the extraneous noises which assists understanding and comprehension.
2. Be sure to be near the student when giving vocal instructions and ask the student to repeat the instructions and prompt when necessary. Provide verbal clues often.
3. Provide a quiet spot for the student to work whenever possible.
4. Speak slowly and deliberately.
5. Provide visual cues - on the blackboard or chart paper.
6. Focus the student frequently and provide step by step directions - repeating when necessary.
7. Use gestures that support understanding.
8. Avoid correcting speech difficulties - this will lead to a weaker self-esteem, it's much more important to model correct speech patterns.
9. Touch base with the speech/language pathologist to ensure the correct accommodations are in place.
10. The learning environment needs to be positive.
11. Capitalize on the student's strengths as much as possible.
12. Be patient when the child is speaking, rushing a child with difficulties magnifies the frustration level.
13. Classrooms should include appropriate and comfortable visual, auditory, and physical access to information for learning. It is very vital to provide an acoustical environment for the speech disordered.

Besides the above mentioned best practices it is recommended to have a speech – language pathology room, equipment and furniture for providing a good learning environment for the speech disordered.

The space provided for speech-language pathology services in a regular school building should be located in the instructional area of the building that houses children of comparable age. It should be located in an area that ensures privacy, confidentiality, and sensitivity to student needs. The room should be used by only one professional at a time and should be designated for the exclusive use of the speech-language pathologist when he or she is scheduled to be in the building.

When services are provided outside the classroom setting, the area should be reasonably exclusive and large enough to provide the full range of evaluation and instructional activities needed to provide services to a caseload. These services may include evaluation and testing of individual students, pull-out treatment for individuals and/or groups, team meetings, and confidential conferences with teachers and parents, as well as activities to prepare for treatment, prepare and maintain assistive technology support, and provide case management services.

Each speech-language area should be readily accessible to nonambulatory students and should accommodate the special needs of students with disabilities. This includes students who are physically challenged, and students with low vision or neurological problems.

The facilities should be adequately heated and cooled, lighted and ventilated, and provided with sufficient electrical outlets and computer accessibility. Speech-language services should be provided in an environment that ensures student safety and welfare; complies with applicable building and safety codes; and includes universal precautions, infection control, risk management, and emergency preparedness

Each speech-language area should be large enough to accommodate the use and storage of special equipment and teaching materials. There should be an adequate number of age-appropriate desks/tables and chairs to meet the physical needs of students and parents, and for preschool, furniture and equipment to provide a developmentally appropriate curriculum.

The facility should be equipped with instructional aids (e.g., mirror, chalkboard/erase board, and bulletin board) that meet the needs of the students' individualized education programs (IEPs) and adequate office equipment and supplies, including a telephone. Speech-language pathologists should be provided with materials, technology devices, Internet access, and computer and technology support, as well as software for providing, managing, and monitoring services.

Each speech-language pathologist should have available current evaluation and instructional materials and equipment appropriate for the age, developmental ability, and disability condition of each student. These should include a variety of multimedia learning/curriculum materials, tests, and equipment, readily available for use to meet the individual interests and learning abilities of the students receiving services.

School districts should make available one portable individual audiometer for the speech-language pathologist to use for screening; this should be checked and calibrated annually in accordance with minimum audiologic standards. Best practice would include impedance screening by a speech-language pathologist trained by an audiologist. Also, one portable tape recorder and a supply of tapes; one portable auditory training unit, computer, and printer; one hearing aid battery tester; and assistive technology devices should be available. There should be adequate maintenance and prompt repair of all special equipment utilized for children with disabilities.

Interior Classroom

In a brief note how the interior structure of the classroom for the speech disordered is as follows:

Ceilings:

A ceiling height of 9–12 feet is optimal for the listening environment. It is important to install acoustical ceiling tile that has a sound absorption coefficient rating that is sufficient to achieve the desired noise and/or reverberation reduction. Banners, student work, and plants suspended from the ceiling can contribute to the reduction of noise and reverberation

Floors:

Although carpeting is an excellent means to reduce noise and reverberation, concerns do exist regarding indoor air quality and allergic reactions that carpeting may generate in a classroom setting. Carpeting, particularly if it is installed over a pad, is the most efficient and effective acoustical modification for absorbing excessive reverberation of high-frequency consonant sounds and dampening noise from students and movement of classroom furniture. The thickness of the pad contributes to the overall decrease in the amount of noise and reverberation.

Windows:

Windows are highly reflective surfaces, and acoustical treatment may be provided by adding draperies, acoustically treated blinds, or shades.

Double-pane windows offer more protection from outside noise than traditional windows, and closed windows allow far less noise to enter the classroom from adjacent or external noise sources.

Walls and Doors:

Reflective wall surfaces may be treated in a variety of ways to dampen classroom noise and reverberation. Interior wall modifications, such as acoustical panels, cork, felt, or flannel bulletin boards, are useful in reducing noise and reverberation time. A well-fitted, solid-core door with a noise lock or doorway treatment will help to lessen noise from external or adjacent sources.

Seating and Furniture Arrangement:

The human body absorbs sound. When desks and tables are staggered, sound will not travel directly to hard reflective surfaces such as walls, chalkboards, and windows. Felt or rubber caps or tennis balls can be used on chair and table legs to help reduce noise in classrooms, particularly if they are uncarpeted. Also, the classroom should be arranged so that instruction occurs away from noise sources (e.g., HVAC systems, aquariums) and to accommodate the teacher's instructional style. This will help reduce noise and the distance between the teacher and the students. Open plan rooms should be avoided whenever possible, particularly for students with hearing loss or other auditory deficits.

Heating, Ventilation, and Air Conditioning Systems:

Supply and return ducts for heating and cooling systems may be treated with acoustical duct lining. If the classroom has an external HVAC system, as is the case with most portable classrooms, the main instructional areas should be planned away from this area if the HVAC system is a source of noise. Noise control devices (e.g., duct silencers, adequate duct length, vibration isolators) can be used in HVAC systems to achieve desirable noise levels in classrooms. When renovation or new construction is planned, careful consideration should be given to the selection and design of the school's HVAC system

Lighting:

Some fluorescent lighting systems emit a constant noise. Regular maintenance should be employed; ballasts can become noisy and create a 60 dB 1000 Hz (or thereabouts) hum. When lighting is housed above the acoustical tile ceiling, the noise level will be lessened.

Special Purpose Areas:

Classrooms for students with hearing loss should be located away from high-noise sources. Mobile bulletin boards and bookcases may be placed at angles to the walls to decrease reverberation in the classroom. In areas where younger children are handling manipulatives or playing with toys, covering the table surface with fabric will reduce noise levels. Study carrels can be lined with acoustic tiles, or rubber pads may be installed underneath equipment (e.g., computer, typewriter) to reduce noise in these areas.

In general Speech Disorders are very fatal and devastating where speech therapy works for regaining the speech but some conditions and diseases cannot be cured and the regaining of the speech may be lost permanently. Therefore early intervention is crucial and the best learning environment is in need for the development of the speech disordered.

References

1. Damico Jack, S., Muller Nicole, and Ball Martin, J., (2010). The Handbook of Language and Speech Disorders, United Kingdom: Blackwell Publishing Ltd, pp.50-51.
2. Umadevi,M.R.,(2010). Special Education: A Practical Approach to Educating Children With Special Needs, Hyderabad: Neelkamal Publications Pvt Ltd, pp.173-182.
3. Williams Dale. F, (2006). Stuttering Recovery: Personal and Empirical Perspectives, London: Lawrence Erlbaum Associates, pp.10.
4. Williams Lynn. A, (2003). Speech Disorders: Resource Guide for Pre School Children, New York: Singular Publishing Group, pp. 30-36.

7

Role of ICT in Educational Transactions

Introduction

The role of teachers is enormous, especially for nurturing children in their formative years, when they begin their schooling. Hence, it is very crucial to have qualified teachers to ensure prefect development of students. The various objectives of the ICT in Teacher Education, are to provide high quality education, monitor Teacher Education as approved by National Council for Teacher Education at all levels in the State, to develop research facilities in Teacher Education; The Tamil Nadu Teacher Education University from 2008, is very much focused to promote quality in Education and to standardize the system of operation. This paper focused on EDUSAT, INSAT, SITE, CAI, Video Conferencing, Virtual Classroom and the equipments and the UGC Tele programmes. Whatever it me, the today's student teachers are tomorrow's Teachers. So that, we are in need of utilization of media and technology in our classrooms and it can used in future for our educational transactions.

Teachers play a vital role in the overall growth and development of students. Teaching as profession is not only restricted to imparting academic knowledge, but also inculcating the right principles and values to the students. The role of teachers is enormous, especially for nurturing children in their formative years, when they begin their schooling. Hence, it is very crucial to have qualified teachers to ensure prefect development of students. Today, there are enormous colleges and universities in India that offer Courses in Education and Teacher Science.

As the needs of primary students are completely different from secondary students, the primary teachers and the secondary teachers are required to take different teachers 'training courses. Hence, most of the prominent Teacher training institutes offer different Courses which include Junior Basic Training or JBT, Basic Training Certificate or BTC, Primary Teachers Training or PTT, Bachelor of Education or B.Ed, Diploma in Education or D.Ed, and many other teachers training courses.

National Council of Teacher Education was established in 1973 by the Govt. of India. It was formed as advisory organization to government, on issues related to the teacher education. The government formed a National Policy on Education in 1986, which was aimed at setting up statutory body to provide quality Teachers' training in country, as step towards producing quality teaching professionals in India. In the year 1995, NCTE was awarded the status of statutory body in the pursuance of the National Council for Teacher Education Act. This Council sets the standards and norms for teachers' training right from primary teacher's education to post graduation teachers education. In the past, a teacher who wanted to display information for a classroom full of students had only a few options at his disposal: writing everything out on the chalkboard manually or projecting it onto a screen using a transparency projector. Today, the liquid crystal display (LCD) technology becoming common in homes has also made its way into the classroom.

We learn

1.0 % through TASTE
1.5 % through TOUCH
3.5 % through SMELL
11.0 % through HEARING
83.0 % through SIGHT

We remember

20 % through HEAR
30 % through SEE
50 % through SEE AND HEAR
80 % through SAY
90 % through SAY AND DO

Utilization of EDUSAT in Schools of Tamil Nadu

The NCERT acts as a major agency for implementing the bilateral Cultural Exchange Programmes with other countries in the field of school education also in addition to research, development, training, extension, and publication and dissemination activities. INSAT (Indian National Satellites) are a series of satellites projected and maintained by ISRO for multipurpose space applications. INSAT-3B, INSAT-3C are satellites in this series.

The ISRO launched a Satellite for education, termed as EDUSAT. With the launch of EDUSAT, TV, Radio and data transfer has become easy for educational institutions situated all over the country. Quality education is to be provided to school students especially in rural areas through this Satellite. This will also enable high quality in-service training to school teachers in the state. Live programmes are being broadcast through the studio at Anna University using EDUSAT. For proper utilization of EDUSAT, a plan of action has been formulated. Satellite Interactive Terminals have been set up in all 29 District Institutes of Education and Training. Satellite interactive terminals will be established in all the BRCs, 215 Urban Cluster Resource Centres and 2000 Government High and Higher Secondary Schools in this academic year 2006-2007 in a phased manner under the aegis of SSA.

Some schools like Delhi Public School and IGNOU are already experimenting with teaching through lessons prepared for distance teaching using multimedia, slides etc. The communication technology based teaching is a viable solution. Any institution which can afford and is willing to put the efforts and costs involved, can utilize the technology. But the technology is still quite expensive and state has to support the venture. Of course the country may look forward to the institutions that have expertise in the related fields at the right time, for the better utilization.

SITE and its Uses

Satellite Instructional Television Experiment (SITE) (1975).This project, one of the largest techno-social experiments in human communication, was commissioned for the villagers and their Primary School going children of selected 2330 villages in six states of India. It started on August 1, 1975 for a period of one year in six states Rajasthan, Karnataka, Orissa, Bihar, Andhra Pradesh and Madhya Pradesh. The main objectives of this experiment were to study the process of existing rural communications, the role of television as new medium of education, and the process of change brought about by the community television in the rural structure with following two type of telecast: (i) Developmental education programmes in the area of agriculture and allied subjects, health, family planning and social education, which were telecast in the evening for community viewing and (ii) The school programmes of 22 ½ minutes duration each in Hindi, Kannada, Oriya and Telugu were telecast on each school day for rural primary school children of 5- 12 years age group to make the children realize the importance of science in their day to day life.

SITE experiment showed that the new technology made it possible to reach number of people in the remotest areas. The role of television was appreciated and it was accepted in rural primary schools as an educational force (IGNOU, 2000). Post-SITE project (1977).The target group for this post SITE project was the villagers of Rajasthan. This was a SITE continuity project and was initiated in March 1977 when a terrestrial transmitter was commissioned at Jaipur. The main objectives of SITE continuity project were to; (i) Familiarize the rural masses with the improved and scientific know how about farming, the use of fertilizers and the maintenance of health and hygiene; (ii) Bring about national and emotional integration; and (iii) Make rural children aware of the importance of education and healthy environment. This project was also successful.

Mass media serve some important functions. They are helpful in teaching large number of people. They are helpful in the spread of compulsory education and adult literacy. Recently their use is being made increasingly in distance education. They are useful in making instructions more effective and meaningful. Mass media play a pivotal role in education. It may be hardware approach like radio, tape recorder, television etc or software approach like newspapers books, magazines etc. Mass media include Computer, Educational satellite, VCR and T.V to meet the tremendous challenges in the educational field using of multimedia is inevitable. In fact it is essential for the ever changing educational field.

The Barriers to Verbal Classroom Communication in the Classroom are;

1) Inaudibility of speech
2) Abnormal speed of speech
3) Unfamiliar pronunciation of the teacher.
4) Use of unfamiliar words and technical terms without explanations
5) Lack of understanding of the basic knowledge of the students known as referent confusion

6) Day dreams on the part of the students on account of their inattentiveness.
7) Unsystematic presentation of the subject matter
8) Lack of scope of immediate feedback
9) Lack of physical facilities in the classroom
10) Socio-economic and cultural difference among the students.

Cai

One of the significant instructional applications of computers is "Computer Assisted Instruction" (CAI). It is nothing but giving instruction with the help of computers. In CAI, the activity of the learner is the most important attribute. The computer can be helping the teacher in the following areas;

i) Evaluation of students performance and classification of children according to abilities;
ii) Preparation of time-table and class schedule;
iii) Allocation of learning materials according to individual needs and interests.
iv) Maintenance of progress cards efficiently and confidentially.
v) Providing information and large data for guidance and reference.
vi) Provision of direct interaction between pupils and subject matter.
vii) Engaging students in tutorial work;
viii) Providing immediate feedback to students for better interaction and motivation
ix) Developing the CAI programmes to teach their students individually.
x) Using the Internet related activities and to take print outs and documentation to their students.

Video Conferencing

Videoconferencing can provide two way interactive teaching-learning facilities where the students can interact with highly qualified faculties from distant locations. This also reduces the costs involved in travel and energy. The visual contents should be used to furnish illustrations during the conferencing of the lecture, to permit pupils to experience the content through the avenues of sight and learning.

Virtual Classroom

Virtualizing is the creation of a three-dimensional, interactive model of a problem or dataset to find a virtual solution that will also work in the real world. Virtual reality also has the flexibility to be a tremendous aid for design in the areas of engineering and manufacturing, architecture and construction, biotechnology and nano pharmacology, chemistry and modeling molecules, medicine and bionics, the apparel sector, and the fine arts. Three-dimensional models of molecules and living structures may be fabricated and handled virtually. Electronics may be fabricated and tested absent creation of a physical prototype. Virtual modeling clay can be shaped into various forms for either aesthetic or practical purposes Computer-artificially constructed objects and worlds should conform with reasonable accuracy to the tangible and other laws that shape such things and environments in the actual world. Some divergence might be relevant for surreal applications, but in case the difference is too great then the sense of believability is lost.

Some of the Virtual Classroom Equipments are;

1. E-D Wireless 3D Glasses for the PC
2. VirtualFX 3D TV Converter
3. 3DPlus 2D to 3D DVD Software
4. 3D Combine 2D to 3D Photo Software
5. 3D DVDs for your PC or TV
6. Long Range Viewing Equipment for Stereo Projection
7. InFocus DepthQ 3D Video Projector
8. 3D Glasses for Samsung and Mitsubishi Televisions
9. Vuzix - VR920 Head Mounted Display

Site

The satellite instructional television experiment was launched in our country in august 1975. The main Objective of the SITE programmes was to help people in their development endeavours. The major educational objective of INSAT television is to promote alternative approaches to education for children, youth and adults.

Insat

INSAT (Indian National Satellites) are a series of satellites projected and maintained by ISRO for multipurpose space applications. INSAT-3B, INSAT-3C are satellites in this series. The objective of the INSAT (Indian National Satellite - 1982) project was aimed at making the rural masses aware of the latest developments in the areas of agricultural productivity, health and hygiene.

Edusat

At present, using EDUSAT, networks for many user agencies like

IGNOU, CEC/UGC, CIET/NCERT, AICTE, Blind People's Association (BPA) or Blind school, Karnataka school network, VTU, YCMOU, Goa University, Amrita VRC, and Kerala/Tamil Nadu are operational for a total of about 1200 terminals or classrooms.

UGC Country wide Classroom

The University Grants Commission (UGC) was formally established only in November 1956 as a statutory body of the Government of India through an Act of Parliament for the coordination, determination and maintenance of standards of university education in India.

CLASS Project

A Pilot Project on Computer Literacy and Studies in Schools (CLASS) was initiated in 1984-85 in 248 selected Secondary/Higher secondary schools. The objective is to acquaint students and teachers with the wide range of computer applications and its potential as a learning medium. By the end of 1988-89 about 2600 schools had been covered. Sixty resource centers had been set up to train school teachers and provide support to the participating schools. Efforts have been made to start generation of indigenous software through NCERT, New Delhi. The project is jointly co-coordinated and supported by the Department of Electronics, the Department of Education, Computer Maintenance Corporation (CMC) and the NCERT.

Learning without Frontiers" (LWF)

It represents UNESCO's pro-active response to addressing the deep social and political problems that confront humanity as they relate to the role of learning in society. It views the processes of engaging in collaborative, multi-channel and innovative learning as being critical for both the development of the individual and the building and linking of culturally diverse communities.

Conclusion

Reliable wireless service is has become an essential tool in both enhancing the education of electronic based teaching learning students as well as increasing operational productivity at Smart schools. Recent advances in Wi-Fi technology dramatically increase the range and reliability of Wi-Fi services by automatically focusing and directing signals over the fastest RF paths as the environment changes. A lot of modern classrooms are replacing classic white boards with "Smart boards". These smart boards are usually touch screen and are connected to a computer. This means that anything on the computer can be shown to an entire class relatively easily. Smart boards do require projectors and can be quite expensive; also environmental effects such as glare through windows can affect use. Everyone should show responsibility towards the LCD projector utility in their classrooms. To fulfill this objective we should educate our all teachers through this electronic technology. The management and authorities should initiates to use videos, documentary films and technology related magazines etc to build LCD projectors knowledge among teachers and develop the educational transactions.

References

1. Edwards, Julie-Ann, M. Hartnell and R. Martin (2002) Interactive Whiteboards: Some Lessons for the Classroom, Micro math, summer 2002, pp 30-33.
2. Gueissaz, Albert. (2002), New Tool, New Actors, New Decisions, European Journal of Education, Vol.37, No.1, p. 16-21.
3. Jo Towers (2007) Using video in teacher education, Canadian Journal of Learning and Technology. Volume 33, No.2 Spring 2007. pp. 54-58.
4. Mark Fischetti (November 2007) Two Technologies Shine, Scientific American, Inc: pp. 110–111
5. Nachimuthu, K. (2007), Mobile learning and Distance Education, Journal of Distance Education, University of Jammu, Kashmir, India, 2007, Vol. XII, No:1, pp. 33-39.
6. Solvie, Pamela A (2004) Digital Whiteboard: A Tool in Early Literacy Instruction. Reading Teacher, Vol. 57, No.5, pp.: 484–487.
7. Vijayakumari, G. et al., (2008), Quality issues and standards of E-content, Journal of Educational Technology, I-Manager Pub, Vol. 04, No. 03, Oct- Dec 2007, pp. 8-11.
8. Wu, C. H. and Lin, T. Y. (2000) Education terms: knowledge economy, knowledge management, Education information and research Journal, Vol.37, pp.100-101.

8

Quality Enhancement in Teaching – Learning Process

Introduction

Using the technology developments is an important thing for teaching learning process. Now a day's the internet and other Medias are doing a vital role for teaching learning process. Using these technologies is easy to understand the concepts of teaching for the students. Digital projectors are the most exciting classroom tool ever. A picture truly is worth a thousand words. Project your laptop or desktop image on the screen for students to see you solve that math problem.

A good teacher is continually learning. Technology makes it easy to extend your learning by offering professional development on demand. Professional development will keep your teaching fresh, current, and will remind you of what it is like to learn something new. Teachers who are continually teach make empathetic teachers they understand how frustrating it can be to learn something for the first time.

Develop a Personal Learning Network on Twitter

Twitter is an excellent place for new teachers to connect, collaborate, share ideas, and struggles with educators around the world. When joining

Twitter, make sure to fill out your profile with information related to education. This will help others in education find you com to find other educators that teach in the same content area(s). Be sure to add your Twitter name to the appropriate list so that other educators can find you.

Keep Students Engaged

Always have engaging activities on hand to keep your students on task and learning. Students will misbehave if they have nothing to do, don't give them the opportunity to be bored. Technology is a great way to fill those extra minutes with critical thinking and problem solving activities. Keep a list or bookmark folder full of great online logic puzzle and problem solving websites for students to refer to when they have extra minutes.

Keep Yourself Organized

During the first year of teaching you will find a lot of new great resources, keep track of all these great finds in one easy to manage location. Delicious.com is a bookmarking website that allows you to bookmark and organize websites and web tools as you find them. Bookmarks can be collected and shared with others educators through Delicious. Be sure to install the Internet browser plug in so that you can easily bookmark a site with the click of a button.

Communicate with e-mail and Blogs

Email facilitates communication with all three members of the academic triangle: the teacher, the student and the parent. The beauty of email is that you can dash off a really short note which will be read. Blogs are a wonderful way to keep an electronic journal which encourages comment and dialog with your students. Anything which helps a student express his thoughts has to be a good thing. Post your assignments on a Web portal. Parents will thank you for this information. They love to be able to review their children's assignments and grades online. The more you can involve parents, the more successful your outcomes will be.

Incorporate a Digital Projector into your Lessons

Digital projectors are the most exciting classroom tool ever. A picture truly is worth a thousand words. Project your laptop or desktop image on the screen for students to see you solve that math problem.

Conclusion

Remember: you are a teacher! You are in the business of igniting the fires of curiosity. Take your own medicine as you probe, inquire and learn about these exciting technologies. The Internet had its birth in the research and academic communities. It was created to allow the free and rapid flow of information to benefit higher learning. Let's recapture that focus in our work, and enrich our teaching in the process.

References

1. Annaraja, P. (2000) "Information technology and Education" in Reflectionson Education, St. Xavier's college of Education, Palaymakotai.
2. Aggarwal,J.C (2008), Principles of Methods and Techniques of Teaching. APH Publishers, New Delhi.
3. Kirshnamacharyulu, V (2004), To be sure teaching for Teacher's Today & Tomorrow.

9

Designing Learning Environment of Tomorrow

Introduction

This paper presents the conclusions of a study, carried out in collaboration with schools in six European countries, which focused on tomorrow's physical learning environments. It resulted in the creation of a learning space model that is flexible, modifiable and sustainable while supporting the teaching and learning processes. It is widely acknowledged amongst today's educators that teachers' roles have changed dramatically since the last century.

In recent years, we have witnessed rapid social and cultural changes, phenomenal advances in communication and information technologies, as well as the introduction of the Internet within schools. These factors have contributed to shape the teaching and operating cultures of schools and created shifts in our expectations of the physical learning environment. Theyhave affected teachers, educators and researchers the world over. These miniature revolutions have given rise to an urgent need for a new generation of facilities to cater for 21st century teaching and learning needs.

Conceptualising the physical learning Environment

The concept of "learning environment" will become increasingly significant as schools of the future become centres of lifelong learning. "Learning environment" is a term used liberally in educational discourse because of the emerging use of information technologies for educational purposes on the one hand, and the constructivist concept of knowledge and learning on the other (Mononen-Aaltonen, 1998).

The OECD (2006) defines "educational spaces" as "a physical space that supports multiple and diverse teaching and learning programmes and pedagogies, including current technologies; one that demonstrates optimal, cost-effective building performance and operation over time; one that respects and is in harmony with the environment; and one that encourages social participation, providing a healthy, comfortable, safe, secure and stimulating setting for its occupants".

In its narrowest sense, a physical learning environment is seen as a conventional classroom and, in its widest sense, as a combination of formal and informal education systems where learning takes place both inside and outside of schools (Manninen et al., 2007). Manninen criticised traditional school teaching for conveying too much theoretical information and for preventing in-depth learning. He claims that inert knowledge is relevant for exams but not for real-world problems. This idea is posing new challenges and exerting pressure to bring about changes in physical learning environments.

The concept of the physical learning environment with respect to physical structures relates to spaces, equipment and tools within the school. Lehtinen (1997, p. 21) suggests that the concept has evolved into an even more complex structure that includes teaching equipment, sources of information and events outside of schools, where students can take part in the learning process both directly and virtually. The term evolved as a result of the recent changes taking place in pedagogy, whereby actual learning has been transposed outside of schools thanks to developments in communication and information technology.

Internet has already brought about significant changes in schools. Both the immense quantity of information available and easy access to social networks have weakened the link between schools and learning and therefore modified the traditional teacher-student scenario. The learning process is becoming more co-operative, changing the teacher into a learner too. Manninen (2007, p. 27) categorises learning according to five different contexts: physical, local, social, technological and didactic. The basic structure of teaching spaces does not seem to have evolved much over the past century. This fact inspired the research team to investigate the reason why, despite the recent changes in pedagogy and the widespread use of information technology inside classrooms and school spaces, the physical learning environment has not yet changed in keeping with this evolution.

In order to plan and construct effective physical learning environments, not only technical specifications need to be elaborated; qualitative aspects also need to be considered (Nuikkinen 2009, p. 64). The concept of "quality design" has become critical the world over. It relates to school construction and, more particularly, defining a quality physical learning environment, measuring it and analysing the results (OECD, 2006). With regard to quality criteria for school building and design, the key actors are students; requirements are determined by specific age groups, in conjunction with societal needs and regulations relating to usability and safety (Heitor, 2005). It has been demonstrated that international comparisons of education can be achieved through comprehensive quality management and quality criteria (Finnish National Board of Education, 2008; OECD, 2006). As a result, the emphasis is shifting from developing physical learning environments using norms and regulations to comparing these environments on the basis of qualitative improvement (OECD, 2009).

Objectives of the Study

With these considerations in mind, a comprehensive study was undertaken of what composes a physical learning environment. This would seem to consist of four learning contexts: social, individual, formal teaching and informal learning processes. These elements form an interactive whole in which the physical learning environment plays a central role in reforming the school's operational culture; it should be analysed and developed holistically. This study approaches the subject by considering the learning space and its operational environment as such. Within it, flexible and modifiable learning spaces and their related learning environments are formed through pairs of dimensions. They are all interactive and totally supportive of one another, as shown below

The study took place between 2007 and 2010. Its objective, which was to contribute to the quality of education, arose from concerns shared by groups of students, teachers and educational administrators about the changes which needed to be implemented in physical learning environments. A school from each of the following countries – Belgium, Finland, Holland, Portugal, Spain and Sweden – participated in the study. They all shared common features such as infrastructure, educational level and socio- economic conditions.The study set out to conceptualise the relationship between educations, the physical learning environment and the facilities needed by its users.

Participants were asked to identify the components that make up good qualitative and modifiable learning spaces: it was commonly agreed that improving educational facilities was key in this regard. It attempted to highlight the qualitative factors and user-oriented design features of physical learning environments. When comparing international physical learning environment criteria and their associate recommendations, we found that expectations relating to changeability, flexibility and sustainability were key factors.

Implementing the Study

Information on users' and school authorities' perceptions was collected from the six countries using different methods: 250 14- and 15-year-old students from the six participating countries were invited to design their ideal model classroom, using a 1:50 scale and including a specific set of furniture and equipment. Students were asked to arrange the furniture to suit their learning needs and according to how they would like tomorrow's classroom to be configured; they were also asked to suggest alternative space solutions. In addition, 65 teachers completed questionnaires and 35 administrative school authorities were interviewed.

We therefore used process simulation, which is a targeted research method used in specific circumstances such as when the physical learning environment is inspected through a co-operative design process (Smeds et al., 2007). This method has been used in Finland to plan large-scale future learning physical environments; it is proving to be an effective design tool because it enhances users' capacity to have an effective impact on the work environment. The process simulation method can be illustrated with the aid of the figure below.

In addition to a phenomenological analysis, which is useful when dealing with verbal answers and pictorial responses, a hermeneutic approach was used to broaden the concepts and find points of convergence. Our study was based on the notion that by describing school authorities' and users' different perceptions; we could reach an accurate overall impression of a high-quality physical learning environment. One element of the study involved evaluating the quality of the latter: this was understood to be a value judgement resulting from users' everyday experiences and their subsequent interpretation of them (Heidegger, 2000; Marton and Booth, 1997).

Study Findings

The results of the study highlighted several key factors relating to a quality physical learning environment, namely the relevance for school users of the teaching space as a whole as well as their specific needs in relation to furniture and equipment. It showed that the physical learning environment is pivotal to users' desire to develop the school's operational environment as well as their need to renew its operational culture. The more meaningful and challenging the operational environment is, the more the user is willing to improve the physical learning environment. The needs of teachers, head-teachers and students call for practical solutions, and these too have an impact on it.

When physical learning environments offer resources and possibilities that support new teaching methods and learning goals, schools are much more prompt to change their operational culture. In other words, they are important when developing school operational culture, as well as work environments. Despite the differences within education systems, the basic principles of using physical learning environments and the concepts behind ideal teaching spaces are very similar. The study's findings indicate that pressure for change in teaching and learning is felt at the national level. Consequently, the expectations for physical learning environments do not differ significantly between countries. Moreover, today's well-educated and committed teachers offer a largely unharnessed resource for planning and implementing future learning environments.

Once the designs by participating students had been examined, a single model was selected. A mock-up of it was made and tested by groups of students. The resulting simulation provided a prime example of a learning space that supports teaching and learning operations, while demonstrating flexibility, sustainability and modifiability. The model is illustrated below.

Future technological advances and developments in social networks and media, as well as different teaching and learning methods, will undoubtedly require dynamic teaching spaces. The design of the proposed model takes these factors into account: the carefully conceived flexible layout and furniture arrangement facilitates individual, pair and group work methods. The simultaneous enhanced interaction between the student and the teacher, on the one hand, and the physical environment, on the other, optimises new information flows (Lehtinen, 1997).Respondents perceived the traditional classroom as a passive area, which hindered the full use of space.

They associated dynamic teaching spaces with flexibility and the possibility of creating different furniture configurations. The latter can be achieved by ensuring that furniture is mobile and that there is free and easy access to information technology.A dynamic teaching space concept is summarised below

The study participants did not decry the traditional classroom as such, but they called for additional spaces of different sizes in optimal locations to support teaching and learning processes. The spaces should offer various possibilities for learning to take place: this can range from individual study to large group activities.

They should also support teacher coaching and individual work. Such flexibility fosters new types of teaching and learning, as illustrated above, which are determined by the demands of the subject or activity. In order to be successful, the sustainable physical learning environment needs to be equipped with both modular workstations and areas with comfortable seating, which contribute to support individual learning. It should be possible to adapt the furniture to different configurations.

Similarly, as teaching and information technology tools facilitate flexible teaching, it should be easy to displace equipment and wireless terminals according to different subjects and work methods. The key operational elements of the teaching space are illustrated in the table below.

Conclusion

Nuikkinen (2009, p. 278) argues that users' expectations and the theoretical concept of what makes a good school building do not match up. In practice, this runs counter – to a certain extent – to traditional planning, which on the whole requires teachers and students, as users of the buildings, to adapt to given environments (Dudek, 2000; Sanoff, 2009).

The research findings were clear: all participants recognised that significant changes must be implemented to the physical learning environment to better support users' needs. Pedagogical and physical structures need to be remodelled in parallel so as to respond to the challenges posed by changes in schools' operational culture. In order for a school to develop into a dynamic physical learning environment, there needs to be a behavioural change in relation to planning and producing spatial solutions. Change cannot occur without input from teachers and students – the main school users. Teachers and students who conceived the study applauded the significant shift away from the traditional classroom and said how much they would like to work in a similar space.If a school provides a quality environment for students, this will facilitate the acquisition of skills that are important for society. The choice of equipment is important: it should be versatile, resistant, durable and easy to repair. User-based innovative processes should be at the heart of designing the physical learning environment of tomorrow's schools. This process should take into account the global needs of students, teachers, school administrators and the community, while respecting the environment. A judicious selection of products and services that minimises Negative Environmental Impacts Will Also Be Of Benefit To All.

References

1. Dudek, M. (2000), Architecture of Schools: The New Learning Environments, Architectural Press, Oxford, p. xiv.
2. Evagorou, M. et al. (2009), "An Investigation of the Potential of Interactive Simulations for Developing System Thinking Skills in Elementary School: A Case Study with Fifth-Graders and Sixth-Graders", International Journal of Science Education, Vol. 31, Issue 5, pp. 356.
3. Heidegger, M. (2000), Oleminen ja aika, translated into Finnish by R. Kupiainen, Vastapaino, Tampere, pp. 33-34, 80, 84.
4. Heitor, T. (2005), "Potential problems and challenges in defining international design principles for school", Evaluating Quality in Educational Facilities, pp. 48, OECD/PEB, www.oecd.org/edu/facilities/evaluatingquality.
5. Lehtinen,E. (1997), Verkkopedagogiikka, Edita, Helsinki.
6. Marton, F. and S. Booth (1997), Learning and Awareness, Lawrence Erlbaum Associates, Mahwah, New Jersey, p. 13.
7. Mononen-Aaltonen, M. (1998), "A Learning Environment – A Euphemism for Instruction or a Potential for Dialogue?", Media Education Publication 8, pp. 163–212.
8. OECD (Organisation for Economic Co-operation and Development) (2006), CELE Organising Framework on Evaluating Quality in Educational Spaces, www.oecd.org/edu/facilities/evaluatingquality.
9. OECD (2009), International Pilot Study on the Evaluation of Quality In Educational Spaces (EQES), User Manual, www.oecd.org/edu/facilities/evaluatingquality.
10. Sanoff, H. (2009), Research Based Design of an Elementary School, Open House International, Vol. 34, No. 1, pp. 9-16.
11. Smeds, R. et al. (2006), "SimLab Process Simulation Method as a Boundary Object for Inter-organizational Innovation", Multidiscip-

linary Research on Simulation Methods and Educational Games in Industrial Management, proceedings of the 10th International Workshop on Experimental Interactive Learning in Industrial Management, Trondheim, Norway, June.

12. Smeds, R. et al. (2007), "Process Simulation for Social Innovation Case: Planning the School for the Future", Multidisciplinary Research on New Methods for Learning and Innovation in Enterprise Networks, proceedings of the 11th Special Interest Group Workshop on Experimental Learning in Industrial Management, 20-22 May, Bremen,Germany, pp. 177–191.

10

Use of ICT for Teaching Psychology

Introduction

ICT enriches the campus by incorporating its role well. This is present paper illustrates the use of ICT in various ways in teaching Psychology for students of B.Ed., Course. An attempt is made to analyze how technology could be best incorporated to the maximum benefit for the students. The purpose of this paper is to create awareness about the advantages of using ICT in a classroom and to illustrate how and when to use them effectively. This information can also be used in developing e-content or module for core paper II of Tamilnadu Teachers Education University B.Ed., syllabus namely Psychology of Learning and Human development.

In the present educational scenario, ICT (Information and Communication Technology) is considered as an important tool in the entire educational system – curriculum, instruction and management. Class room instruction forms the basis for majority of educational processes. Hence it should aim at making the teaching learning process interesting, effective and goal oriented. In current scenario of a classroom there is a paradigm shift in the focus from teacher centered approach to child centered approach, autocratic classroom climate to democratic climate, lecture method to constructive activity, stress full learning to joyful learning, general learning to customized learning, teacher or instructor to facilitator. The advantages of using ICT are dealt with under the broad four categories, namely 1. As an aid-to augment the learning process 2. As an administrative tool-to effectively undertake other curricular transactions like administrating tests, evaluation, maintenance of records and many more. 3. As a subject per see to learn about ICT, though it is only incidental in psychology class 4. As a medium of knowledge management – use a range of strategies and practices to create, identify, represent and distribute insights and experiences. The present study elaborate some ways and means to convert a traditional B.Ed., Psychology class room in to a smart class and mentions the advantages associated with it.

ICT as a Learning Process

In the B.Ed., Psychology syllabus prescribed by Tamilnadu Teachers Education University there are ten units. The uses of multimedia are discussed here unit wise. In the first unit concepts about the various methods and branches of psychology can be easily illustrated by preparing power points by downloading pictures and images from the internet. Pictures, images or schemes are available in plenty for topics on S-R conditioning, Thorndike's puzzle box and Pavlov's classical conditioning. If the teacher is persistent enough she could get picture with beautiful animation too. The only problem the teacher face is the problem of plenty which could be easily overcome by the teacher developing a scanning eye with practice. Using visual perception it become easier for the students to distinguish conditioned stimulus from unconditioned stimulus, conditioned responds from unconditioned responds. Various website offer a large number of methods of psychology. For example a more look at the simple figure, the student is able to graphs the importance of the whole against the parts. The ice berg model of personality structure of Sigmund Freud's Psychoanalysis theory is well illustrated in many website. All that the teacher requires to do is to cut and past these figures and make a presentation with notes of explanations. There are websites which offer Transactional Analysis well illustrated by schematic representations which rarely finds a place in many of the popular text books followed in B.Ed., colleges.

Another strategy to improve the understanding ability of the students is that different unit of Educational Psychology can be compared easily using a table with the Colum heading as' unit wise objective, concept, variation, main ideas and method adopted'. The topic of the units of Psychology namely "Nature ofEducational Psychology, Human Growth and

Development, CognitiveDevelopment, Social, Emotional and Moral Development, Learning,Intelligence and Creativity, Motivation and Group Dynamics, Personality andAssessment, Mental Health and Hygiene and Guidance and Counseling from the row headings this table will provide the summary of all units the Educational Psychology. To add value to this table, pictures of the ten units can be pasted. It would serve as the ready beckoner for the exam oriented students.

Once the various approaches in psychology are made clear to the students by making use of ICT enabled instructional materials the major difficulties in getting through the other concepts in the minds of the students become easier for the teacher on one hand .On the other hand the students can easily go through this comprehensive table understand, appreciate, recall and recite. Since these are objectives most often tested in our present system of examination this in our present system of examination this would serve them the purpose similarly, the concept of Identical twins. Fraternal Twins, Mendelism, Sex determination in human being and the difference between positive reinforcement, negative reinforcement and punishment all these can be made easy by an ingenious teacher. One may argue that good books are available with excellent illustrations and figures. But most of the time a single book will not be giving the best illustration for all the concepts. But teacher can collect the best illustration, best images and best tables from the various freely downloadable sites and make her own presentation in a LCD projector. Over and above, already prepared PowerPoint's are also available for many of the topics which the classroom teacher can alter according to the needs of the students. In this context the uses of the free open source community based tool 'Moodle' cannot be overemphasized. This tool can be used effectively to speed up the process of learning among the students.

ICT- as an Administrative Tool

The uses of computer especially the packages MS office is tremendous in a classroom as an administrative tool. It is a boon to the classroom teacher. It is used for marking the attendance register, calculating the attendance percentage for issue of hall tickets, giving roll numbers or register numbers, preparation of question papers, preparation of key, entry of marks, maintaining rank card or progress report or a cumulative record.

ICT as a Subject

Even though it is in the purview of Engineering and technology students, the basic operations of the computer, knowledge about various tools, utilities and sites available are a must for any teacher. By using modern gadgets as tool in a classroom the students are bound to learn about them. Though incidental in the process learning psychology, the fundamental knowledge about ICT is an added advantage for students as well as teachers.

ICT as a Medium of Knowledge Management

We are in an information society. This does not mean that there is lot of data in the society. It means we have easier access to information today than ever before. Data is just a number or figure. With context defined a data becomes meaningful information. Knowledge management is employing various strategies and practices combining information gathered by technology or any other means with our past experiences and insights to attain the goal. Modern technology provides for knowledge management also. Internet, email, social websites like blog, twitter etc., help us to manager our knowledge.

Conclusion

The above cited illustrations of uses of ICT in a Psychology class are not exhaustive. The scope is very wide. Everything depends on the ingenuity and interest of the teacher. Suitable conditions should be ensured in schools and teacher education Institutes to implement effectively ICT integration. Only then we can achieve our target in converting our classrooms to totally smart classes.

References

1. Tamilnadu Teachers Education University, prescribed syllabus for Bachelorof Education (B.Ed.) Course 2011-12.
2. Computer Assisted Instruction (CAI) www. Wikieducator.org
3. Anna Martinkova (2009), Intactive ICT in Education.

11

Traditional Classroom Vs Flipped Classroom

Introduction

Flipped classroom is a form of blended learning in which students learn new content online by watching video lectures, usually at home, and what used to be homework is done in class with teachers offering more personalized guidance and interaction with students, instead of lecturing.Teachers can deliver this instruction by recording and narrating screen casts of work they do on their computers, creating videos of themselves teaching, or creating video lessons from trusted Internet sites. Students can watch the videos or screen casts as many times as they need to, enabling them to be more productive learners in the classroom. Since direct instruction is delivered outside the group learning space, teachers can then use in-class time to actively engage students in the learning process and provide them with individualized support. The traditional pattern of teaching has been to assign students to read textbooks and work on problem sets outside school, while listening to lectures and taking tests in class. In flip teaching, the students first study the topic by themselves, typically using video lessons prepared by the teacher. Flipping changes teachers from "sage on the stage" to "guide on the side", allows them to work with individuals or groups of students throughout the session.

Key elements of the flipped classroom are to provide a mechanism to assess students understanding. Provide an opportunity for students to gain first exposure prior to class, an incentive to students to prepare for the class and also promote in-class activities that focus on higher level cognitive activities. By providing an opportunity for students to use their new factual knowledge while they have access to immediate feedback from peers and instructor, the flipped classroom helps student learn to correct misconceptions and organize their new knowledge such that it is more accessible for future use. More over the immediate feedback that occurs in the flipped classroom helps students recognize and think about their own growth in understanding.

Originally developed in 2000 by Wes Baker at Cedarville University in Cedarville, Ohio, the flipped classroom model has gained widespread traction across the country as a means to integrate computer and online resources with day-to-day coursework. The flipped classroom is a pedagogical model in which the typical lecture and homework elements of a course are reversed. Short video lectures are viewed by students at home before the class session, while in-class time is devoted to exercises, projects, or discussions. The video lecture is often seen as the key ingredient in the flipped approach, such lectures being either created by the instructor and posted online or selected from an online repository. While a pre-recorded lecture could certainly be a podcast or other audio format, the ease with which video can be accessed and viewed today has made it so ubiquitous that the flipped model has come to be identified with it.

Flipped Classroom

Flipped classroom is a form of blended learning in which students learn new content online by watching video lectures, usually at home, and what used to be homework is done in class with teachers offering more personalized guidance and interaction with students, instead of lecturing. This is also known as backwards classroom, reverse instruction, flipping the classroom and reverse teaching.

The flipped classroom approach has been used for years in some disciplines, notably within the humanities. The students gain first-exposure learning prior to class and focus on the processing part of learning like synthesizing, analyzing and problem- solving in the class. To ensure that students do the preparation necessary for productive class time, an assignment-based model in which students produce work prior to class. The students receive productive feedback on the students' work.

Traditional Vs Flipped Teaching

The traditional pattern of teaching has been to assign students to read textbooks and work on problem sets outside school, while listening to lectures and taking tests in class. In flip teaching, the students first study the topic by themselves, typically using video lessons prepared by the teacher. In class, students apply the knowledge by solving problems and doing practical work. Complementary techniques include differentiated instruction and project-based learning.

Flipped classrooms free class time for hands-on work. Students learn by doing and asking questions. Students can help each other, a process that benefits both the advanced and less advanced learners. Flipping also changes the allocation of teacher engages with the students who ask questions-but those who don't ask tend to need the most attention. We refer to 'silent failers,' said one teacher, claiming that flipping allows her to target those who need the most help rather than the most confident. Flipping changes teachers from "sage on the stage" to "guide on the side", allows them to work with individuals or groups of students throughout the session.

Significance of Flipped Classroom

1. In a traditional lecture, students often try to capture what is being said at the instant the speaker says it. They cannot stop to reflect upon what is being said, and they may miss significant points because they are trying to transcribe the instructor's words.
2. By contrast, the use of video and other pre-recorded media puts lectures under the control of the students: they can watch, rewind, and fast-forward as needed.
3. Lectures that can be viewed more than once may also help those for whom English is not their first language. Devoting class time to application of concepts might give instructors a better opportunity to detect errors in thinking, particularly those that are widespread in a class.
4. At the same time, collaborative projects can encourage social interaction among students, making it easier for them to learn from one another and for those of varying skill levels to support their peers.
5. Concept engagement takes place in the classroom with the help of the instructor. Educational Technology and activity learning are two key components of the flipped classroom model.

How does it work?

There is no single model for the flipped classroom the term is widely used to describe almost any class structure that provides pre-recorded lectures followed by in-class exercises. In one common model, students might view multiple lectures of five to seven minutes each. Online quizzes or activities can be interspersed to test what students have learned. Immediate quiz feedback and the ability to rerun lecture segments may help clarify points of confusion. Instructors might lead in class discussions or turn the classroom into a studio where students create, collaborate, and put into practice what they learned from the lectures they view outside class. As on-site experts, instructors suggest various approaches, clarify content, and monitor progress. They might organize students into an ad hoc workgroup to solve a problem that several are struggling to understand. Because this approach represents a comprehensive change in the class dynamic, some instructors have chosen to implement only a few elements of the flipped model or to flip only a few selected class sessions during a term.

Implications on Teaching and Learning

The flipped classroom constitutes a role change for instructors, who give up their front of the class position in favour of a more collaborative and cooperative contribution to the teaching process. There is a concomitant change in the role of students, many of who are used to being cast as passive participants in the education process, where instruction is served to them. Activities can be student-led, and communication among students can become the determining dynamic of a session devoted to learning through hands-on work. What the flip does particularly well is to bring about a distinctive shift in priorities from merely covering material to working toward mastery of it.

Key Elements of the Flipped Classroom

1. Provide an opportunity for students to gain first exposure prior to class.
2. Provide an incentive for students to prepare for the class.
3. Provide a mechanism to assess students understanding.
4. Provide in-class activities that focus on higher level cognitive activities.

Steps in Flipping the Classroom

1. Click on “Find and flip”.

2. Find YouTube videos for your lessons.
3. Click to select that video then click on flip this video.
4. Listed/unlisted.
5. Title/description.
6. Customize your video lesson.
7. Click on finish flip when you are done you can also preview it before saving it.
8. Share
9. Lesson starts.

Advantages

Students take control of their learning:

1. The expectation of spending time doing homework should be clear
2. Student can develop foundation of factual knowledge.
3. Students can understand facts and ideas in the context of a conceptual framework.
4. They can enrich their knowledge in ways that facilitate retrieval and application.
5. It saves time. Teacher may spend more time with students.

Conclusion

Meta-cognitive approach to instruction can help student learn to take control of their own learning by defining learning goals and monitoring their progress in achieving them. Although students thinking about the own learning is not an inherent part of the flipped classroom, the higher cognitive functions associated with class activity, accompanied by the ongoing peer/instructor interaction that typically accompanies them, can readily lead to the meta-cognition associated with deep learning.

References

1. Wesley, Baker.J (2000), The classroom flip: using web course management tools to become the guide by the side
2. Tucker, Bill (Winter 2012), "The Flipped Classroom", Education Next.
3. Pierce Richard, Fox Jeremy (20 Dec 2012), Vodcasts and active-learning exercises in a "flipped classroom" model of a renal pharmacotherapy module.
4. "Flipping the classroom", The Economist, 17 Sep 2011

12

Characteristics of Authentic Learning Environments

Introduction

Over the past decade, expert opinion and design recommendations for teacher professional development have moved steadily away from traditional workshop models and toward models that involve various types of professional collaboration among teachers. Whether expressed as the peer coaching model in the 70's and 80's, Professional Development Schools in the 80's through the present, or current day professional learning communities, collaboration is increasingly central to emerging models for professional development. Rigorous research on the impact of collaboration on teachers and teaching practices is just beginning to emerge. Literally no rigorous research is available directly linking collaborative professional development practices to improvements in student achievement or other student outcomes. Studies suggested that collaboration, in combination with specific configurations of professional development, may result in increased student learning and it is emphasized that authentic teaching learning environments will provide the fruitful results. The characteristics of learning environments are discussed in this article.

The influence of technology spreads its' wings to every sphere of life and life becomes so crucial and complicated. The educational principles and philosophies have changed drastically and online teaching learning becomes the order of the day. Unless we use this technology effectively the next generation will suffer with a number of confusion in utilizing the technology. Despite the intuitive appeal of authentic learning environments, and much anecdotal evidence that they are effective in promoting higher order learning, such complex learning environments appear to be used only rarely in higher education courses. Authentic learning designs have the potential to improve student engagement and educational outcomes. It is essential to provide an authentic environment for online teaching-learning which should facilitate students' learning in all the possible way.

Characteristics of a Situated Learning Environment

1. An authentic context that reflects the way the knowledge will be used in real life:In designing online learning environments with authentic contexts, it is not enough to simply provide suitable examples from real-world situations to illustrate the concept or issue being taught. The context needs to be all-embracing, to provide the purpose and motivation for learning, and to provide a sustained and complex learning environment that can be explored at length (e.g., Brown, Collins, & Duguid, 1989; Honebein, Duffy, & Fishman, 1993; Reeves & Reeves, 1997).
2. Authentic activities: The learning environment needs to provide ill-defined activities which have real-world relevance, and which present a single complex task to be completed over a sustained period of time, rather than a series of shorter disconnected examples (Bransford, Vye, Kinzer, & Risko, 1990; Brown, Collins, & Duguid, 1989; Reeves & Reeves, 1997; Lebow & Wager, 1994).
3. Access to expert performances and the modelling of processes: In order to provide expert performances, the online learning environment needs to provide access to expert thinking and the modelling of processes, access to learners in various levels of expertise, and access to the social periphery or the observation of real-life episodes as they occur (Collins, Brown, & Newman, 1989; Brown, Collins, & Duguid, 1989; Lave & Wenger, 1991). The facility of the World Wide Web to create global communities of learners who can interact readily via email, also enables opportunities for the sharing of narratives and stories.
4. Multiple roles and perspectives: In order for students to be able to investigate the learning environment from more than a single perspective, it is important to enable and encourage students to explore different perspectives on the topics from various points of

view, and to 'criss cross' the learning environment repeatedly (e.g., Collins, Brown, & Newman, 1989; Honebein, Duffy, & Fishman, 1993; Spiro, Feltovich, Jacobson, & Coulson, 1991).

5. Collaborative construction of knowledge: The opportunity for users to collaborate is an important design element, particularly for students who may be learning at a distance. Consequently, tasks need to be addressed to a group rather than an individual, and appropriate means of communication need to be established. Collaboration can be encouraged through appropriate tasks and communication technology e.g., discussion boards, chats, email, debates etc. (e.g., Brown, Collins, & Duguid, 1989; Collins, Brown, & Newman, 1989; Hooper, 1992; Reeves & Reeves, 1997).
6. Reflection: In order to provide opportunities for students to reflect on their learning, the online learning environment needs to provide an authentic context and task, as described earlier, to enable meaningful reflection. It also needs to provide nonlinear organisation to enable students to readily return to any element of the site if desired, and the opportunity for learners to compare themselves with experts and other learners in varying stages of accomplishment (e.g., Boud, Keogh, & Walker, 1985; Kemmis, 1985; Collins & Brown, 1988).
7. Articulation: In order to produce a learning environment capable of providing opportunities for articulation, the tasks need to incorporate inherent—as opposed to constructed—opportunities to articulate, collaborative groups to enable articulation, and the public presentation of argument to enable defence of the position (e.g., Edelson, Pea, & Gomez, 1996; Collins, Brown, & Newman, 1989; Lave & Wenger, 1991).
8. Coaching and scaffolding: In order to accommodate a coaching and scaffolding role principally by the teacher (but also provided by other students), the online learning environments needs to provide collaborative learning, where more able partners can assist with scaffolding and coaching, as well as the means for the teacher to support learning via appropriate communication technologies (e.g., Collins, Brown, & Newman, 1989; Greenfield, 1984).
9. Authentic assessment: In order to provide integrated and authentic assessment of student learning, the online learning environment needs to provide: the opportunity for students to be effective performers with acquired knowledge, and to craft polished, performances or products in collaboration with others. It also requires the assessment to be seamlessly integrated with the activity,

and to provide appropriate criteria for scoring varied products (e.g., Wiggins, 1993; Reeves & Okey, 1996; Linn, Baker, & Dunbar, 1991; Duchastel, 1997; Bain, 2003).

Authentic tasks

Authentic tasks are an integral component to situated learning environments, and it was felt important to investigate and describe their design more fully in order to explore their effective use in online learning environments. A literature review and study was undertaken where examples of online courses were investigated. The courses needed to use complex and sustained tasks that comprised an entire semester's work, so that in completing a single task, students would fulfil the requirements of the course. Such courses have been described in face-to-face and on-campus courses. Ten characteristics of authentic tasks were distilled from a review of papers on authentic learning environments from the literature and the characteristics were used to select cases for investigation:

1. Authentic tasks have real-world relevance: Activities match as nearly as possible the real world tasks of professionals in practice rather than decontextualised or classroom-based tasks (e.g., Brown, Collins, & Duguid, 1989; Jonassen, 1991; Lebow, 1993; Oliver & Omari, 1999; Cronin, 1993; Young, 1993; Winn, 1993; Resnick, 1987; Cognition and Technology Group at Vanderbilt, 1990a)
2. Authentic tasks are ill-defined, requiring students to define the tasks and sub-tasks needed to complete the activity: Problems inherent in the activities are ill-defined and open to multiple interpretations rather than easily solved by the application of existing algorithms. Learners must identify their own unique tasks and sub-tasks in order to complete the major task (e.g., Lebow & Wager, 1994; Bransford, Vye, Kinzer, & Risko, 1990; Cognition andTechnology Group at Vanderbilt, 1990a)
3. Authentic tasks comprise complex tasks to be investigated by students over a sustained period of time: Activities are completed in days, weeks and months rather than minutes or hours, requiring significant investment of time and intellectual resources (e.g., Bransford, Vye, Kinzer, & Risko, 1990; Lebow & Wager, 1994; Cognition and Technology Group at Vanderbilt, 1990b; Jonassen, 1991)
4. Authentic tasks provide the opportunity for students to examine the task from different perspectives, using a variety of resources: The task affords learners the opportunity to examine the problem

from a variety of theoretical and practical perspectives, rather than a single perspective that learners must imitate to be successful. The use of a variety of resources rather than a limited number of preselected references requires students to detectrelevant from irrelevant information (e.g., Young, 1993; Spiro, Vispoel, Schmitz, Samarapungavan, & Boeger, 1987; Bransford, Vye, Kinzer, & Risko, 1990; Cognition and Technology Group at Vanderbilt, 1990b)

5. Authentic tasks provide the opportunity to collaborate: Collaboration is integral to the task, both within the course and the real world, rather than achievable by an individual learner (e.g., Lebow & Wager, 1994; Young, 1993; Gordon, 1998)
6. Authentic tasks provide the opportunity to reflect: Activities need to enable learners to make choices and reflect on their learning both individually and socially (e.g., Young, 1993; Myers, 1993; Gordon, 1998)
7. Authentic tasks can be integrated and applied across different subject areas and lead beyond domain-specific outcomes: Activities encourage interdisciplinary perspectives and enable diverse roles and expertise rather than a single well-defined field or domain (e.g., Jonassen, 1991; Bransford, Sherwood, Hasselbring, Kinzer, & Williams, 1990)
8. Authentic tasks are seamlessly integrated with assessment: Assessment of activities is seamlessly integrated with the major task in a manner that reflects real world assessment, rather than separate artificial assessment removed from the nature of the task (e.g., Reeves & Okey, 1996; Young, 1995; Herrington & Herrington, 1998)
9. Authentic tasks create polished products valuable in their own right rather than as preparation for something else: Activities culminate in the creation of a whole product rather than an exercise or sub-step in preparation for something else (e.g., Barab, Squire, & Dueber, 2000; Gordon, 1998; Duchastel, 1997)
10. Authentic tasks allow competing solutions and a diversity of outcomes: Activities allow a range and diversity of outcomes open to multiple solutions of an original nature, rather than a single correct response obtained by the application of rules and procedures (e.g., Duchastel, 1997; Bottge & Hasselbring, 1993; Young & McNeese, 1993; Bransford, Vye, Kinzer, & Risko, 1990; Bransford, Sherwood, Hasselbring, Kinzer, & Williams, 1990).

BEST (Beginning and Establishing Successful Teachers)

Conclusion

There are many teachers who employ authentic learning approaches in online courses. Widespread research at the practitioner level would add substantially to the knowledge we have about the advantages and disadvantages, affordances and limitations, and benefits and problems associated with authentic learning. The use of development research or design-based research studies would importantly contribute not only empirical knowledge about the veracity of the approach, but also design principles to inform theory and practice in education (Reeves, Herrington, & Oliver, 2004). Instructional designers and learning designers should perform an important role in this regard by considering the authentic principles of online learning thereby they can serve the student community in a better manner.

References

1. Bain, J.D. (2003). Slowing the pendulum: Should we preserve some aspects of instructivism? In P.Kommers & G. Richards (Eds.), World Conference on Educational Multimedia, Hypermedia and Telecommunications 2003 (pp. 1382-1388). Honolulu, Hawaii: AACE.
2. Barab, S.A., Squire, K.D., & Dueber, W. (2000). A co-evolutionary model for supporting the emergence of authenticity. Educational Technology Research and Development, 48(2), 37-62.
3. Gulikers, J.T., Bastiaens, T.J., & Martens, R.L. (2005). The surplus value of an authentic learning environment. Computers in Human Behaviour, 21, 509-521.
4. Herrington, A., & Herrington, J. (Eds.). (2006). Authentic learning environments in higher education. Hershey, PA: Information Science Publishing.
5. Herrington, J., & Herrington, A. (1998). Authentic assessment and multimedia: How university students respond to a model of authentic assessment. Higher Education Research and Development, 17(3), 305-322.
6. Kantor, R.J., Waddington, T., & Osgood, R.E. (2000). Fostering the suspension of disbelief: The role of authenticity in goal-based scenarios. Interactive Learning Environments, 8(3), 211-227.
7. Oliver, R., & Herrington, J. (2000). Using situated learning as a design strategy for Web-based learning. In B. Abbey (Ed.), Instructional and cognitive impacts of web-based education (pp. 178-191). Hershey, PA: Idea Group Publishing.

8. Reeves, T.C. (2000). Socially responsible educational research. Educational Technology, 40(6), 19- 28.
9. Reeves, T.C., Herrington, J., & Oliver, R. (2004). A development research agenda for online collaborative research. Educational Technology Research & Development, 52(4), 53-65.
10. Taylor, J.A. (2003). Managing staff development for online education: A situated learning model. Journal of Higher Education Policy and Management, 25(1).
11. Wiggins, G. (1993). Assessing student performance: Exploring the purpose and limits of testing. San Francisco: Jossey-Bass.
12. Winn, W. (1993). Instructional design and situated learning: Paradox or partnership. Educational Technology, 33(3), 16-21.
13. Young, M.F. (1993). Instructional design for situated learning. Educational Technology Research and Development, 41(1), 43-58.
14. Young, M.F. (1995). Assessment of situated learning using computer environments. Journal of Science Education and Technology, 4(1), 89-96.

13

Preparing the Academy of Today for the Learner of Tomorrow

Introduction

Predicted to be America's first generation to exceed 100 million persons, the wave of Net Geners entering colleges and universities brings a blend of behaviors, attitudes, and expectations that creates opportunities—as well as challenges—for higher education. Opportunities arise from students' familiarity with technology, multitasking style, optimism, team orientation, diversity, and acceptance of authority. Challenges, on the other hand, include the shallowness of their reading and TV viewing habits, a comparative lack of critical thinking skills, naïve views on intellectual property and the authenticity of information found on the Internet, as well as high expectations combined with low satisfaction levels. Not surprisingly there is an increasing gap between most institutions' IT environments and the technologies the Net Gen uses. These factors lead, in turn, to the greatest challenge for higher education leaders, faculty, and staff—nearly all of whom belong to earlier generations: to understand the Net Generation learner and through this understanding provide the learning environments, services, and facilities needed to help these students achieve their potential.

Most institutions profess intense interest in the academic, social, and personal needs of their students. Yet, generational differences are not often used to gain a better understanding of students' behaviors, attitudes, and expectations. Change and adaptation within the academy proceed at a slow, deliberate pace. Planning is complicated because personal characteristics are not homogeneous within generational groupings. Unfortunately, the generational literature fails to predict the characteristics of future generations. Institutional leaders need to find ways to think about generations in designing campus and individual student initiatives, as well as to discern trends that will allow future-directed planning.

Generations and Technology

The technologies available as a generation matures influence their behaviors, attitudes, and expectations. People internalize the technologies that shape information access and use, as well as the ways they communicate. Matures (born 1946–1964) were exposed to large vacuum-tube radios, mechanical calculators, 78 rpm records, dial telephones, and party lines. Baby Boomers grew up with transistor radios, mainframe computers, 33? and 45 rpm records, and the touchtone telephone. Gen-Xers matured in the era of CDs, personal computers, and electronic mail. For the Next Generation, the prevailing technologies are MP3s, cell phones, and PDAs; they communicate via instant messaging, text messaging, and blogs. For each successive generation "technology is only technology if it was invented after they were born."

Technology has experienced its own series of generations. In computing, the nexus has shifted from the mainframe to the minicomputer to the personal computer, and now to mobile devices. In line with Moore's Law, computing and communication devices have radically decreased in size and increased in performance. Connectivity has experienced a similar transition across generations, from no connectivity to proprietary device-to-device cabling, to globally interconnected local area networks, and now to wireless. Computers were initially developed as number crunching devices. The early emphasis on processing numbers, then words, has been joined by multimedia: graphics, images, video, sound, and interactive games. Prevalent among today's applications are interpersonal and group communication tools. The use of early computers was batch-processing-oriented and required programming skills and arcane commands. Today's graphical user interfaces and the Web make the operation of computers highly interactive and achievable by nearly anyone. The Internet has led to the kind of global village of information and communication.

Behaviors of the Net Generation are expressed through technologies to an extent not observed in previous generations. At one level, Net Geners are the beneficiaries of decades of technological development that preceded them; at another level, as students they use these technologies in new ways, and in so doing are redefining the landscape in higher education and perhaps beyond. To a great extent, the behaviors of the Net Gen are an enactment of the capabilities afforded by modern digital technologies.

According to a report from the Pew Internet & American Life Project, one in five of today's college students began using computers between the ages of 5 and 8; by the time they were 16 to 18, all of them used computers. Nationwide, nearly 90 percent of college students have gone online, compared with about 60 percent of the general population. Use of the Internet or campus networks is nearly universal in higher education. Eighty-five percent or more of college students own a computer, and nearly all of the rest have ready access to one. Sixty percent of college students regularly play computer or online games, and they are twice as likely to have downloaded music as the general population. The Net Generation students exhibit technology-related behaviors that may be unfamiliar to many in the academy: social networking, photo sharing, swarming, blogging, instant messaging, and text messaging. Four out of five students believe that Internet use has had a positive impact on their academic experience, and three out of four say they use the Internet for research more than they do the library.

Students are very familiar with the top online commercial sites such as amazon. com and ambercrombie.com; they hold these sites to be the standard against which they judge colleges' online services. And, of all of the generational groups, the Net Generation is least satisfied with their higher education experience. Net Geners have access to affordable multifunctional devices (for example, cell phones equipped with digital cameras and Web browsers that can play digital audio and video recordings, as well as send and receive e-mail and text messages) that readily support their interpersonal communication needs and multitasking behaviors. Between classes, students bustle about with cell phones attached to their ears. Silberman described the prevalence of cell phones among Net Geners in Finland, and how cell phones' voice and short messaging capabilities allow them to move in synchronization "like schools of fish ... on currents of whim." This behavior has since become well established in America, where it is known as social swarming or smart mobs.

Emerging Patterns

The mobility enabled by wireless communication, combined with an expanding class of wireless-equipped portable computers and PDAs, is leading to new instructional and social patterns. No longer do students need to go to a specific place, or even be seated, to use a computer. An array of multifunctional PDAs capable of wireless communication is allowing such devices to follow their users wherever they go, serving as "prosthetics for information, memory, or creativity." This is challenging the very definition of learning spaces because learning can now occur both in and out of the classroom, in both formal and informal settings, and by lone scholars or among groups. Net Gen students not only use technology heavily, they also trust it implicitly. They are as likely to get their news online as from a newspaper and conduct research through Google as visit a library. Their belief that anything accessible online should be free leads many to download or share music, movies, or software they have not purchased. The extent of this activity has surprised many institutions; campus networks often became saturated when students returned to school in the fall. In some cases this is followed by copyright violation notices from organizations such as the Recording Industry Association of America. The interactive and exploratory way the Net Generation uses technology is also a break with the past. The Net Gen approaches computers and other technologies as environments for communication, socialization, learning, and game playing, not as machines to be programmed. To be sure, today's students are avid users of Web, e-mail, telephones, and other IT resources; however, their rapid adoption of instant messaging, cell phones, blogs, wikis, social networking Web sites, and other resources that are not generally part of the core campus infrastructure leads to a host of new concerns. There is increased potential for incompatibilities between the technologies adopted by students and campus standards. The real opportunity lies in observing and talking to today's students to learn more about how they conceptualize and use these new tools. With this knowledge institutions can create contexts for technology use that enhance learning, improve student services, and enrich students' social lives.

Assessing the Generations in Online Learning

The Research Initiative for Teaching Effectiveness (RITE) at the University of Central Florida (UCF) regularly conducts formative and summative surveys of students' online learning experiences. These data become transformative because they are instrumental in modifying the organization, structure, and processes of our distributed learning initiative. We believe that both qualitative and quantitative research yield a more valid assessment of students in the online learning environment. When we ask respondents to complete objective statements followed by a reflective narrative, we obtain a more authentic characterization of their attitudes, beliefs, and behaviors. In the latest survey conducted at UCF, students used a series of 5-point Likert-scale questions to evaluate their online learning experience around two components previously identified through extensive numerical work. The first domain—learning engagement—encompassed six items where students indicated there:

?Overall satisfaction with online learning

?Ability to integrate technology into their education

?Ability to control their own learning

?Ability to study efficiently

?Ability to meet their educational objectives

?Willingness to take another online course

The second domain—interaction value—asked students to evaluate their online learning experience in regard to:

?Ease of interaction

?Amount of interaction with students

?Quality of interaction with students

?Amount of interaction with the instructor

?Quality of interaction with the instructor

Excellent Teaching

From our exploration of generational issues, an important question evolved: Can students distinguish characterizations of excellent teachers independent of generation, learning style, course modality, and technological sophistication? Data collected at UCF, with more than half a million student responses, suggest an answer. We have identified six characteristics that students attribute to the best faculty—characteristics that are independent of age, gender, and academic achievement. Interestingly, these characteristics correspond to the seven principles of good practice in undergraduate education and to the national study of student engagement. Although students' behaviors, attitudes, and expectations are generally shaped by their generation, what constitutes good teaching appears to be universal across these generations. Students believe that excellent instructors:

?Facilitate student learning

?Communicate ideas and information effectively

?Demonstrate genuine interest in student learning

?Organize their courses effectively

?Show respect and concern for their students

?Assess student progress fairly and effectively

This seemingly paradoxical way in which students determine teaching excellence through the lens of their instructors clarifies how universities must accommodate students' needs, realizing that these needs are universal, yet greatly mediated by the Net Generation.

Conclusion

The Net Generation possesses sophisticated technological adaptability and a remarkable capacity to incorporate multitasking into day-to-day academic activities. However, there is also a growing discrepancy between institutional infrastructure and these students' personalized facility with information. Freeland described a corresponding trend emerging in higher education that he called practice-oriented education—the combination of liberal and professional studies. He foreshadowed the students' tendency to learn through bricolage and the university's reticence to respond: "After 1945 it [the academy] became steadily more open... [but] as its clientele became more 'modern,' higher education became more traditional." As we move into the next decades, the resolution of that polarization compels colleges and universities to examine, and perhaps redesign, their strategic direction. Possibly, by studying how students interacted (politically, economically, culturally, socially, and technologically) with institutions' instructional climate in the past. From an instructional design perspective, we realize that knowing our students gives us many more options for engaging them in the learning process. The audacity with which the Net generation has burst on the academic scene has accelerated our need to understand its learning characteristics. A conundrum accompanies that solution, however: adaptation for the present generation may not be adequate for the next.

References

1. Neil Howe and William Strauss, Millennials Rising: The Next Greatest Generation (New York: Vintage Books, 2000).

2. Alan Kay quoted in Marc Prensky, Digital Game-Based Learning (New York: McGraw- Hill, 2000), p. 38.
3. Marshall McLuhan and Bruce R. Powers, The Global Village: Transformations in World Life and Media in the 21st Century (New York: Oxford University Press, 1999).
4. Steve Jones et al., "The Internet Goes to College: How Students Are Living in the Future with Today's Technology" (Washington, D.C.: Pew Internet & American Life Project, September 15, 2002), <http://www.pewinternet.org/reports/toc.asp?Report=71>.

14

Effectiveness of Edu-digital Skill Among Higher Secondary Students

Introduction

The end of the 20th Century and beginning of the 21st Century witnessed very exciting changes, one of them being in the field of Information and Communication Technology. Educators have begin to realize that in the fast changing world of today, the students have to be prepared to cope intelligently with the social, economic and technological changes. The educational environment is changing rapidly as a consequence of ICT and will continue to change. Information and Communication Technologies (ICT) are electronic and/or computerized devices and associated human interactive materials that enable the user to employ them for a wide range of teaching and learning processes in addition to personal use. Around the world, educational systems are under increasing pressure to use the new information and communication technologies to teach students the knowledge and skills they need in the 21st Century. With the emerging new technologies, the teaching profession is evolving from an emphasis on teacher-centered, lecture-based instruction to student-centered, interactive learning environments. The present study aims to find out the effectiveness of edu-digital skill among higher secondary students in Coimbatore District. A samples of 100 higher secondary students selected randomly were studied. A questionnaire method of survey was used to find out the effectiveness of edu-digital skill higher secondary students. The data were collected by using questionnaire as an instrument. Primary data were collected by conducting direct structured interview using questionnaire. All the respondents were asked the same questions in the same fashion and they were informed the purpose of study. t-test, Regression and correlation analysis were applied to test the hypotheses. The findings and observations are the result and outcome of the interpretations made during the study of analysis. The result found that edu-digital skill is positively correlated with higher secondary students.

Education, the foremost weapon for social reform, is now under the forces of change. Newly formed branches of knowledge and techniques of education facilitate the physical, mental and emotional development of the learners. Schools have an unavoidable role in acquainting the students with the nature of changing field of education and in making necessary changes in the instructional techniques. In the modern world of technological innovations, all educational institutions are trying to improve their quality in terms of facilities and academic outputs.

Scientific knowledge is exploding every day. Knowledge available to mankind today is emerging in the form of science and technology. There is no limit or end to the accumulation of scientific knowledge. It also satisfies the intellectual thirst of human beings. Science education is a bridge between science and education, using psychology. It links the most powerful concepts of science to the growing minds of children through active experimental pedagogy. Science education plays a prominent role in Indian educational system. It has, as its objective, the aim of providing individual learners a firm grasp of the concepts and processes of science as also to impart the ability to use scientific method of problem-solving. As a result of it, every aspect of human civilization has been influenced to a very great extent.

The present world is the world of science and technology. Science is the most inexhaustible storehouse of knowledge. Continuous advances in scientific and technological research have led to the growth and greater application of science in contemporary society. The purpose of science education is to give individuals a firm grasps of the concepts and processes of science and to develop scientific attitude, scientific reasoning, problem solving ability and scientific temper and to impart them the ability to use the scientific method to other situations in life. Hence science education has been included in school curriculum at all levels. It is however necessary that science teaching be impressive so as to inculcate its values in young minds.

The increasing importance of informatics in day-to-day life has resulted in the emergence of computers in education at the international level. The worldwide recognition gained for the importance of computers has compelled educationists to revise the existing curricula to include informatics components. Even the developing countries have realized that unless they invest heavily in computer education, they will be left behind in the informatics revolution. Computers are being used in education to prepare the children for the informatics future by training them in programming and related skills for work in the informatics industry. They are also being used as educational aids to improve children's skills in academic subjects at all levels of education. Introduction of computers in education has brought out changes in the content and methods of education. However, lack of resources remains one of the main obstacles to the introduction and development of informatics in education in a large way in developing countries.

The most striking innovation in the field of educational technology is the use of computers. Computer is included in the hardware approach of educational technology. It is one of the machines of automation in teaching and learning and is used for presenting individualized instruction.

The main objective of teaching through computer is to provide the needed flexibility for individualizing the educational process. It meets the specific needs of the student in a way in which is almost impossible to do in a face-to face student-teacher relationship.

Computers should have a major role in the teaching-learning process. Computers have become an essential class room tool for the acquisition, analysis, presentation, and communication of data in ways that allow students to become active participants in research and learning. The computers offer students very important resources for learning concepts through simulations, graphics, sound, data manipulation and model building. Computers can improve scientific learning and facilitate communication of ideas and concepts.

There are three roles for computer in education. First, it functions as a tutor for students by presenting material, evaluating responses, and depending on the basis of the evaluation, deciding what to present next. Second, it is a tool that helps students perform calculations, analyze data, keep records, or write papers. Third, it functions as tutee by having told what to do through programming.

A computer program can be designed to create models for experimental purpose. Students, that particularly in higher education, have the benefits of using computer as a computational tool. They learn a programming language and write a program to solve some of their course work problems treating the computer as an aid in much the same way as a slide rule or a set of mathematical tables. Computers are capable of giving almost instant feedback, tirelessly, no matter how many learners 'get it wrong' and it is equally well known that human tutors have limited value when it comes to learners repeatedly getting things wrong.

Review of Literature

Dalacosta et al. (2009) developed and studied the effectiveness of Multimedia application with animated cartoons in teaching science in elementary education.The results of the study provide evidence that the use of animated cartoons significantly increases the young students' knowledge and understanding of specific science concepts, which are normally difficult to comprehend and often cause misconceptions to them.

Jian Hu et al. (2009) investigated the effects of introducing a software program, named the Dental 3D Multimedia System (D3DM), into the education of a group of junior dental students in their preclinical practice. One group received their training program in the traditional way, unassisted by 3D technology. The second group received their training program in the traditional manner, but also used the D3DM to supplement their education. The results showed that the D3DM-assisted group achieved higher scores and also indicated that the usage of 3D multimedia PC software had a positive impact on several aspects of subjects' performance.

Kanmani and Radha (2009) studied the Effectiveness of CAI package in basic electronics teaching. There was a significant difference between the control and the experimental group students in attainment of knowledge level, understanding level, and application level objective in the gain scores. Hence, the experimental group students were better than the control group students in attainment of knowledge level, understanding level, and application level objective in the gain scores. It was inferred from the finding that the experimental treatment is effective to the students.

Korakakis et al. (2009) made a study on the "3D visualization types in multimedia applications for science learning for 8th grade students in

Greece". The aim of the study was to determine whether the use of specific types of visualization (3D illustration, 3D animation, and interactive 3D animation) combined with narration and text, contributes to the learning process in science courses. The results indicated that multimedia applications with interactive 3D animations as well as with 3D animations do in fact increase the interest of students and make the material more appealing to them.

She, Hsiao-Ching and Chen, Yi-Zen (2009) examined how middle school students constructed their understanding of the mitosis and meiosis processes at a molecular level through multimedia learning materials presented in different interaction and sensory modality modes. The dependent variables included subjects' pre-test, post-test, and retention-test scores, showing their understanding of mitosis and meiosis process at molecular level. The results of the study showed that the group which used multimedia learning material has a greater amount of visual attention and consistent with their long term retained learning than the group which did not use the same. This study adds empirical evidence of a direct correlation between the length of eye fixation behavior and the depth of learning. Moreover, it provides insight into the multimedia effect on students' cognitive process through the use of eye fixation behavior evidence.

Anboucarassy (2010) studied the effectiveness of Multimedia in Teaching Biological Science to IX Standard students. The results of the study revealed that experiment group performed better than the control group due to the exposure of multimedia based learning. Thus multimedia helps the students to sustain their interest and also their retention power compared to the traditional method of teaching. The constant use of multimedia will make students understand more and achieve more in their academic achievement. Hence it was concluded that the multimedia approach is considered to be one of the best techniques for biology teaching at IX standard level.

Ponraj and Sivakumar (2010) studied the effectiveness of Computer-Assisted Instruction in Teaching Zoology in Relation to Learners' Personality. The major findings of the study indicated that achievement scores of experimental group students were higher than the control group students after the treatment.

Yusuf, Mudasiru and Afolabi, Adedeji (2010) investigated the effects of computer assisted instruction (CAI) on secondary school students' performance in biology. The findings of the study showed that the performance of students exposed to CAI either individually or cooperatively were better than their counterparts exposed to the conventional classroom instruction. Based on the research findings recommendations were made on the need to develop relevant CAI packages for teaching biology in Nigerian secondary schools.

Objectives

1. To know the edu-digital skill among higher secondary students in Coimbatore district.
2. To find out the effectiveness of Multimedia Programme in teaching among higher secondary students.

Methodology

Research may be termed as a systemic inquiry of verified knowledge; it is an organized deliberate effort to collect information, to analyze it, to put it together and finally to evaluate it. This research paper on methodology describes elaborately, the sample that was chosen, research design, objectives of the study, data collection, statistical techniques used for data and analysis.

Population

Population selected for this study was 100 higher secondary students in a selected school at Coimbatore District.

Attitude Scale towards Multimedia Programme

The attitude scale was used to measure the level of attitude towards Multimedia programme. The scale was constructed and validated by the investigator.

The attitude scale towards multimedia programme, consisting of 40 items, was designed by the investigator and was given to experienced teachers who were handling Computer Science in higher secondary schools, professors of Computer Science and Education and Educational psychologists. On the basis of the suggestions of above experts, some items were restructured and some were eliminated. Finally 25 items were selected for this test. The scale for measuring the higher secondary student's attitude towards multimedia programme in the study is of the Likert type. This scale has as many as 25 statements of which 20 are favourable towards multimedia programme and the remaining are unfavourable towards it.

Scoring

In the Likert type of scale, against each statement, five alternatives namely "Strongly agree", "Agree", "Undecided", "Disagree", and "Strongly disagree" are given. The subjects have to indicate their choice by putting a tick-mark (") under one of the five columns against each statement.

For favourable statement weightage of 4,3,2,1 and 0 were given from strongly agree to strongly disagree in that order. For unfavourable statements the scoring was reversed. Thus the strongly agree response will get 0 and the strongly disagree response will get 4. Here the weightage of 0,1,2,3 and 4 were given from strongly agree to the strongly disagree in that order.

Thus the score value lies between 0-100. The content validity of the tool was established based on the opinion given by the experts. The reliability of the tool was established by Split-Half method. It was found to be 0.83 which was significant.

Data Collection

Primary data, required for the present research work were collected by conducting direct interviews using questionnaire. All the respondents were given sufficient information about the Project work. These respondents were provided with the same questionnaires. They were also informed that they have to answer in the same fashion.

Hypothesis

- There is no significant difference between the pre and post-test mean scores of experimental group students in their attitude towards multimedia programme.

Administration of retention test

The Attitude Scale towards Multimedia Programme was constructed and validated by the investigator and was administered to the subjects of the experimental group. The pre test scores on attitude towards multimedia programme were collected. Thus pretestand post test scores on attitude towards multimedia programme were computed for analysis.

Analysis and Interpretation

To find out the significance of the difference between the pre and posttest mean scores of experimental group students in their attitude towards multimedia programme the 't' test was used.

Table 1

Distribution of 't' value between the pre and posttest mean scores of experimental group students in their attitude towards multimedia programme

Group	N	Mean	S.D	't' value	Level of Significant
Pre test	50	42.08	10.42	24.47	p<0.05
Post test	50	93.58	2.57		

There is no significant difference between the pre and posttest mean scores of experimental group students in their attitude towards multimedia programme.

The obtained 't' value is statistically significant since it is greater than the table 't' value 1.96 at 0.05 level of significance. Hence the null hypothesis is rejected. It shows that there is significant difference between the pre and post test mean scores of experimental group students in their attitude towards multimedia programme. It is therefore concluded that the experimental group students show more favourable attitude towards multimedia programme in the post test than the pre test.

Table 2

Showing the Stepwise regression analysis predicting factors influencing effectiveness of edu-digital skill among higher secondary students and demographic variables

Sl.No	Step/Source	Unstandardized Coefficients Beta	Std. Error Beta Beta	Standardized Coefficients	Step t	P
1.	Gender	1.144	0.156	0.242	7.324	0.01
2.	Father education	1.254	0.359	0.163	3.495	0.01
3.	Mother education	2.615	0.462	0.361	5.661	0.01
4.	Monthly Income	2.175	0.402	0.280	5.410	0.01
5.	Father Occupation	1.022	0.513	0.137	1.992	0.01

*P<0.01

Five variables viz Gender, Father Education, Mother Education, Monthly income and Father Occupation have significantly contributed for predicting the factors influencing effectiveness of edu-digital skill among higher secondary. The first variable Gender seems to be 7.324, Father Education seems to be 3.495, Mother education seems to be 5.661, Monthly income seems to be 5.410 and Father Occupation seems to be 1.992. The predictive value of these variables separately is 0.01.

Table 3

Showing the correlation between the effectiveness of edu-digital skill among higher secondary students and demographic variables

Factors	Effectiveness of edu-digital skill among higher secondary students
Gender	0.920**
Father education	0.849**
Mother education	0.914**
Monthly Income	0.880**
Father Occupation	0.855**

* Significant at 0.01 level

Effectiveness of edu-digital skill among higher secondary students is positively and significantly related to Gender (0.920), Father education (0.849), Mother education (0.914), Monthly income (0.880) and Father occupation (0.855). So, the direct relationship between the effectiveness of edu-digital skill among higher secondary students and selected demographic variables.

Conclusion

Computer and multimedia technology for education offers a number of benefits. They allow the teacher to structure and present the information with varying special effects to the students. They can also be used for the storage of audio-visual information of various types. Multimedia programmes provide a lot of benefits. The benefits for learners include flexibility of scheduled instruction at a location convenient to learners, reduced student time, assured progress in skill development, increased achievement and increased retention and continuous report to the learners of progress and accomplishments, specified performance criteria, good response and feedback.

The application of multimedia programme would definitely create a good learning environment in classroom, sustaining attention and motivating the students to learn effectively. The application of multimedia may create a congenial learning climate in schools and can bring real life situations.

The investigator has chosen the topic for the present study in order to address the problem faced by teachers, teaching science, to foster involvement in new teaching approaches, to get a feeling of satisfaction through learning in the classroom, to create joyful learning environment and to stimulate active information processing for effective learning, in a vast country like India, enormous work is now being done in the field of education, but it is still not possible to equip each and every school with all the facilities for teaching science. Secondary schools need high quality teaching aids. Multimedia, as a teaching aid, is very much effective with colour, sound and graphics, which are found in the audio, video movie media. Any diagram can be explained in detail with 3D effects, which helps the students understand clearly. The students can get a live vision of life's aspects and scientific factors. Multimedia includes use of computer.

The present study has found out that the multimedia programme is very effective in higher secondary level. As the present teaching-learning process in higher secondary classes is very rigid, time bound and outmoded, it was proposed to use multimedia programme.

As multimedia programme develops a favourable attitude towards multimedia programme, motivates the students to involve in the process of learning, attracts students' attention in learning, accelerates the students' understanding of concepts of subjects, increases the retention power and that it is highly suitable for all categories of students ranging from low to high achievers, it is suggested that this multimedia programme be widely adopted and implemented in educational institutions as computer laboratory facilities are available in all the schools and colleges to enable the learners to learn the subjects of their choice according to their own pace and ability. Learning through multimedia programme is very easy, understandable and comfortable to all categories of students for all types of subjects.

References

1. Anboucarassy, B. (2010). Effectiveness of Multimedia in Teaching Biological Science to IX Standard students. EDUTRACKS, 9(5): 37-38.
2. Dalacosta, K., Kamariotaki-Paparrigopoulou, M., Palyvos, J.A., & Spyrellis, N. (2009). Multimedia application with animated cartoons for teaching science in elementary education. Computers & Education, 52(4): 741-748. Retrieved March 20, 2010 http://www.linkinghub.elsevier.com/retrieve/pii/S0360131508001905
3. Jian Hu, Hao Yu, Jun Shao, Zhiyong Li, Jiawei Wang & Yining Wang (2009). Effects of dental 3D multimedia system on the performance

of junior dental students in preclinical practice: a report from China. Advances in Health Sciences Education, 14(1): 123–133.

4. Kanmani, M., & Radha, M. (2009). "Effectiveness of CAI package in basic electronics teaching", Journal of All India Association for Educational Research, 21(1): 47-50.
5. Korakakis, G., Pavlatou, E.A., Palyvos, J. A., & Spyrellis N. (2009). 3D visualization types in multimedia applications for science learning: A case study for 8th grade students in Greece. Computers & Education, 52(2): 390-401. Retrieved March 21, 2010 http:// portal.acm.org/citation.cfm?id=1480558
6. Ponraj, P., & Sivakumar, R. (2010). Computer-Assisted Instruction in Zoology in Relation to Learners' Personality. EDUTRACKS, 9(6): 34-37.

15

Students Attitude Towards Audio-visual Aids used by the Teachers

Introduction

Audio Visual aids or Graphic aids are the form of visuals that are represented on plane surface. The subject matter areas that are represented in Audio Visual aids or Graphic aids are in an abridged and easily understandable form. They convey meaning mainly through relatively conventionalized symbols that are nearer to reality perceptually than verbal symbols. They secure the attention of the pupils by their attractive format and simplicity of layout. They convey the expected message by combination of visual and pictorial message made meaningful by suitable captions. Pictures and words blended in harmony deliver the required information. The idea conveyed by any graphic aid should be a single concept. The layout and words should not be complicated so as to puzzle the viewer and make him lose interest in the same. The statement "one good visual which can secure and maintain attention and educate the viewer in the desired area is worth a thousand words" is quite correct. Graphics could be truly considered as the shorthand language of the idea presented. The criteria for good graphics are that they should be simple, bold, legible, brief and have adequate margins. Graphics are only two-dimensional and should be carefully planned to offset the limitation. An Audio Visual aids or a graphic aid by eliminating non–essentials and by using bold symbolic representations with attractive portrayal should be able to create interest and secure the attention of the pupils. Since the message to be conveyed pertains to a single concept and hence brief, the viewer will not get perplexed on being exposed to the visual but will try to read and understand what is implied (visual and words).Audio Visual aids or a graphic aids could easily be prepared by and teacher using simple materials that are easily available and stored for future use. Making graphics should form an integral part of the teacher's preparation for teaching. Almost any material involving illustrations is basically graphic in nature. There can be an infinite variety of graphic materials. It is difficult to give a rigid list of these materials. The present study aims to find out the students attitude towards audio-visual aids used by the teachers in Coimbatore district. A samples of 100 respondents selected randomly were studied. An interview schedule method of survey was used to find out the attitude towards audio-visual aids. Primary data were collected by using a structured interview scheduled. All the respondents were asked the same questions in the same fashion and they were informed the purpose of study. ANOVA, t-test and regression analysis were applied to test the hypotheses. The data collected through questionnaires have been tabulated. The findings and observations are the result and outcome of the interpretations made during the study of analysis.

Graphs, Diagram, Posters, Maps, Comics, Cartoons, Charts, Globes, Display Board, Peg Boards, Hook and loop board, felt board, magnetic board, marker board, chalk board, bulletin board, models, Epidiascope, slight projector, overhead projector (OHP), fields trips, excursion, exhibition, museums, radio, Television, Tape recorder, Video Caste Record VCR and Computers. By using audio visual materials in accessible process, materials givens objects changes in time, speed and space could easily be brought to the class. Audio visual aids can helps to imaginative teachers to solve the communication problems. It also helps to extend human experience. It can provide effective substitutes for direct contact of students with environment-social and physical. It also adds an expected change in attitude and behaviour of the students. It can provide integrated experiences varying from abstract to concrete. It helps in to secure and retain to attention as well as develop the communication skills. It could be used to motivate and stimulate interest of students to gain further knowledge. Lastly, in a conventional teaching method teacher is the centre of attention and the primary sources of information.

An attitude is a mental state of readiness exerting directive or dynamic influence upon individual's response to all objects and situations with which it is related. Therefore if we can have some judgement about the attitude of an individual towards a specific thing or activity then we can have a fair idea as to whether the individual can be persuaded to participate in a particular thing or activity and whether he shall adopt it with interest and sincerity or not.

The attitude is the degree of positive or negative effect associated with some psychological objects namely institution, ideal, symbol, phrase, slogan, job or idea towards which people can differ with respect to positive or negative effect (Thurstone, 1946). The attitude is a dispositional readiness to respond to certain situations, persons, objects in a consistent manner which has been learnt and has become one's typical mode of response (Free Mann, 1950). According to Guild (1950) attitude is a tendency of individual to favour or not to favour some type of situation. The attitude may be considered as motivational perceptual states, which direct perceptions and predispose a person to act in accordance with perceptions (Allport, 1955). The attitudes are learnt pre-dispositions to respond positively to certain objects, situations, institutions, concepts or other persons (Aiken, 1979).

Review of Literature

Glee Harrah Cady and Pat Mc Gregor (2005) describe that "Internet is a network of network and the internet mostly connects network of computers".

Barry (2006) studied the relationship between students perceptions of their science class room learning environment and attitude to four different scores of scientific information experiments, books, promote positive attitude towards experiment as a source of information, while less favorable environment promoted more positive attitude to the more authoritarian sources of information.

Schafer (2007) compared third and fourth grade students using ESS units with students using laid low science serious on classification skills, science achievements and science attitudes. No achievement or classification skill different were noted but ESS students had more favorable attitudes.

Williams (2008), "Attitude of high school pupils towards general science and its relationship with achievement and its subjects". In her study it is found to examine if there are any differences among the different groups of students such as boys and girls. Rural school pupil and urban school pupils in respect of their achievement in science, attitude towards science and attitude forwards science education.

Martis Anandi (2009) developed the test on scientific attitudes (TOSA), taking the point of view that attitudes must be inferred from the behavior of students. They developed a multiple – choice format test. The developed behavioral definitions of eight attitudes: (1) critical mindedness, (2) suspended judgment (3) Respect for evidence (4) Honesty, (5) Objectivity, (6) Willingness to change opinions, (7) Open – mindedness and (8) Questioning attitude. The behavioral definitions to these eight attitudes were used to develop items.

Mohanty Ajay Kumar (2010) investigated attitudes towards education, critical thinking ability and specific effective behavious of (1) Students who had studied, the BSCS environmental models "Investing your Environment" (IYE), (2) Those students using one of BSCS biological science version and (3) Those studying models of Biology. He found that the ability of students who had experienced BSCS Biological science was significantly increased but no other differences were found among the students on any of the other variables.

Objectives

1. The present study attempts to investigate the attitude towards Audio-visual aids used by the teachers.

Methodology

Methodology is an important aspect of any research work. There are different methods followed at various stages of any investigation. The details of methods followed in this study such as selection of tools, sample frame, collection of data, and analysis of data are involved in this research paper. The study has been designed with the students attitude towards Audio-visual aids used by the teachers achievement. The major aim of the present study is to determine the students Audio-visual aids used by the teacher.

Method of data collection

The investigator personally distributed the questionnaires to each member of the randomly selected sample. They were requested to answer the items in the booklet as per the instructions provided at the beginning of each questionnaire. Confidentiality of response was assured. The questionnaires were collected by the investigator from the employees. The responses were scored as per the scoring key of the respective questionnaire. Then the results were tabulated, analysed and discussed.

Sample

A sample is a finite number of observations (or) cases in a particular universe of which it is a pat (Good 1952). The investigator prepared a representative random sample of students studying VIII & IX standard in different schools at Coimbatore District. A sample of 100 students was finally selected

Hypothesis

2. Students have favourable attitude towards use of Audio Visual Aids in Coimbatore district school.

Nature of the Tool

The inventory contained general instruction for the students and information about bio data. In addition to that the specific instruction ware given to on the first page of the inventory. Space for collecting personal data like students name type of school, locality of the school, class, gender, community, religion, group, medium of instruction, birth order of the child and parental literacy.

Data Processing

The collected data were analysed using appropriate statistical techniques. The descriptive statistics such as mean and S.D, t-ratio were computed. In order to study the functional dependencies to indicate the likelihood of causal relationships between the variables, inferential statistical techniques of ANOVA and Percentage analysis were computed.

Analysis and Interpretation

Table 1: Showing Mean, SD and t-test for respondent about students attitude towards audio visual aids used by the teachers on the basis of type of the school.

Types of the school	N	Mean	SD	t-value	LS
Government	62	70.48	6.50	2.78	0.01
Private	38	73.30	10.33		

Hypothesis 1: Students do not differ in their students attitude towards audio visual aids used by the teachers on the basis of types of the school.

The calculated t-value (2.78), which is significant at 0.01 level, confirms that there is a significant difference in student audio visual aids on the basis of type of the school. Hence the stated hypothesis is rejected. So government students have high level of audio visual aids than private school students.

Table 2: Showing Mean, SD and t-test for respondent about students attitude towards audio visual aids used by the teachers on the basis of locality of the school.

Locality of the school	N	Mean	SD	t-value	LS
Urban	74	72.24	8.11	1.07	NS
Rural	26	71.14	9.19		

Hypothesis 2: Students do not differ in their students attitude towards audio visual aids used by the teachers on the basis of locality of the school.

The calculated t-value (1.07), which is not significant at 0.05 level, confirms that there is no significant difference in their audio visual aids on the basis of locality of the school. Hence the stated hypothesis is accepted.

Table 3: Showing Mean, SD and t-test for respondent about students attitude towards audio visual aids used by the teachers on the basis of Gender.

Gender	N	Mean	SD	t-value	LS
Male	74	70.97	7.41	1.85	NS
Female	26	72.90	9.89		

Hypothesis 3: Students do not differ in their students attitude towards audio visual aids used by the teachers on the basis of gender.

The calculated t-value (1.85), which is not significant at 0.05 level, confirms that there is no significant difference in their audio visual aids on the basis of gender. Hence the stated hypothesis is accepted.

Table 4: Showing Mean, SD and t-test for respondent about students attitude towards audio visual aids used by the teachers on the basis of group.

Group	N	Mean	SD	t-value	LS
Arts	56	69.19	5.37	5.58	0.01
Science	44	74.58	10.37		

Hypothesis 4: Students do not differ in their attitude towards audio visual aids used by the teachers on the basis of group.

The calculated t-value (5.58), which is significant at 0.01 level, confirms that there is a significant difference in student audio visual aids on the basis of group. Hence the stated hypothesis is rejected. So science students have high level of audio visual aids than art students.

Table 5: Showing Mean, SD and F-ratio for students attitude towards audio visual aids used by the teachers on the basis of medium of instruction.

Medium of instruction	N	Mean	SD	F-ratio	LS
Hindi	50	70.20	9.64		
English	30	71.75	4.19	6.49	0.01
Kannada	20	75.00	11.60		
Total	100	71.78	8.58		

Hypothesis 5: Students do not differ in their attitude towards audio visual aids used by the teachers on the basis of medium of instruction.

The calculated F-ratio (6.49), which is not significant at 0.05 level, confirms that there is a significant difference in students attitude of audio visual aids on the basis of medium of instruction. Hence the stated hypothesis is rejected.

Table 6: Regression for student demographic characters and their attitude towards audio visual aids used by the teachers

Model Summary

Model	R	R Square	Adjusted Square	R Std. Error of the Estimate
1	.436[a]	.190	.159	7.87

a. Predictors: (Constant)

ANOVA[b]

Model	Sum of Squares	df	Mean Square	F	Sig.
Regression	.4189.756	11	380.887	6.155	.000[a]
Residual	17821.724	88	61.881		
Total	22011.480	99			

a. Predictors: (Constant)

b. Dependent variable

Coefficients[a]

Model	Unstandardized Coefficients		Standardized Coefficients	t	Sig.
	B	Std. Error	Beta		
Name of the school	58.979	4.376		13.477	.000
Type of the school	2.387	1.116	.139	2.139	.033**
Locality of the school	-1.000	1.005	-.058	-.995	.320
Class	-.500	1.046	-.028	-.478	.633
Gender	1.989	1.052	.115	1.891	.060
Community	-1.365	.422	-.190	-3.233	.001**
Religion	.757	.627	.068	1.208	.228
Groups	5.255	.947	.306	5.548	.000**
Medium of instruction	2.183	.649	.191	3.365	.001**
Birth order of the child	-9.11	1.032	-.001	-.009	.993
Parental literacy (Father)	-.143	1.003	-.008	-.143	.887
Parental literacy (Mother)	-.585	.955	-.033	-.612	.541

a. Dependent Variable: Attitude towards Audi visual aids

** Significant at 0.01 level

According to the regression result it is known that the demographic variables are influenced nearly 19 per cent to measure their attitude towards audio visual aids. This is proved by the obtained r square value (0.19).

Further the calculated F-value (6.15) also significant at 0.01 level. It indicates that there is a significant influence between students demographic characters and their attitude towards audio visual aids.

Also from the obtained t- values the demographic variables such as type of school, community, group studied and medium of instructions the students studied are significant at 0.01 level. So it is concluded that there is a significant difference regarding attitude towards audio visual aids on the basis of these variables.

Conclusion

Audio Visual aids or graphic aids are the form of visuals that are represented on plane surface. The subject – matter areas that are represented in Audio Visual aids or graphic aids are in an abridged and easily understandable form. They convey meaning mainly through relatively conventionalized symbols that are nearer to reality perceptually than verbal symbols. They secure the attention of the pupils by their attractive format and simplicity of layout. They convey the expected message by combination of visual and pictorial message made meaningful by suitable captions. Pictures and words blended in harmony deliver the required information. The idea conveyed by any graphic aid should be a single concept. The layout and words should not be complicated so as to puzzle the viewer and make him lose interest in the same. The statement "one good visual which can secure and maintain attention and educate the viewer in the desired area is worth a thousand words" is quite correct. Graphics could be truly considered as the shorthand language of the idea presented. The criteria for good graphics are that they should be simple, bold, legible, brief and have adequate margins.

Findings of the study

1. Based on the results that students do not differ in their audio visual aids on the basis of types of the school
2. From the calculation that students do not differ in their audio visual aids on the basis of locality of the school
3. Based on the results that students do not differ in their audio visual aids on the basis of gender
4. Based on the results that students do not differ in their audio visual aids on the basis of group
5. From the analysis that students do not differ in their audio visual aids on the basis of medium of instruction

Discussion

Audio visual aids a process of inward journey to unravel the hidden potentialities of a being. It helps an individual to develop ones personality. A systematic approach of Audio visual aids helps an individual to see the all-around development at physical, mental, intellectual and emotional level. The practice of use of audio visual aids makes an individual perfect. It removes the unwanted elements in the mind of the learner. It improves concentration and brings mental stability. Audio visual aids arean essential tool for students to achieve higher score in their studies as if improves concentration, memory and skills. The present study clearly indicates and recommends the students to use of audio visual aids as to develop positive attitude towards everything in their life which helps to excel themselves in their studies. The entire study concluded reveals that the use of audio visual aids has high achievement and expressed more favourable attitude.

Educational Implications

Audio-visual aids are very important and useful aids for teaching. As well as it creates high interest among the students to learn the subjects. So, the department of education shall take steps to implement the latest audio-visual aids to all the school and colleges for teaching purpose.

For self-learning, these types of aids are very helpful to the students. Also students are very much interested in using latest technologies such as computers and internet. In internet lot of facilities are there to learn new information with visual appearance. From that students are also get more interest to use that.

In the case of teaching, in older days teachers follow interactive methods and oral demonstration. But these are not creating much interest. In order to create interest and attention audio-visual aids are highly useful. So, the concerned educational institution tries to provide these facilities. So that teachers and students get benefited.

Suggestions

The following suggestions are arrived from the research findings. Research found that use of audio visual aids will contribute more in student's achievement. Also the result reveals that use of audio visual aids increases the memory power, concentration. Further it sharpens the intelligence. Apart from that it reduces misconception in learning. Further due to use of audio visual aids the sensory expression would be more exercised. So, the present research suggested that in all schools and colleges, the students advised to use of audio visual aids compulsory. The education department forms a rule for that and advises the educational institutions make a step to establish separate infrastructure for this one. Also the Government take a step to use audio visual aids effectively students in their academic. This will definitely help the students to be a good learner imbibing the concepts.

Conclusion

The present study attempted to identify the student's attitude towards audio-visual aids used by the teachers. For that the researcher framed some objectives. On the basis of objectives, a questionnaire is framed. After framing the questionnaire, these are circulated to the selected samples. 100 samples were selected randomly. The responses were collected and coded using computerised. To test the hypotheses and characteristics of the data, some standard statistical tools were used. The statistical tools such as t-test, F-ratio and correlation were used. From the analysis the result concluded that the students have positive attitude towards audio-visual aids used by the teachers.

References

1. Glee Harrah CadyandPat Mc Gregor (2005) "Internet is a network of network and the internet mostly connects network of computers". Journal of research in science teaching.
2. Barry (2006) "Relationship between students perceptions of their science class room learning environment and attitude", Journal of Educational Research.
3. Schafer (2007) vargo students science attitudes and self-concept in science as a function of rose specific pupil/teacher interpersonal compatibility", San Francisco, California, National association for research in science teaching.
4. Williams (2008), "Attitude of high school pupils towards general science and its relationship with achievement and its subjects". Journal Community and Guidance.
5. Martis Anandi (2009), in test on scientific attitudes (TOSA), taking the point of view that attitudes must be inferred from the behavior of students, Journal of All India Association for Educational Research, Vol.17, Nos. 1 & 2, March & June.
6. Mohanty Ajay Kumar (2010), Attitudes towards education, critical thinking ability and specific effective behavious, Journal of all India Association for Educational Research, Vol.14, Nos.3 & 4.

16

Transitive Cloud Computing for Teaching-learning Process

Introduction

This paper is an introduction to the terms, characteristics and services associated with internet-based computing, commonly referred to as cloud computing. The primary business service models being deployed, such as software, platform and infrastructure as a service - and common deployment models employed by service providers and users to use and maintain the cloud services, such as private, public, community, and hybrid clouds are discussed. Cloud computing is not something that suddenly appeared overnight: in some form it may trace back into our time when computer system remotely shared computing resources and applications. Some of the notable challenges associated with Cloud computing is that it not delivers more services in the cloud; it also can provide opportunities, if resolved with due care and attention in the planning. Lack of standard-clouds have documented inter faces; however, no standards are associated with these, and thus it is unlikely that most clouds will be interoperable. The open grid forum is developing an open Cloud computing interface to resolve this issue and the open cloud consortium is working on Cloud computing standards and practices. An important function of the Cloud is that it automatically saves content, making it impossible to lose or delete any valuable material. This means that even if a computer crashes, all documents and content will remain safe and accessible in the cloud. Any data stored in the Cloud can easily be accessed from almost any device including mobile devices such as phones or tablets. With the availability of content online, it is no longer necessary for teachers to spend time and resources printing or copying lengthy documents or lesson plans. Now, students are able to access homework assignments, lesson notes, and other materials through online.

The term "cloud" as used in this white paper, appears to have its origin in network diagrams that represented the internet, or various part of it, as schematic clouds. "Cloud computing" was coined when applications and services were moved into the internet "Cloud". Cloud computing is not something that suddenly that appeared overnight: in some form it may be traced back into our time when computer system remotely shared computing resources and applications. Cloud computing refers to many different types of services and applications being delivered in the internet cloud and the fact that in many cases the device used to access these services and applications do not require any special applications.

How Cloud Computing is used in Education?

Cloud computing take education to the next level. There is no surprise that cloud computing education is a necessary tool for many companies and even schools. In this type of calculation, this should not be confused with others such as grid computing, utility computing or autonomic computing. Even if you are not completely familiar with cloud computing, you are certainly in touch with it on a regular basis, such as in use in computer applications like Skype. The interesting part about cloud computing is that entire systems can be set on a rental basis. Rather than more commonly owned tools to be engaged, it is true that cloud computation is another form of resource where teaching can take place. Most people use it to teach through social networking sites such as Face book and MySpace, email systems like Hotmail, gmail etc...

Cloud Computing is an umbrella term used to describe Cloud Computing services that are hosted on a network (typically the internet) and used by the PCs (or other devices) without mentioning specific servers or systems for teaching.

Characteristics of Cloud Computing

Shared infrastructure – uses a virtualized software model which enables the sharing of physical services, storage and networking capabilities. The cloud infrastructure regardless of deployment model seeks to make the most of the available infrastructure across a number of users.

Dynamic provisioning – It allows for the provision of service based on current demand requirements. This is done automatically using software automations enabling the expansions and contraction of service capability as needed. This dynamic needs to be done while maintaining the high level of reliability and security.

Network access – needs to be accessed across the internet from a broad range of devices such as PCs, laptops and mobile devices, using standard based APIs (For e.g., ones is based on http). Deployments of services in the cloud include everything from business applications to the latest applications on the newest smart phones.

Managed Metering – uses metering for managing and optimizing the services and to provide reporting and billing information. In this way consumers are billed for services according to how much they actually use during the billing period.

SERVICE MODELS

Software as a service (SaaS) - consumers purchase the ability to access and use an application or service that is posted in the cloud.

Platform as a service (PaaS) - consumers purchase access to the platforms, enabling them to deploy their own software and applications in the cloud.

Infrastructure as a services(IaaS) - consumers control and manage their systems in terms of the operating system, applications, storage, and network connectivity, but do not themselves control the cloud infrastructure.

Deployment Models

Deploying Cloud computing can differ depending on requirements, and the following four development models have been identified:

Private cloud-the cloud infrastructure has been deployed, and is maintained and operated for a specific organization. The operation may be in-house or with the third party on the premises.

Community cloud- the cloud infrastructure is shared among the number of organizations with similar interest and requirements.

Public cloud- the cloud infrastructure is available to the public on the commercial basis by a cloud service provider.

Hybrid cloud- the cloud infrastructure consists of a number of clouds of any type, but the clouds have the ability through their interfaces to allow their data and/or applications to be moved from one cloud to another.

Advantages

1. **Back Up:** An important function of the Cloud is that it automatically saves content, making it impossible to lose or delete any valuable material. This means that even if a computer crashes, all documents and content will remain safe, saved, and accessible in the cloud.
2. **Storage:** The Cloud allows its users to store almost all types of content and data including music, documents, eBooks, applications, photos, and much more.
3. **Accessibility:** Any data stored in the Cloud can easily be accessed from almost any device including mobile devices such as phones or tablets.
4. **Collaboration:** Because the Cloud allows multiple users to work on and edit documents at the same time, it enables effortless sharing and transmission of ideas. With this feature, group projects and or collaborative lesson plans can be optimized for both teachers and students.
5. **Resource and Time Conscious:** With the availability of content online, it is no longer necessary for teachers to spend time and resources printing or copying lengthy documents or lesson plans. Now, students are able to access homework assignments, lesson notes, and other study materials online.
6. **Assignments:** I love the Cloud to allow teachers to post assignments online. Students are able to access these assignments, complete them, and save them in a folder to be reviewed later.

Benefits

1. Cost savings
2. Scalability or flexibility
3. Reliability
4. Maintenance
5. Mobile accessible

Challenges

Security and privacy - perhaps two of the more "hot button" issues surrounding Cloud computing relate to storing and securing data, and monitoring the use of the cloud by the service providers. These issues are generally attributed to slowing the deployment of cloud services.

Lack of standards - Clouds have documented inter faces; however, no standards are associated with these, and thus it is unlikely that most clouds will be interoperable. The open grid forum is developing an open Cloud computing interface to resolve this issue and the open cloud consortium is working on Cloud computing standards and practices. The findings of these groups will need to mature, but it is not known whether they will address the needs of the people deploying the services and the specific interfaces these services need.

Continuously evolving - user requirements are continuously evolving, as are the requirements for interfaces, networking and storage. This means that a "cloud," especially a public one, does not remain static and is also continuously evolving.

Conclusion

As cloud computing is achieving increased popularity, concerns are being voiced about the security issues introduced through adoption of this new model· The effectiveness and efficiency of traditional protection mechanisms are being reconsidered as the characteristics of this innovative deployment model can differ widely from those of traditional architectures. Any data stored in the Cloud can easily be accessed from almost any device including mobile devices such as phones or tablets. With the availability of content online, it is no longer necessary for teachers to spend time and resources printing or copying lengthy documents or lesson plans. Now, students are able to access homework assignments, lesson notes, and other materials through online.

References

1. Dan Sullivan (2014-01-14). "Cost of the Cloud: A Developer's Guide to Reducing Your AWS Bill". PragTech Publishing. Retrieved 2014-11-27.
2. "Cloud Computing: Clash of the clouds". The Economist. 2009-10-15. Retrieved 2009-11-03
3. Semple, Bryan. (2011-07-14) "Five Capacity Management Challenges for Private Clouds," Cloud Computing Journal.
4. Cloud Computing Grows Up: Benefits Exceed Expectations According to Report. Press Release, May 21, 2013.
5. Burns, Paul (2012-01-02). "Cloud Computing in 2012: What's Already Happening". Neovise.

17

Integrating ICT in Education: Examining Needs, Barriers and Recommendations

Introduction

Information Communication Technologies are the power that has changed many aspects of the lives. The education is a socially oriented activity. It plays vital role in building the society. The quality education traditionally is associated with strong teachers having high degrees. Using ICTs in education it moved to more student –centered learning As world is moving rapidly towards digital information, the role of ICTs in education becoming more and more important and this importance will continue to grow and develop in 21st century. This paper highlights various impacts of ICT on contemporary education and also discusses the major barriers faced in the process of integration. The paper argues the role of ICT in transforming teacher-centered learning to competency based learning. It also explores some recommendations to overcome those barriers.

Information and Communication Technologies (ICT) that are becoming increasingly pervasive in societies around the world are also reaching schools. With numerous global advancements in ICT it is essential that educators have a thorough working knowledge of these media and their influence on the performance and engagement of their students. There is no firm agreement on the definition of ICT, as these technologies evolve almost daily. The 21st Century Society is an entrepreneurial Society- A century of knowledge and century of mind. Knowledge explosion, communication revolution, technology advancement, application of science to all aspects of life and above all rising aspirations of the society are the hallmarks of this century.

Use of Ict in Teaching Learning

Teaching at School, mostly, concentrates on giving information which is not the sole objective of Teaching. Along with giving information, the other objectives are:

1. Developing understanding and application of the concepts
2. Development of reasoning power and decision making ability
3. Improving comprehension, speed and vocabulary
4. Developing self-concept and study habits
5. Developing proper study habits
6. Developing tolerance, risk taking capacity, scientific temper, etc.

In India with the present infrastructure, class size, availability of teachers, quality of teachers, training of teachers, etc., it is difficult to realize all the objectives. As the objectives are multi-dimensional in nature, multiple methods should be used in an integrated fashion in teaching learning. At present ICT may be of some use. It is a well-known fact that not a single teacher is capable of giving up to date and complete information in his own subject. The ICT can fill this gap because it can provide access to different sources of information.

Use of Ict in Diagnostic Testing &Remedial Teaching

Computer Based Diagnostic Tests will help the teachers as well as students in identifying the gray area of each and every student. This can be put on the website of the school and the student can access to it from home also. The student can learn the topic and can take the test to find exactly what he has not understood. The teacher cannot do this manually. The student progress can be monitored and his performance can be improved. This will develop confidence in students and may change their attitude towards the subject. It may also help in reducing the suicidal tendency among students. Students may start enjoying learning. The Remedial Teaching can be done by the teacher if some common mistakes are identified. It may not be feasible to organize remedial programme for individual students.

Use of Ict in Evaluation

At present the paper pencil tests are conducted for evaluating the academic performance of students. The content coverage is poor and students cannot use them on their own. These tests are evaluated by the teachers and they may not give feedback immediately to each and every student. It may be due to this that students are unable to know their weakness and do not make any attempt to improve upon them. The ICT can be made use in the evaluation. The test can be used by individual student to evaluate his learning. The student can instantaneously get the feedback about the status of his understanding. It goes a long way in improving the learning and teacher has no role to play in it. Such tests can be uploaded on the website for wider use. The students from other institutes can also make use of it. Not only the students even the teachers can also use it to assess their own understanding of the subject.

Use of Ict in Psychological Testing

The psychological testing is laborious and involves money and time. This is the age of digital technology. It can be used to digitalize all the psychological tests including the scoring and evaluation. The same may be available on the website and students and teachers can use them whenever required. Even student can use it individually and can share the result with the teacher who can help the student to improve his academic performance. The digitalized psychological tests will be easy to use and economical also.

Use of Ict in Developing Virtual Laboratory

If the Virtual Laboratory is developed, it can provide lots of freedom to students. The students can manipulate any attribute or variable related to the experiment and can see how it affects the outcome. The Virtual Laboratory can be developed using ICT. It may be made available at the door step of each and every student by uploading it on the Website.

Use of Ict in Online Tutoring

Online tutoring makes the students stay at their home. They logs in to their tutor through the use of Internet and software. It will make the academic life of many students easy. This is also how the knowledge power available in India can be made use of other countries.

Use of Ict in Developing Instructional Material

There are many teachers who are well known for their specialties in the subject. Their lectures should be digitalized and made available to all the users. It will enhance the quality of instruction in the classrooms. The teacher can use them in the classrooms and can organize discussion after it wherein the new points can be added both by the teacher as well as students. It will make the teaching effective, participatory and enjoyable.

Barriers of Integration of ICT in Education

Teacher Level Barriers

1. Several researchers indicate that one barrier that prevents teachers from using ICT in their teaching is lack of confidence. Beggs (2000) asserted the teachers "fear of failure" caused a lack of confidence.
2. The second teacher level barrier is the lack of knowledge and skills to use computers in their teaching process.
3. Resistance to change and negative attitudes towards ICT is one of the important teacher related barriers.

School Level Barriers

1. Lack of time for teachers in many aspects of their work as it affects their ability to complete tasks, with some of the teachers specifically stating which aspects of ICT require more time.
2. There are not enough training opportunities for teachers in the use of ICT's in a classroom environment. Lack of opportunities for professional development obstructed them from integrating technology in certain subjects such as science and maths.
3. Lack of access to resources in schools discourages teachers from integrating new technologies into education.
4. Lack of Technical support was found to be a major barrier for teachers in the integration of ICT in education.

Government commitment to the use of ICT in schools in india

India has one of the lowest "pupils to computers ratio" in the world. Much investment is required for the provision of dedicated ICT rooms where pupils would gain 'hands on' experience of using Excel, Word, PowerPoint, Video conference, Internet etc. The poor investment by the government to the schools in integrating the ICT is seen in India.

Barriers in the Process of Preparing the Teachers

In the majority of teacher education programme offered in India, the syllabi exhibit less weight to practical than theoretical aspects. Since the nature of ICT subjects is more practical and application-oriented, there needs to be more practical than theoretical input in our curriculum related to teacher education.

Recommendations in the integrating the ICT in education

Recognizing the importance of ICT in education, ICT has been included as a core course at the B.Ed level in the colleges. Teacher Trainees need more structured support of ICT development from their educational institutions. There must be congruence between the school curriculum andteacher training curriculum. Otherwise, teachers are not ready to utilize their knowledgeto effectively design teaching/learning processes, project work, and assignments. In addition to offeringICT as a compulsory and special course, integrated approaches need to be studied along with methodscourses. This will help pupil-teachers to develop the concept of 'techno pedagogy' to a greater extent.

Enrolling the teachers for online professionally development courses. There are many websites offering free training modules. Enrolling for the best commercially available ICT training programs. The teachers should attend the ICT related courses, seminars, conferences and workshop for their professional development.

The schools which are committed to preparing students for the future information society empower them to become more active learners constructing their own learning situations. In this learning mode, ICT applications become vital and more user-oriented. In this case the physical environment is made more suitable for learning individually and in small groups.

Government cooperation is necessary for implementing the ICT programmes to have substantial impact and be sustainable. The active participation of the Government is essential to ensure the sector-wise introduction of ICT. Prioritizing and Planning Access to Remote Areas and Special consideration should be given to ICT connectivity and accessibility for educational purposes.

Conclusion

The role of ICTs in the education is recurring and unavoidable. Rapid changes in the technologies are indicating that the role of ICT in future will grow tremendously in education. ICT also focuses modification of the role of teachers. In addition to classroom teaching, they will have other skills and responsibilities. Teachers will act as virtual guides for students who use electronic media. Ultimately, the use of ICT will enhance the learning experiences of students. Also it helps them to think independently and communicate creatively. It also helps students for building successful careers and lives, in an increasingly technological world.

18

Educational-digital Skill

Introduction

There is a tremendous revolution in science and technology. Information in communication technologies has a deep Cultural Revolution changing. There is a need to make a realistic assessment of what technology cannot do to reach a plateau of productivity when the technology consistently delivers to realistic goals.

The impact of science and technology among students:-

Digital skill is a vast technique used by all people. Educational technology and mobile learning, multi- media learning are all digital skill. Science is a boon. Man has discovered many wonderful things from the treasure of developing every day. It has made our life easier, happier and more secure. Science and technology has conquered time and space. It has made very good communication and made the transport easier. With the help of science and technology, modern medicine and medical treatments, the doctors save the life of sick people from the jaws of death. Many organs are now transplanted. It is used in the field of agriculture. The impact of science and technology among students in the field is both good and bad.

Science laboratory, space centre ISRO are taken in the highest form. Television, telecommunication, type- recorder, films, LCD projectors, digital and white board, e- learning, e-teaching, teleconferencing, teaching machine cell phones such as all types of multimedia are boons to us. But the students are affected by this because of misusing. So they blamed science. We cannot blame science. It is a wonderful boon.

Digital skill in website

By the wrong use of face book, web site, web-camera, especially cell phones, net connection, lab top etc. Science and technology become down. But once for all where we use science and technology in proper, correct and perfect way it is a boon to us otherwise it is curse and demon to us.

A secondary Information and Communication Technology curriculum should contribute to the building up of teams of professionals with these new competencies. The use of Information and Communication Technology cuts across all aspects of economic and social life. Technological developments in Information and Communication Technology are very rapid. Technology quickly becomes obsolete requiring new skills and knowledge to be mastered frequently. Adaptation is only possible when based on a sound understanding of the principles and concepts of Information and Communication Technology.

Review of Literature

Lei, Jing (2010) studied on Quantity versus Quality: A New Approach to Examine the Relationship between Technology Use and Student Outcomes. It is found that that to examine the relationship between technology use and student outcomes, the quality of technology use—how, and what, technology is used—is a more significant factor than the quantity of technology use—how much technology is used. This argument was exemplified by an empirical study that used both angles to examine the association between technology use and student outcomes. When only the quantity of technology use was examined, no significant association was observed. However, when the quality of technology was examined by investigating the specific types of technology uses, a significant association was identified between technology use and all student outcomes. Furthermore, different types of technology use showed different influences on specific student outcomes. General technology uses were positively associated with student technology proficiency, while subject-specific technology uses were negatively associated with student technology proficiency. Social-communication technology uses were significantly positively associated with developmental outcomes such as self-esteem and positive attitude towards school. Entertainment/exploration technology use showed significant positive association with student learning habits. None of these technology uses had significant influence on student academic outcome.

Chen, Rong-Ji (2010) studied on Investigating Models for Preservice Teachers' Use of Technology to Support Student-Centered Learning. The study addressed two limitations of previous research on factors related to teachers' integration of technology in their teaching. It attempted to test a structural equation model (SEM) of the relationships among a set of variables influencing preservice teachers' use of technology specifically to support student-centered learning. A review of literature led to a path model that provided the design and analysis for the study, which involved 206 preservice teachers in the United States. The results show that the proposed model had a moderate fit to the observed data, and a more parsimonious model was found to have a better fit. In addition, preservice teachers' self-efficacy of teaching with technology had the strongest influence on technology use, which was mediated by their perceived value of teaching and learning with technology. School's contextual factors had moderate influence on technology use. Moreover, the effect of preservice teachers' training on student-centered technology use was mediated by both perceived value and self-efficacy of technology. The implications for teacher preparation include close collaboration between teacher education program and field experience, focusing on specific technology uses.

Eisenberg, Mike; Johnson, Doug; Berkowitz, Bob (2010) studied on Information, Communications, and Technology (ICT) Skills Curriculum Based on the Big6 Skills Approach to Information Problem-Solving. There is clear and widespread agreement among the public and educators that all students need to be proficient technology users. Technology literacy is among the attributes that appear in nearly every set of "21st Century Skills." However, while districts spend a great deal of money on technology, there seems to be only a vague notion of what technology literacy really means. Defining and describing technology skills is only a first step to assure all children become proficient information and technology users. Other critical elements will include a teacher-supported scope and sequence of skills, well designed projects, and effective assessments. Equally essential is fruitful collaboration among classroom teachers, teacher librarians, and technology teachers in order to present students with a unified and integrated approach to ensure that all children master the skills they will need to thrive in an information-rich future. This article presents the

"Information, Communications, and Technology (ICT) Skills for Information Problem Solving" curriculum which defines technology capabilities and identifies associated skills based on the Big6 Skills Approach. The Curriculum describes levels of technology proficiency, and in so doing, promotes the skills and concepts basic to information and technology. In an information society, it is essential that students are technologically productive and able to solve information problems effectively and efficiently. This curriculum requires more than teaching computer skills, technology hardware, and software programs in an isolated approach. An effective technology curriculum must be integrated across content areas and grade levels to improve the learning process. Technology is successfully integrated when it seamlessly supports curricular goals. Students learn and refine their technology skills when they work on projects that require them to solve problems and make decisions.

Savage, Robert S.; Erten, Ozlem; Abrami, Philip; Hipps, Geoffrey; Comaskey, Erin; van Lierop, Dea (2010) studied on ABRACADABRA in the Hands of Teachers: The Effectiveness of a Web-Based Literacy Intervention in Grade 1 Language Arts Programs . Each teacher chose to use the program in qualitatively distinct ways that corresponded to the first three stages of Sandholtz, Ring staff, and Dwyer's (1997) technology integration model, namely: "Entry," "Adoption" and "Adaptation." Growth in literacy between pre- and post-test revealed significant differences associated with technology integration style across all measures of literacy and related language skills. The largest and most-widespread effects were evident for the "Adaptation" group that linked technology content to wider learning themes in the classroom. In terms of overall growth in standardised literacy scores across all six such measures used, Adaptation proved to be 60% more effective than Adoption. Results suggest that explorations of exactly how teachers use technology have important implications for practice as well as for the interpretation of field-based studies of the effectiveness of educational technology.

Jun, Han; Zhuzhu, Wang (2010) studied on Capability Building in Educational Technology for Teachers in China. This paper gives a brief introduction to the project called Education Technology Capacity Building Plan for All Primary and Secondary Teachers now being implemented in China. Because information and communication technology skills training cannot match the demand of teachers' professional development, the Chinese Ministry of Education established the education technology standard for teachers and launched the project. This paper introduced the features of standard training and testing, and discusses the output and influence of the project.

McGarr, Oliver (2010) studied on Education for Sustainable Development in Technology Education in Irish Schools: A Curriculum Analysis. This paper explores the integration of Education for Sustainable Development (ESD) in technology education and the extent to which it is currently addressed in curriculum documents and state examinations in technology education at post-primary level in Ireland. This analysis is conducted amidst the backdrop of considerable change in technology education at post-primary level. The analysis of the provision of technology education found, that among the range of technology related subjects offered, the study of Technology and Society is only addressed in one in a comprehensive manner. The paper discusses the implications of this limited integration, examines the factors inhibiting greater integration of ESD and outlines opportunities for future development.

Waring, Scott M. (2010) studied on The Impact of a Technology Coordinator's Belief System upon Using Technology to Create a Community's History. As it has been shown that teachers of social studies content are less likely than teachers of other content areas to utilize technology in their classroom, this study focuses on one instructional technology coordinators' beliefs towards technology, instruction, and students and how these beliefs impacted how technology was utilized during a technology-enriched community history project with a group of fourth-grade students. It was determined that the instructional technology coordinators' beliefs included the following: (a) technology should serve as a tool and should be seamlessly integrated into the curriculum; (b) the teacher should construct meaningful experiences that allow students to become engaged in the learning process; however, before guiding student discovery, the teacher needs to explicitly teach basic technological skills; (c) and all students are able to learn and are capable of engaging in independent problem solving and critical thinking at some level. Her beliefs manifested themselves daily, particularly in the way that she approached instruction and integrated technology seamlessly into the curriculum. Through this study, it was found that the technology coordinator's beliefs toward technology, instruction, and her students directly impacted how technology was used in her classroom.

Jun, Han; Zhuzhu, Wang (2010) studied on Capability Building in Educational Technology for Teachers in China. This paper gives a brief introduction to the project called Education Technology Capacity Building

Plan for All Primary and Secondary Teachers now being implemented in China. Because information and communication technology skills training cannot match the demand of teachers' professional development, the Chinese Ministry of Education established the education technology standard for teachers and launched the project. This paper introduced the features of standard training and testing, and discusses the output and influence of the project.

Ruzic-Dimitrijevic, Ljiljana; Dimitrijevic, Maja (2010) studied on Challenges IT Instructors Face in the Self-Education Process. We find that the earlier the instructors graduated, the smaller is the chance they studied the technologies similar to the ones they teach. We found that none of the surveyed instructors who graduated before 1979 teach a technology they studied. The analysis of the survey also supports the second hypothesis. The results show that 70% of the IT instructors have to change the course syllabus every 2-3 years due to the technology changes. We also found that the majority of the instructors primarily use textbooks and online tutorials to self-teachnew technologies, which support the third hypothesis. By comparison, they take courses given by others and work on real life projects far less often. In contrast, most instructors agree that taking courses and working on projects would greatly help them in their self-education. Most instructors (16 out of 20) assert that the lack of time stops them from doing so, which according to the survey is found to be one of the major challenges they face in the process of self-education, supporting the fourth hypothesis. Considering the results of our research, as well as our own experience, we have identified a list of activities that make the process of self-education more efficient and/or effective for IT instructors. These activities include taking on-line tutorials, creating software programs using the environment/ language/tools covered in the courses, working on real life projects, taking organized courses, attending IT/CS conferences, seminars, and workshops, collecting experience from industry people, and using the help of advanced students. However, in order to create the time for IT instructors to apply the self-learning methods and stay on top of the new technologies, we conclude that it may be necessary that the university policy include the time for self-learning as a significant part of IT instructors' everyday duties, i.e., as a part of their "job description".

Larson, Lotta; Kuhn, Cyndi Danner; Collins, Royce Ann; Balthazor, Gerri; Ribble, Mike; Miller, Teresa Northern (2009) studied on Technology Instruction: Fixing the Disconnect. High school students spend much of their educational journeys immersed in "old" literacies of paper, pencil, and print books. But outside of the classroom, they are exposed to information and communication technologies—such as blogs, wikis, Internet browsers, multimedia, social networking sites, and a wide range of software—each of which demand new literacies. This disconnect is a serious problem for schools because it reflects a decline in school's relevancy to students' futures, and the gap between how schools teach and how students learn will only grow over time. The first step in updating a school's technology and instruction is to revisit and revise current vision statements by facilitating conversations with all stakeholders about expectations for student skills upon graduation. Vision setting must include the new literacies. Teachers and education leaders must model expectations and support visionary teaching and learning through technology. To make that happen, they need instructional technology specialists who not only have a strong knowledge of hardware, networks, and equipment maintenance but also understand the art of teaching and how to enhance and enrich the daily curriculum by integrating technology. To do this, instructional technology staff members and those creating the curriculum must engage in ongoing dialogue to ensure that computer language is translated into the language of teaching and is directly related to what teachers want to do in their classrooms. For schools to successfully integrate technology, leaders must encourage and support strong relationships between teachers and technology support staff members. Schools must also provide easy access to technology in classrooms so that teachers can effectively integrate technology into the curriculum. Limited resources and complicated check-out procedures often contribute to lack of use. In addition, frustrations over blocked sites or limited access to online resources prevent teachers from integrating technology. Leaders, teachers, and technology staff members need ongoing communication with one another to share needs, frustrations, and solutions. Schools must move ahead quickly. It may be understandable for teachers and leaders to be a bit behind in the use of technology, but it is no longer adequate or appropriate to hold students back. Students today will be leaders in a global society, and technology can connect them to that world in ways that were unimaginable 10 years ago. School leaders need to join students in their world—which includes all of the new literacies—so that everyone can function and contribute to the future.

Objectives

1. To study the level of teachers attitude towards using new technology in teaching

2. To find out whether there is any significant relationship between teachers attitude towards the use of new technology and their interest in teaching.

Methodology

The methodology adopted for the study is explained in detail. The sampling technique, size of the sample, variables of the study, description of the tool used and administration of tool are elaborated.

Sample

The study was conducted on 100 school teachers, Coimbatore district, Tamil Nadu.

Data Collection

Primary data, required for the present research work were collected by conducting direct interviews using questionnaire. All the respondents were given sufficient information about the study. These respondents were provided with the same questionnaires. They were also informed that they have to answer in the same fashion.

Analysis and Interpretation

Gender and attitude towards the use of new technology

Null Hypothesis No. 1

There is no significant difference between male and female teachers attitude towards the use of new technology.

Table 1

The Significance of the difference ('t' value) between mean scores of male and female teacher'sattitude towards the use of new technology

Gender	N	Mean	SD	't' value	Level of Significance (0.05)
Male	50	100.30	11.81	4.89	Significant
Female	50	107.30	12.57		

It is evident from the table the calculated 't' value is 4.89 is significant at 0.05 level. Hence, the framed null hypothesis is rejected and research hypothesis is accepted. It is inferred that there is significant difference found between male and female teachers attitude towards the use of new technology.

Qualification and attitude towards the use of new technology

Null Hypothesis No. 2

There is no significant difference between undergraduate and post graduate teachers with respect to their attitude towards the use of new technology.

Table 2

The significance of the difference ('t' value) betweenundergraduate and post graduate teachers with respect to their attitude towards the use of new technology.

Qualification	N	Mean	SD	't' value	Level of Significance (0.05)
Under graduate	35	103.64	11.44	0.28	Not Significant
Post graduate	65	103.23	13.53		

It is evident from the table the calculated 't' value is 0.28 which is not significant at 0.05 level. Hence, the framed null hypothesis is accepted. It shows that there is no significant difference between undergraduate and post graduate teachers with respect to their attitude towards the use of new technology.

Locality of the School and attitude towards the use of new technology

Null Hypothesis No. 3

There is no significant difference between rural and urban school teachers attitude towards the use of new technology.

Table 3

The Significance of the difference ('t' value) between ruraland urban school teachers attitude towards the use of new technology

Locality of the school	**N**	**Mean**	**SD**	**'t' value**	**Level of Significance (0.05)**
Rural	65	103.42	11.23	0.06	Not Significant
Urban	35	103.33	14.15		

It is evident from the table the calculated 't' value is 0.06 which is not significant at 0.05 level. Hence, the framed null hypothesis is accepted. It shows that there is no significant difference between rural and urban school teachers attitude towards the use of new technology.

Type of School and attitude towards the use of new technology

Null Hypothesis No. 4

There is no significant difference between private and government school teachers attitude towards the use of new technology.

Table 4

The Significance of the difference ('t' value) between private and government school teachers attitude towards the use of new technology

Type of School	N	Mean	SD	't' value	Level of significance (0.05)
Private	65	104.79	11.54	1.26	Not Significant
Government	35	102.78	13.01		

It is evident from the table the calculated 't' value is 1.26 which is not significant at 0.05 level. Hence, the framed null hypothesis is accepted. It shows that there is no significant difference between private and government school teachers attitude towards the use of new technology.

Level of teaching and attitude towards the use of new technology

Null Hypothesis No. 5

There is no significant difference between secondary and higher secondary school teachers attitude towards the use of new technology.

Table 5

The Significance of the difference ('t' test) between secondary and higher secondary school teachers attitude towards the use of new technology

Level of teaching	N	Mean	SD	't' value	Level of Significance (0.05)
Secondary School	60	102.12	12.12	1.85	Not Significant
Higher secondary School	40	104.82	13.03		

It is evident from the table the calculated 't' value is 1.85 which is not significant at 0.05 level. Hence, the framed null hypothesis is accepted. It is inferred that there is no significant difference between secondary and higher secondary school teachers attitude towards the use of new technology.

Teaching Experience and attitude towards the use of new technology

Null Hypothesis No. 6

There is no significant difference among teachers who have different years of teaching experience with respect to their attitude towards the use of new technology.

Table 6

The Significance of the difference ('F' test) among school teachers with respect to their attitude towards the use of new technology

Teaching Experience	Sum of Squares	Mean Squares	df	'F' Value	Level of Significance (0.05)
Between Groups	2281.690	1140.845	2		
Within Groups	45273.227	152.435	97	7.48	Significant
Total	47554.917	-	99		

It is evident from the table the calculated 'F' value is 7.48 which is significant at 0.05 level. Hence, the framed null hypothesis is rejected and research hypothesis is accepted. It is inferred that there is significant difference among teachers who have different years of teaching experience with respect to their attitude towards the use of new technology.

Table 7

The Significance of the difference ('t' test) between teachers who have different years of teaching experience with respect to their attitude towards the use of new technology

Teaching experience	N	Mean	SD	't' value	Level of Significance (0.05)
Below 10 years	49	109.33	11.05	3.06	Significant
10-20 years	20	103.03	12.80		
Above 20 years	31	101.67	12.47	4.16	Significant

Teaching experience	N	Mean	SD	't' value	Level of Significance (0.05)
Below 10 years	49	109.33	11.05		
10-20 years	20	103.03	12.80	0.81	Not Significant
Above 20 years	31	101.67	12.47		

From table, it is revealed that there is significant difference between teachers who have below 10 years of teaching experience and 10-20 years of teaching experience and teachers who have above 20 years of teaching experience and below 10 years of teaching experience. Whereas no significant difference is found between teachers who have above 20 years of teaching experience and 10-20 years of teaching experience.

Correlation Analysis

Correlation Analysis between teachers attitude towards the use of new technology and interest in teaching

One of the important objectives of the present investigation is to study the significant relationship between teacher's attitude towards the use of new technology and interest in teaching. For this purpose, the investigator applied the co-efficient of correlation ('r'). The computed values are given in the table. The investigator also framed a null hypothesis for testing the relationship between teacher's attitude towards the use of new technology and interest in teaching.

Null hypothesis No. 8

There is no significant relationship between teacher's attitude towards the use of new technology and interest in teaching.

Table 8

Co-efficient of Correlation between teacher's attitude towards the use of new technology and interest in teaching

Correlation	N	'r' value	Level of Significance at 0.05 level
Teacher's attitude towards the use of new technology and interest in teaching	100	0.56	Significant

It is evident from the table the computed correlation coefficient 'r' for entire sample is 0.56, which is significant at 0.05 level. Hence, the framed null hypothesis is rejected. It is inferred that there is significant relationship found between teacher's attitude towards the use of new technology and their interest in teaching.

Suggestions

The present study gives a clear-cut view about the present position of teachers attitude towards the use of new technology and their interest in teaching. Based on the important findings stated earlier the following recommendations are suggested.

1. Teachers must be provided with adequate opportunities to enhance their knowledge in new technologies and equipments. The government should provide more effective environment through schools for them to improve their skills in application of new technologies in teaching.
2. Periodical in-service training programmes should be organized to keep their interest and quest in teaching.
3. The finding of the present study reveals that the teachers have neutral attitude towards the use of new technology in teaching and low interest in teaching. This indicates that the Heads of the institutions must look into the varied problems that influence the interest of teachers and find amicable solutions to their difficulties.
4. More activities should be planned in the curriculum to bring forth different modes of creative expressions which will provide competition and generate interest of teachers in teaching.
5. Sincere work and involved performances of teachers must be recognized and honoured by the authorities. And application of innovative methods and technologies in instruction must be encouraged.
6. In addition with the above recommendation the government and all the other concerned authorities should realize the problems of experienced teachers and provide conductive environment of growth and mutual help of teachers should be ensured.

Conclusion

The present study is conducted on teachers attitude towards the use of new technologies in teaching and their interest in teaching. The findings of the present study revealed that the teachers have neutral attitude towards the use of new technology and low interest in teaching. Therefore, the authorities and government should find suitable measures to improve the interest of teachers in teaching and the application of innovative technologies in Teaching Learning Process.

References

1. Larson, Lotta; Kuhn, Cyndi Danner; Collins, Royce Ann; Balthazor, Gerri; Ribble, Mike; Miller, Teresa Northern (2009) Technology Instruction: Fixing the Disconnect. Principal Leadership, v10 n4 p54-58.
2. Chen, Rong-Ji (2010) Investigating Models for Preservice Teachers' Use of Technology to Support Student-Centered Learning. Computers & Education, v55 n1 p32-42.
3. Eisenberg, Mike; Johnson, Doug; Berkowitz, Bob (2010) Information, Communications, and Technology (ICT) Skills Curriculum Based on the Big6 Skills Approach to Information Problem-Solving. Library Media Connection, v28 n6 p24-27.
4. Jun, Han; Zhuzhu, Wang(2010) Capability Building in Educational Technology for Teachers in China British Journal of Educational Technology, v41 n4 p607-611.
5. Lei, Jing (2010) Quantity versus Quality: A New Approach to Examine the Relationship between Technology Use and Student Outcomes. 2010.
6. Lesisko, Lee J.; Wright, Robert J.; O'Hern, Brenda (2010) Technology Integration: A Best Practice Perspective. Online Submission, Paper presented at the Annual Meeting of the Eastern Educational Research Association (Savannah, GA, Feb 10-13, 2010).
7. McGarr, Oliver (2010) Education for Sustainable Development in Technology Education in Irish Schools: A Curriculum Analysis. International Journal of Technology and Design Education, v20 n3 p317-332.
8. Ruzic-Dimitrijevic, Ljiljana; Dimitrijevic, Maja (2010) Challenges IT Instructors Face in the Self-Education Process. Journal of Information Technology Education, v9 pIIP-35-IIP-48.
9. Savage, Robert S.; Erten, Ozlem; Abrami, Philip; Hipps, Geoffrey; Comaskey, Erin; van Lierop, Dea (2010) ABRACADABRA in the Hands of Teachers: The Effectiveness of a Web-Based Literacy Intervention in Grade 1 Language Arts Programs . Computers & Education, v55 n2 p911-922.

10. Shapley, Kelly; Sheehan, Daniel; Maloney, Catherine; Caranikas-Walker, Fanny (2010) Effects of Technology Immersion on Teachers' Growth in Technology Competency, Ideology, and Practices. Journal of Educational Computing Research, v42 n1 p1-33.
11. Waring, Scott M. (2010) The Impact of a Technology Coordinator's Belief System upon Using Technology to Create a Community's History. Computers in the Schools, v27 n2 p76-98.

19

Progress of Open and Distance Learning

Introduction

Education is not acquiring bookish knowledge but it is a lifelong process for self-development and at a large scale it is the development of the country. Besides curricular instructions, the life skills need to be integrated in the education system of India. Life skills are abilities for adaptive and positive behavior that enable individuals to deal effectively with the demands and challenges that facilitate the physical, mental and emotional well-being of student. Knowledge and life skills education imparted to the students are likely to be passed on their own children, thus influencing future generations. This is possible with the system like open and distance education learning.

Open and Distance Learning

Open and Distance Learning (ODL) system is a system wherein teachers and learners need not necessarily be present either at same place or same time and is flexible in regard to modalities and timing of teaching and learning. ODL system in India consists of State Open Universities (SOUs), Institutions and Universities offering education and includes Correspondence Course Institutes (CCIs) in conventional dual mode universities. At present there are 13 State Open Universities in India, which provide education only in the distance mode.

The mission of distance learning includes greater dimensions of openness, flexibility, and access. “Open” means the removal of constraints of face to face conventional classroom method, flexibility for students who need an alternative to the conventional system and scale with equality. “Distance” means teacher and student have a space and time division or distance, and also involves e-learning, open learning, flexible learning, on-line learning, resource-based learning, and technology-mediated learning.Distance learning is described as “a process to create and provide access to learning when the source of information and the learners are separated by time and distance, or both”

History Of ODL

1840 - Modern distance learning initially relied on the development of postal services and has been practiced since Isaac Pitman taught shorthand in Great Britain via correspondence.

The University of London claims to be the first university to offer distance learning degrees, establishing its External Program. This program is now known as the University of London International Programs and includes Postgraduate, Undergraduate and Diploma degrees created by colleges such as the London School of Economics, Royal Holloway and Goldsmiths.

1892 - In the United States William Rainey Harper, first president of the University of Chicago developed the concept of extended education, whereby the research university had satellite colleges of education in the wider community, he also encouraged the concept of correspondence school courses to further promote education, an idea that was put into practice by Columbia University (Levinson, 2005, p. 69).

1911- In Australia, the University of Queensland established its Department of Correspondence Studies. (White, 1982, p. 262).

1968 - Charles Wedemeyer of the University of Wisconsin–Madison is considered significant in promoting methods other than the postal service to deliver distance education in America. The Carnegie Foundation funded Wedemeyer’s Articulated Instructional Media Project (AIM) which brought in a variety of communications technologies aimed at providing learning to an off-campus population.

1974 - Germany's Fern Universidad in Hagen followed and now there are many similar institutions around the world, often with the name Open University (in English or in the local language). All "open universities" use distance education technologies as delivery methodologies and some have grown to become "mega-universities" (Daniel, 1998, p. 15) a term coined to denote institutions with more than 100,000 students.

History of ODL in India

Open and distance learning in India started around 1960s. By the 1980s there were 34 Universities offering correspondence education through departments designed for that purpose. The first single mode Open University was established in Andhra Pradesh in 1982, followed by the Indira Gandhi National Open University (IGNOU), and subsequently in Bihar, Rajasthan, and Maharashtra, Madhya Pradesh, Gujarat, Karnataka, West Bengal, and Uttar Pradesh (established throughout the 1980s and 1990s). The establishment of these single mode distance education universities was stimulated by the government's intention to democratize education and make it lifelong. The initiative did not discourage the expansion at the same time of correspondence programs in dual mode universities.

The year 1995 witnessed the enrollment of 200,000 students in open and distance learning, accounting for 3% of total higher education enrollment. Most open and distance learning universities in India follow the model of the UK Open University.

Need for ODL

There is a need to bring changes in the existing system where the learning time, learning style, and the pace of learning, and the evaluation system is such that it does not create any pressure and stress on the learners. The focus of the education should be on life skill development rather than making the students bookworms. The learners should be made capable of using their potential and capabilities for a happy and stress free life. For this they should be provided with an open and free environment at home as well as in the schools and colleges.

Every year 5.5 million students pass out of class X of which 3.3 million go to Class X1, leaving 2.2 million out of the educational system. By 2020, about 220 million students will pass out from school, out of which, about 150 million will not enroll for college education. ODL is needed to provide second chance to those who miss the education.

Distance Education Council

Distance Education Council (DEC) is founded in 1992. DEC is responsible for the promotion, co-ordination, and the maintenance of quality and standards. A range of factors including emerging ICTs, liberalization, privatization and globalization have amplified the demand for open and distance learning.

The DEC provides technical and financial support to the Open and Distance Education Institutes in the country. The technical help includes development of technological infrastructure, institutional reform, professional development and training, student support services, computerization and networking of improvement of quality of education. The DEC's financial help includes financial assistance to State Open Universities (SOUs) and other institutions of open and distance learning like CCIs, research grant on topics of contemporary relevance, travel grants to individuals to attend international conferences and funds for organizing seminar to institutions.

Significance

The potential impact of distance learning on all education has been emphasised by the development of Internet-based technologies, particularly the World Wide Web. Significance of distance learning are balancing inequalities between age groups, geographical expansion of education access, delivering education for large audiences, offering the combination of education with work or family life. Distance learning increases access to learning and training opportunity, provides increased opportunities for updating, retraining and personal enrichment, improves cost effectiveness of educational resources, supports the quality and variety of existing educational structures, enhances and consolidates capacity.

Another advantage of distance learning is its convenience because many of the technologies are easily accessible from home. Many forms of distance learning provide students the opportunity to participate whenever they wish, on an individual basis, because of distance learning flexibility. This kind of education is quite affordable, as many forms of distance learning involve little or no cost. Distance learning is also multi-sensory. Introverted students who are too shy to ask questions in class will often "open up" when provided an opportunity to interact via e-mail or other individualized means (Franklin, Yoakam & Warren, 1996, p. 126).

Distance Learning Methods

The methods of learning used in distance learning are divided into two basic groups: synchronous and asynchronous learning. The term synchronous learning is a mode of delivery where all participants are present at the same time. It resembles traditional classroom teaching methods despite the participants being located remotely. It requires a timetable to be organized. The asynchronous learning mode of delivery is where participants access course materials on their own schedule and so is more flexible. Students are not required to be together at the same time.

Distance Learning Technologies

The various technologies used in distance learning are print, computer, audio and video. Print materials may serve as the primary source of instruction, or they may be supplemental. As a primary source, distance students use a textbook. As a supplement to instruction, text materials may take the form of worksheets or study guides that are used in conjunction with video or voice technologies. Supplemental print materials may be disseminated via regular mail or over the Internet. In addition, fax machines are often used to transmit the print materials back and forth between the students and the teachers.

Other technologies, such as e-mail, could then be used to ask questions and send assignments back to the teacher. Audio or voice technologies offer cost-effective ways to enhance distance learning courses. The audio component of a distance learning course can be as simple as a telephone with voicemail, or it can be as complex as an audio conference with microphones, telephone bridges and speakers. Audio files and CDs are inexpensive, easily duplicated and very versatile and it is used to deliver lectures, panel discussions, or instructions for the distant learners.

Telephone conversations can be used to monitor individual students or to reach numerous students simultaneously via a conference call. Podcast is a method for making digital audio and video files available on the Internet in such a way that others can set their computers to automatically download new episodes in a series as they are posted online.

Concepts and Models

James Taylor's Models of distance education are as follows

The "examination preparation" model

The correspondence education model

The multiple (mass) media model

The group distance education model

The autonomous learner model

The network-based distance teaching model

The technologically extended classroom model

The "examination preparation" model

This model was institutionalized when the University of London was founded in the middle of the 19th century for the benefit of those persons who could not afford to be enrolled at Oxford or Cambridge University or of those persons who could not attend any university as they lived in the colonies of the British Empire. This university supported the students only by informing them about the examination regulations and sometimes by offering special reading lists. Presently, this model is being developed and practiced by the Regents of the University of New York.

The correspondence education model

This is the oldest and most widely used model. This model is simple and relatively cost-effective since the teaching texts can be mass-produced by the printing press. This model is still used extensively – in spite of the worldwide interest in the digitalization of distance education. It is also used to a great extent by distance teaching universities which take pride in announcing that they are multiple media and open universities.

The multiple (mass) media model

This model was developed in the seventies of our century. Its characteristic feature is the regular and more or less integrated use of radio and television together with printed matter in the form of pre-prepared structured course material. It designates a new era in the development of distance education, namely the second generation of this particular form of academic teaching and learning. It initiated and supported the movement towards open learning and open universities.

The group distance education model

This model is similar to the multiple media model as radio and television are used permanently as teaching media, especially for transporting lectures held by professors. However, these lectures are as a rule not received by individual students but rather by groups of students attending obligatory classes where they follow the explanations of an instructor, discuss what they have heard and watched, do their assignments and take their tests. No special printed teaching material is developed and distributed with the exception of the customary "lecture notes".

The autonomous learner model

This model provides for freedom to develop independent learning. Its goal is the education of the autonomous learner, which is, an ambitious, demanding, but also a very promising goal. The students do not only organize their learning themselves as, e.g., in the correspondence or multiple mass media model, but they tackle also the curricular tasks, they are responsible for determining the aims and objectives, for selecting the contents, for deciding on the strategies and media they want to apply and even for the measurement of their learning success. Here, the long tradition of expository teaching comes to an end.

The network-based distance education model

This model is presently emerging as part of the digital transformation. It provides for the possibility to work in a digitized learning environment. This is a most convenient learning situation. The students have access to even the remotest teaching programmes and databases carrying relevant information. They may work off-line or on-line or use CD-ROMs. They may take part in virtual seminars, workshops, tutorial and counseling meetings, tuition or project groups and chat with their fellow students. The greatest pedagogic advantage, however, is that the students are challenged to develop new forms of learning by searching, finding, acquiring, evaluating, judging, changing, storing, managing and retrieving information when needed. This model is certainly a complex and demanding one. But it is promising as it opens up new dimension of pedagogical endeavour in distance education.

The technologically extended classroom teaching model

This model has been developed in the USA. In this model one teacher teaches a college class or a studio class – and his presentation is transmitted to two or more other classes by cable or satellite TV or with the help of a video conference system. In this way one teacher may teach several classes making the process more economical.

Implementation of ODL

The twentieth century saw the creation and evolution of technologies beyond imagination a century ago. The acceptance of these technologies has led to a new alternative for providing education and training i.e. distances learning. Despite initial concerns that distance learning might lower the quality of instruction, studies shown that its benefits are clear and demonstrable and many forms of distance learning are quickly gaining acceptance (Belanger & Jordan, 2000, p. 17).

The implementation of distance learning and its supporting technologies requires careful planning. This process includes four basic steps: conduction of needs assessment, outlining instructional goals and producing instructional materials, providing training and practice for instructors and facilitators and implementing the program.

Conducting the needed assessment includes course, audience instructor and technology analysis. The course analysis is to identify content areas that could be enhanced, through distance learning techniques. Distance learning needs facilitators and technical support teams who will ensure that all equipment is functioning. Instructors, facilitators and technical support staff should be trained for such purpose. Distance learning can be delivered through different technologies. Selecting the most appropriate technology depends on the content area, student's learning styles and existing hardware and software.

The technology solutions may be impacted by the geographic locations of the teachers and students. A well-structured distance learning course must place instructional objectives foremost. In this case the technology is just another tool that teachers can use to effectively transmit the course content and interact with students.

Once the goals and objectives are outlined, instructional materials can be designed and developed. Materials must be accurate, appropriate and structured to maximize the benefits for students and to minimize the limitations. Teacher training programs are important to acquaint the teachers with the use of technology as well as to help with the re-design of the instructional strategies.

The program can be implemented after the training has been completed and after a pilot test of supporting technologies has been carried out satisfactory. It is important to include structured activities. Timelines, deadlines and feedbacks motivate students and provide the framework students need to function in a flexible environment. The implementation phase should also emphasise interactions. Through the development and implementation, formative evaluation takes place. In selecting distance learning applications factors such as physical location, size and specialization are important for data system creation which supports distance learning.

Conclusion

Distance learning is a contributing force to social and economic development. In developed and developing countries distance education is becoming an essential part of the mainstream of educational systems. The globalization of distance learning provides many opportunities for countries for the realization of their education system-wide goals. The growing needs for continual skills upgrading and retraining and the technological advances have led to an explosion of interest in distance learning.

Reference

1. Ashok K Gaba, Professor, IGNOU, Global Skills Summit 2011 presentation.
2. Bates A.W, The impact of Technological change in IDL: In Distance Education 1997, Vol 18, p. 93-109.
3. Madhava Menon Report on ODL, 2010.
4. Saima Ghosh, Journal of Global Research in Computer Science, April 2012, p.53-57.
5. Viplav Baxi, Report on ODL in India, April 14, 2012.
6. UGC Annual Report 2010 – 2011.
7. www.mhrd.gov.in.
8. http://www.c3l.uni-oldenburg.de/cde/found/peter98b.htm
9. http://www.slideshare.net/missan/open-and-distance-learning-history-status-and-trends.

20

Blended Learning in Teacher Education

Introduction:

Educator's seem to have the most interest in blended learning, gives learners and teachers a potential environment to learn and teach more effectively than any other method of teaching. Because of this much of the research on blended learning has been based around classroom situations. All levels of education have been researched width blended learning; from the elementary school grades up to graduate school Educator's interests in blended learning are common to most effective and efficient teachers.

Blended learning provides a 'good mix of technologies and interactions, resulting in a socially supported, constructive, learning experience, this is especially a significant given the profound effect that it could have on teacher education learning.

Objectives

1. To understand the different approaches to Blended learning.
2. To attain knowledge of the various models of teaching
3. The institutional capacity available at present for all levels of school education

4. Understand the different components levels of teaching
5. The teacher face while designing a blended learning is to determine the balance between online and face to face instruction.

Blended Learning

A blended learning approach combines face to face classroom methods.A thoughtfully designed.integration of live and online materials and methods in the post digital materials have served in a supplementary role helping to support face to face instruction for students of all ages and levels of learning.The best aspects of online instruction students in advanced interactive experiences. Meanwhile, the online portion of the course can provide students with multimedia rich content at any time of day anywhere the students has internet access from computer labs. This allows for an increase in scheduling flexibility for students Hence it is necessary for the educators to utilize the Blended learning approach in teaching learning process to be more effective for classroom instruction.

1. The institution enhance under enrolled programs, computer faculty teaching loads.
2. Blended learning across the curriculum by blending the boundaries of knowledge.
3. Creative thinking processes are developed with in a meaningful context in lifelong earning
4. Students can participate at any time
5. Class goals can easily to meet.
6. Increase the quality of communication between the instructor and learner.

Technology in Blended Learning

Technology in education leads to achieve a milestone in the field of education like

Self-learning

1. Life-long education
2. Learning at one's own convenience and choice
3. Multimedia learning

Models of Blended Learning

Blended learning can be group into models based on the difference in teacher roles. Physical space delivery methods and scheduling the models of blended learning is,

1. Face to face driver
2. Online lab
3. Self-Blend
4. Online communications
5. Flex
6. Rotation
7. Self-faced learning
8. Online driver

Benefits of Blended Learning

1. Blended learning combines online and classroom learning activities and resources to reduce in-class seat time for students in a face to face learning
2. It can be a tremendous for a university
3. Multiple learning sources
4. Equal opportunity to obtain education and information
5. Promote technology literacy of all students
6. Many more innovation in teaching and learning methodology.

Importance of Blended learning

Learning quite different for each learner in that we have to consider differences in

1. Importance of aptitudes
2. Interest spans
3. Preservation of knowledge
4. Creation of interesting learning situation
5. Achievements and motivation

Conclusion

The Blended learning approach used consists of face to face instruction, from textbooks and developed teacher education is one of the special professional courses designed for the post higher graduate students learning.The study involving the blended learning approach have shown that students demonstrate positive perceptions towards learning.A blended learning should describe a planned and deliberate educational activity that integrate students-centred learning salesroom based teaching and learning based on individual learners and their specific needs.

Reference

1. http://www.kneulton.com/blended-learning/

2. http://www.blended learning now.com/
3. http://en.wikipedia.org/wiki/blended learning
4. http:\\weblearning.PSU.edu/blended-learning initiative/blended learning.

21

An Assessment of Edu Digital Skills Among Teachers in Namakkal District

Introduction

Teacher is an ideal personality whose knowledge and skill play a major role in the development of the nation to the global standard education in general and tapping the potentialities of students to the maximum extent in particular. Teachers are expected to learn forever to withstand the innovations in teaching and updating the knowledge and widen the clarity of the conceptual framework of the subject of specialization too. Unless and until the teachers prepared to meet the requirements and challenges, the dream and purpose of education will not be fulfilled. Nowadays the system of education has assumed the character which involves more students' participation and student centric which is highly enabled through the application of various educational technologies. Edu - digital skills is considered prerequisite for all teachers teaching for nursery to doctorate scholars. 21st century school curriculum has been enriched to meet the demands of world requirements of quality. Communication, collaboration, critical thinking, problem solving, creativity, invention, information and technology literacy and self-direction will facilitate the achievement of aims and objectives of education. Teachers of 21st century are expected to equip themselves with modern technology application in teaching and learning process. A paradigm shift has happened to meet the demands of gen y and z learners which require innovative, explorative and interesting approach in teaching and learning. The curriculum will need withstand the futuristic vision for the global scenario. At this juncture the teachers of today should be enthusiastic to update their knowledge and skills forever in order to keep young to the youngest generation whom they meet and it may also be emphasized greatly as the professional ethics. This study has been attempted to assess the knowledge and skills of teachers in the field of information and communication technology which a teacher necessarily possess in the digital world.

Educational Digital Skills

It is mentioned that in order to thrive in a digital economy, students will need digital age proficiencies. It is important for the educational system to make parallel changes in order to fulfill its mission in society, namely the preparation of students for the world beyond the classroom. Therefore, the educational system must understand and embrace the following 21st century skills within the context of rigorous academic standards.

The 21st Century Literacy Summit (2002) contends that "the explosive growth of technology in every aspect of society offers us a unique opportunity to engage our citizens in economic and civic life" The report further states that to take advantage of this opportunity, we must continually acquire and develop new knowledge and skills. Summit participants noted "Information and communication technologies are raising the bar on the competencies needed to succeed in the 21st century, and they are compelling us to revisit many of our assumptions and beliefs" The sheer magnitude of human knowledge, world to technology necessitates a shift in our children's education - from plateaus of knowing to continuous cycles of learning. Therefore, policymakers and educators alike must define 21st century skills, highlighting the relationship of those skills to conventional academic standards. As they do so, they must also recognize the need for multiple assessments to measure these skills within the context of academic standards, evaluating their application to today's technological and global society.

Technological Literacy

Demonstrate a sound conceptual understanding of the nature of technology systems and view themselves as proficient users of these systems. Understand and model positive, ethical use of technology in both social and personal contexts. Use a variety of technology tools in effective ways to increase creative productivity. Use communication tools to reach out to the world beyond the classroom and communicate ideas in powerful ways. Use technology effectively to access, evaluate, process and synthesize information from a variety of sources. Use technology to identify and solve complex problems in real-world contexts have been considered as Technological Literacy

Information Literacy

Before Accessing Information one should determine what is known and what is needed forproblem solving,identify different sources of information, including text, people, video, audio, and databases andprioritize sources based on credibility and relevance. When Accessing Information one need identify and retrieve relevant information from sources and use technology to enhance searching. Revise information-gathering strategies that prove to be in effective when understands how information retrieved does or does not address original problem, evaluate information in terms of credibility and know what are the social, economic, political, legal, and ethical issues that may impact it to facilitate to use technology for evaluation. After Information is extracted, using retrieved information to accomplish a specific purpose, present information clearly and persuasively by using a range of technology tools and media and evaluate the processes and products of these activities have here been considered essential to assure one to be Literate in information.

Global Awareness

Global awareness is knowledge about the connectedness of the nations of the world historically, politically, economically, technologically, socially, linguistically, and ecologically and understand that these interconnections of positive benefits and negative consequences too. The ability to recognize, analyzes, and evaluates major trends in global relations and the interconnections of these trends with both their local and national communities. Participate in the global society by staying current with international news and by participating in the democratic process.

Objectives of the Study

To find the level of Edu-digital skill among school teachers and find whether there is significant different exist among them in relation to their personal variables such as sex, Age, Educational Qualification, Area of Residence, Management of the Institution, Subject of Specialization and the Location of the School.

Research Question

What is the level of educational digital Skills of School Teachers? Is there any Significant Difference Exists among them with respect to their Personal Variables?

Research Methodology

A Normative Descriptive Method of study has been attempted to assess the level of Educational Digital Skills among the School Teachers in Namakkal District

Population, Sample and Sampling Technique of the Study

All teachers who teach in school education are the population of the study and the sample of the study has been chosen from teachers work in Namakkal district only and the sample was taken by stratified random sampling technique which consists of 250.

Tools and Technique of Data Collection

A tool consisted of 24 items related to some basic skills necessary for adopting computer enabled teaching technology, using internet connection which will benefit students to gain knowledge, understand the concept better, improve the critical thinking, problem solving ability, creativity and to enhance their communication skill and appropriate application of the knowledge gained for the betterment of himself and to the society. The scope of this study extent all teachers who teach in the classroom from kindergarten to plus two levels. The questionnaire has dimensions of using the computer for retrieving useful information via internet, knowledge about various search engines, and preparation of effective PowerPoint materials, video clippings, software package application, audio recording, connecting to virtual classroom and the facilities to publish the students works in internet. Knowledge and the application of MS word, Excel format, mobile for teaching and learning purpose and the ability to set ready LCD, mike and arrange show in the smart classroom and the application of social media in education have also been taken for assessing.

Scoring Procedure & Statistical Tools Used

The Questionnaire used in the study has five point scale of the level of skill of the respondents in relation to their digital skill hence it has five options of known very well, known, moderately known, known little and Unknown which scored as 5, 4,3,2 and 1 respectively.

SPSS package has been used to analyze the data and the percentage analysis and the differential analysis have been used to describe and infer the details pertaining to the research question formulated for the study.

Table -1

An Analysis of Edu Digital Skills among Teachers in Namakkal District

Items	Very well Known		Well Known		Moderately Known		Known Little		Unknown		Total
	F	%	F	%	F	%	F	%	F	%	
Information Retrieval	41	16.4	59	23.6	62	24.8	75	30	13	5.2	250
Power point preparation	52	20.8	67	26.8	53	21.2	60	24	18	7.2	250
Efficient use of Windows operating system	35	14	48	19.2	75	30	81	32.4	11	4.4	250
Connecting to the Online Teaching of World Classroom	15	6	20	8	39	15.6	116	46.4	60	24	250
Skill in make it work well of LCD mike screen view	15	6	26	10.4	77	30.8	114	45.6	18	7.2	250
Knowledge about E learning material preparation	21	8.4	15	6	27	10.8	129	51.6	58	23.2	250
Account in social networking sites like Face-book, twitter	22	8.8	36	14.4	74	29.6	12	4.8	106	42.4	250
Using of videos and computer games in teaching	19	7.6	29	11.6	55	22	85	34	62	24.8	250

Items	Very well Known		Well Known		Moderately Known		Known Little		Unknown		Total
webmail											
Application of Virtual classrooms and chat rooms in teaching and learning	13	5.2	18	7.2	17	6.8	56	22.4	146	58.4	250
Application of documentary film in deliverance of the instructional objectives	51	20.4	60	24	41	16.4	31	12.4	67	26.8	250
Using of web-Camera in virtual interaction	16	6.4	41	16.4	27	10.8	71	28.4	95	38	250
Application of white Board in teaching	25	10	16	6.4	19	7.6	43	17.2	147	58.8	250
Safety and security issues in using	17	6.8	39	15.6	90	36	70	28	44	17.6	250
Security Challenges in instant messaging	15	6	35	14	78	31.2	98	39.2	24	9.6	250
Application of iPod and tables in teaching	11	4.4	23	9.2	67	26.8	80	32	69	27.6	250
Application of Video conferencing for teaching and learning	32	12.8	24	9.6	71	28.4	90	36	33	13.2	250
Application of YouTube	49	19.6	86	34.4	55	22	62	24.8	38	15.2	250
Application of Flicker & Picasa	19	7.6	25	10	62	24.8	104	41.6	40	16	250
Application of mobile phone for transferring data of video	21	8.4	27	10.8	80	32	90	36	32	12.8	250
Application of mobile phone for transferring data of voice	22	8.8	33	13.2	76	30.4	81	32.4	38	15.2	250
Application of mobile phone	187	74.8	46	18.4	3	1.2	9	3.6	5	2	250

Items	Very well Known		Well Known		Moderately Known		Known Little		Unknown		Total
webmail for transferring data of text											
Assessment of students performance through online	25	10	52	20.8	58	23.2	105	42	10	4	250
Application of learning Management System - LMS	11	4.4	21	8.4	37	14.8	57	22.8	15	6	250
Application of Video-recording	17	6.8	26	10.4	51	20.4	78	31.2	78	31.2	250

Majority of teachers have necessary in Skill and knowledge in the application of MS office, Mobile technology in teaching and learning, information retrieval system from online resource centre but the majority teachers have moderate and least knowledge about e-content preparation, application of social media, and security issues in web mails, various learning management system and efficient use of ICT in teaching

Table -2

Significance of Difference in Edu-Digital Skill of Teachers

Demographic Variables	P Value	Level of Sig.
Sex	0.153	S
Area of Residence	0.104	S
Location of the School	0.214	S
Teaching Experience	0.098	S
Educational Qualification	0.521	S
Management of the School	0.021*	
Subject of Specialization	0.001**	

There is no significant difference exist among the respondents in their Educational digital skill in relation to their personal variables of Sex, Area of Residence, Location of the School, Teaching Experience and their educational qualification. But the statistical report of analysis shows that there is significant difference exist among the sample in relation to their management of the school and their subject of specialization.

Educational Implications

1. Teacher Education curriculum should emphasize the ICT enabled education in B.Ed program

2. Workshops need to be conducted for B.Ed program in the practical application of ICT and training program can be organized for E-content preparation
3. Orientation and Refresher courses for the teachers in schools should be conducted frequently to enable teachers to facilitate them in the efficient use of ICT in teaching and learning environment
4. Collaborative Approach should be made in integrating ICT in education

Conclusion

Teachers are the forerunner of all developments and growth of the nation and the world; they play a significant role in bringing desirable outcome in the world with their adaptability and their ever learning behavior of updating knowledge and skills in any field. No technology can replace the teacher in any period of time but the teacher needs possess skills in the application of technology which facilitate desirable educational outcome in the field of education.

References

1. Felix.A & Jahitha Begum (2011) "An Awareness of E-resources related to ICT and Education among M.Ed Students and M.Phil Scholars" ICT in teaching and learning, APH Publishing Corporation, New Delhi, p.169
2. Nagarajan .K (2009) "Educational Innovations and Management" Ram Publishers, Chennai. Pp.135-185.
3. Natchimuthu.K (2012), "Need of E-Content Development in Education Today" APH Publication Corporation, New Delhi. P.76.
4. Rangarajan. P & Senthilnathan.S (2012) "Teacher Educators Attitude towards E Learning" Edutracks, Vol.No.12 No.1 pp. 21-32.
5. www.educatorstechnology.com/2012/06/33-digital-skills-every-21st-century.htm
6. http://www.educatorstechnology.com/2013/07/the-8-digital-skills-students-need-for.html

22

Learning Without Limit-kinds of Learning

Introduction

"'Creating Learning without Limits' takes on one of the most important issues in education today. In the last decade schools in have taken a path towards putting all children into boxes, attaching a level to their heads and deciding what they are capable of achieving. The possibility of a different educational path, one in which all students are encouraged to achieve the greatest they can. Importantly the book also documents ways in which courageous teachers can do this - promoting fair and engaging learning environments for all students. This is a must-read for educators, policy makers and parents alike. "This will undoubtedly turn out to be amongst the most important educational books of the decade. Our capacity to respond, both individually and collectively, to its key insights and messages will profoundly affect not just the quality of our schools, but of our society for years to come. It reminds us why people come into education - to make a difference for children. To make a deep difference we have to organize education differently. It describes a school that vibrates with learning in an atmosphere of deep humanity and care. Its practices are light years away from the measuring, labeling, targeting, and testing structures that have become our recent national norm. The school as a whole community transforms people.The self-confidence that comes from a profound faith in the capacity of every child to be a passionate and engaged learner. This in the face of powerful and societal dominant messages that explicitly or more insidiously tell a different and more deterministic tale: that children (and schools) are fit and proper subjects for classification, measurement and management. And there's more - the careful scholarship on which this story is based prevents this book from being merely a description of what happens when a unique constellation of propitious circumstances meets a charismatic leader: this 'other way' is open to all who will take it - but it will demand the laying of solid and value-rich foundations, the exercising of autonomy for staff and pupils, the rethinking of relationships, a focus on learning (letting performance come as a secondary gift), and the taking of collective action. It's become a cliché to say of a book that it 'should be read by every teacher (or parent or whoever...).' This one, and its predecessor 'Learning withoutLimits' 'meritsthatinjunction."

Many students would likely cite a desire to learn. Students assume that, because they have read their text and memorized facts, they have learned something. Definition of 'learn' in a dictionary step, Step1. To acquire knowledge of a subject or skill through education or experience, Step2. To gain information about somebody or something. Step3. To memorize something. This definition is not particularly insightful, although it reminds us that the word can be used to describe the acquisition of both knowledge and skill, and that acquisition can be by a variety of means. Including education experience, or memorization.

The Current Situation

The American education system is considered among the best in the world. More than 50% of our nation's high school graduates continue on to college and each year our universities and colleges enroll thousands of students from other countries. Despite these statistics, several recent studies have shown that many college seniors have neither good general knowledge nor the necessary skills for reasoning in today's society. At the end of the course, the test scores of those students who had completed the economics course were only 20% better than those who had not taken the course, and this difference dropped to less than 10% seven years after completion of the course. The results and many others, strongly suggest that our current instructional practices are not working and that many students are not learning, or retaining what they do learn.

Need for New Kinds of Learning

There have been calls for new kinds of learning from many different parts of society. College teachers have expressed frustration about attendance in class, uncompleted reading assignments, and students focus on grades rather than learning. Student surveys indicate that courses are not interesting, that students fail to recognize the value of what they are learning, and that many faculties rely too heavily on lectures for transmitting information. The 1996 National Science Foundation report on shaping the future urges faculty to promote new kinds of learning that include developing skills in communication, teamwork, and lifelong learning. Gardiner (1994) compiled a list of critical competencies for citizens and workers from leaders in business, industry and government.

1. Personal responsibility.
2. Ability to act in principled, ethical fashion
3. Skill in oral and written communication
4. Interpersonal and team skills
5. Skills in critical thinking and problem-solving
6. Respect for people different from oneself,
7. Ability to change
8. Ability and desire for lifelong learning.

Society and individual learners now have different needs, both in terms of what people need to learn and how they can and should learn. It is a great nuisance that knowledge can be acquired only by hard work-Somerset Maugham.

Implement learning strategies and evaluate learning outcomes;-

Effectively communicate orally, visually in writing and in a second language.

Understand and employ Quantitative and Qualitative analysis to solve problems.

Intellectual Skills

The human imagination, expression, and the products of many cultures.

Means of modeling the natural, social and technical words

Different kinds of thinking and learning

In cognitive theory and education have used Bloom's (1956) taxonomic of learning. Bloom and colleagues identified three learning domains. The cognitive domains involve thinking of all sorts. The affective domain includes feelings, emotions, attitude, values and motivations.

The psychomotor domain of learning includes physical movement, coordination, motor, and sensory-skills. When a learning experience has a profound effect on a student, it can result in a greater sense of caring for the subject, for them, other or learning in general. Greater caring can lead to new interests, energy for learning, or a change in values. 'To learn how to learn' this includes learning how to diagnose one's own need for learning and how to be a self-learner. Then type of learning enables students to continue learning with greater effectiveness and is a particularly important skill with the recent explosion of knowledge and technology.

Learning and the Brain

Many people both young and old enjoy solving problems. These observations suggest that the human brain has a fundamental need to solve problems and understand its surroundings. New understanding of the working of the brain.

1. Learning changes the physical structure of the brain.
2. Learning organized and reorganizes the brain.
3. Different parts of the brain may be ready to learn at different stages of development.

Experience equate to learning, the brain is a dynamic organ. Learning in individual and social contexts actually results in new pattern of organization and improved functioning of the brain.

Intellectual development

One goal of college education should be to develop more sophisticated approaches to thinking.

1. Dualism(authority)
2. Multiplicity(opinion)
3. Relativism (perspective)
4. Commitment (understanding)

Critical Thinking

" A tool for everyone" Critical thinking is so central to sound reasoning that it deserves special attention. The methods of critical thought arc by no means limited to thinking in science, but have also been applied in virtually all other disciplines. They involve both cognitive and affective components. Critical thinking is the intellectually disciplined process of actively and skillfully conceptualizing, applying, analyzing, synthesizing and evaluating information gathered from or generated by observation experience, reflection, reasoning or communication as a guide to belief and action.

Thinking about one's own Thinking and Learning

Intentional thought about one's own thinking is generally regarded as an essential component of successful thinkers and learners monitor their understanding and progress during problem solving. I went to a bookstore and asked the sales-woman, "Where's the self-help section?" She said if she told me, it would defeat the purpose-George Carlin

Effective Learning and Learning Styles

Best learning occurs when students are engaged in active learning- when they are doing things instead of sitting passively and listening. In a recent review of the effectiveness of active learning, Prince(2004) found extensive, widespread support for active learning approaches, especially when activities were designed around important learning outcomes and promoted thoughtful engagement. Many instructors recognize that active learning results in significant improvements in student knowledge retention, conceptual understanding, engagement, and attitudes about learning.

A commonly used approach in active learning is cooperative learning. An enormous body of research confirms the effectiveness of cooperative learning. Compared with more traditional individualized and competitive models of learning, students who learn in cooperative group's exhibit markedly improved individual achievement.

Conclusion

There are many different ways of modeling the way of learning. No one model provides a complete description of learning, and no single learning style is superior to another. However, it is important to be aware of your own learning style preferences so that you can make the necessary adjustments to maximize your learning. Unfamiliar pedagogies example active learning, cooperative learning. These have largely been designed to teach to a wide variety of learning styles and to facilitate learning the content and skills encompassed within significant learning. Some of these new instructional approaches keep an open mind and try to understand the objectives of each pedagogical approach. If you have questions about classroom methods, ask your instructor. Most teachers are happy to discuss instructional practices with their students.

Bibliography of Learning

1. AACU,2002, Greater Expectations: A New Vision for Learning as a Nation Goes to College: National panel Report, American Association of Colleges and Universities, Washington,DC62p.
2. Atkinson,R.L Atkinson R.C Smith, E.E and Bem D.J., 1993, Introduction to Psychology, Harcourt Brace Jovanovich, Fort Worth, TX, 11 th edition
3. Cuesta College, 2004, Characteristics of a Successful Student: Cuesta College. Available at:http://academic. Cuesta.edu/accasupp/as/201.HTM.
4. Johnson, D.W., Johnson, R.T., and Smith, K., 1991,Active Learning: Cooperation in the College Classroom Interaction Book Company,Edina,MN.
5. Krathwohl, D.R.Bloom, B.S, and Masia,B.B., 1964, Taxonomy of Educational objectives. The classification of Educational Goals, Handbook II: Affective Domain. David McKay Company,Inc
6. Teaching Goals Inventory,2004, Available form: http://www.uiowa.edu/-centeach/tgi/.
7. Williams,John,H., 1993, Clarifying grade expectations. The Teaching Professor, August/September.

23

Implications of Multimedia in Teaching

Introduction

The computer has revolutionized the whole society overwhelmingly inclusive of all human activities especially those of education. The computer is changing the total educational system namely, content, methodology, learner participation learning process, teacher roles, curricular implication etc. "The computers are very powerful instructional media that enhance quality of instruction". By programming the subject of study in computers, teaching and learning become full of contexts and situations. The student can take his own time to learn the contents because they are individualized instructional situation. The performance of the student in instruction as well as in test will automatically record in the computer. The present study aims to find out the implications of multimedia in teaching economics with special reference to higher secondary education in Chennai. A samples of 155 samples selected randomly were studied. A questionnaire method of survey was used to find out the implications of multimedia in teaching economics. The data were collected by using questionnaire as an instrument. Primary data were collected by conducting direct structured interview using questionnaire. All the respondents were asked the same questions in the same fashion and they were informed the purpose of study. t-test, ANOVA and Correlation analysis were applied to test the hypotheses. The findings and observations are the result and outcome of the interpretations made during the study of analysis.

In 1965, Lorence settler and Danieal Davis[5] developed most complicated teaching process in which computer was used for presenting instruction in place of teacher. They divided the teaching process of the computer in two parts.

1. Pre-tutorial phase
2. Tutorial phase.

In the first phase, computer assisted instruction is given to the pupils to achieve the specific objectives on the basis of his entry behaviour. In the second phase instructing material is presented accordingly. The pupil is evaluated. After presenting the instruction, computer also controls it. It also provides reinforcement to the pupils.

In the modern age, the use of computers in the field of education, made in the following areas.

3. All the researches do all analytical tasks with the help of computers in the research work.
4. Computers are also used in educational guidance and counseling.
5. Remedial teaching of the pupils is also done by the computers.
6. Computers help in sought for preparing the results of the examinations.

Learning with aid of computer through computer, aided instruction, computer simulation etc. It is a self-learning strategy in teaching learning process. Students learnt their subjects at their own pace.

Internet is worldwide computer network that contains a large collection of information which could be made available to you on your computer. The person having internet connection can retrieve any information on individual interest. Purves, A.C.[6] (1998) says that, the internet is the abbreviation of inter network system. The internet is the name for a vast, worldwide system consisting of people, information and computers. It is also described as a network of networks because these are more than one lakh readily accessible through the Internet. Internet is the largest and most complete learning tool for a group of people with varied educational background and interests. Teachers, students, businessmen and other educators can share ideas instantly across vast distances. For scientific and research community, internet is an essential and indispensable tool. Through Internet scientist can gain and enjoy instant access to the world's most advanced research facilities and discuss their research problems with others, working in the same field.

Review of Literature

Coyne, Margaret Ann[17,] Ed.D., (2006), in their paper "Emerging literacy Assisted parents to scaffold the emerging literacy skill of their pre-school-aged children through the use of electronic storybooks", reported that, that importance of parents reading to their young child is well supported by research (Health, 1986). However, Edwards (1989) found that parents whose own literacy skills are emerging have difficulty supporting the emerging literacy skills of their young children through storybook reading.

The development of a new paradigm, Universal Design for Learning (UDL) (Meyer & Rose, 1998 and 2002) provides a framework for the use of computer technology to support learning. Drawing on Vygotsky's (1978; 1986) socio constructive theory of learning and the latest advances in the neurosciences, UDL investigates how technology can support diverse learners. This study examined whether UDL –based technology might help parents who are themselves emerging readers support their children's literacy development.

When parents use of targeted storybook reading behaviours increased if their children's pre-intervention scores on language measures were below age-level, the children's scores on post-intervention measures improved to age-level or above. In addition, the children's scores on measures of story retelling and print knowledge improved.

BEABVIS C.[18], Deakin University, Literacy and the new technologies in the middle years. (2006) This paper explores young people's textual engagements with electronic and other forms of popular culture, and the changing nature of literacy in the context of COM modification, mass marketing and the new technologies. Building on school based studies exploring computer games in the classroom and the Poke on phenomenon, it examines ways in which popular texts are read, and narrative and generic elements incorporated into the curriculum and into students' spoken and written texts. Drawing on Green's model of cultural, critical and opal dimensions of (technological) literacy, it examines issues of literacy and culture, identity and critique for teachers and students in the middle years, and their implications for constructions of literacy and curriculum.

BERRY L. and CHAPMAN E,[19] University of Sydney Effects of Background Information and Audiovisual Presentation Modes on

Students' Attention Styles and Enjoyment in Listening to Unfamiliar Music.(2006) Research has indicated that students typically do not enjoy or engage with unfamiliar pieces of music. This is discouraging and puzzling to music educators who wish to introduce their students to a diverse range of musical genres. This study explored the effects of two factors on students' initial reactions to an unfamiliar Shakuhachi piece. Using a 2 by 2 crossed-factor design, 438 students in grades 9-11 were assigned at random to listen to the piece in either audio-only or audiovisual form, and with or without verbal background information.

Results indicated that while the provision of information significantly ($p<0.05$) increased students' enjoyment of the music and their interest in hearing more of the same kind of music, it had no effect on their listening attention styles (e.g., focusing on the melody or idiomatic details of the piece). Conversely, use of the audiovisual presentation mode significantly impacted on one aspect of students' attention styles (focus on idiomatic details) and perceived familiarity with the piece, but had only a marginally significant effect on their enjoyment or interest. Implications of these results for the introduction of unfamiliar music to high school students will be discussed.

BLACKMORE J., JOHNSON R., WARREN W.[20], (2006) States that the potential of new learning technologies for transforming teaching and learning, and indeed the organization of schooling. Much has also been written about teacher responses to new learning technologies-how they resist, ignore, or innovate. A number of recent reports indicate a gap between policy, practice and the capacity of organizations to provide the conditions and resources sin schools to creatively use new learning technologies. Few of these discourses draw upon theories of educational change, in particular those which relate to the dissonance between attitudes and feelings about radical change, and how it impacts on teacher work identity with respect to learning technologies. Much of the literature has focused upon the technical aspects, the hardware and software, but not the 'warm ware', so critical to sound pedagogical practice. This paper draws from the Learning in New Environments Research Group action research project, a pilot study in a large metropolitan secondary college, which is exploring the social implications of new learning technologies for changing relations between students, between teachers and students, between teachers and between family and school. The paper draws from the first round of data collection from the teachers in an ongoing action research project in a region with a high level of socio-economics and cultural diversity.

It draws on concepts of Lieberman's notion of learning networks and Wenger's notion of communities of practice, as well as past research on the reception of gender equity reform in educational organizations, which focuses upon emotional aspects of professional work identity and organizational change.

Joseph Kacharayll$_{25}$ (2006) – "Suitability of colleges for Web Bases Learning" reported that Web based learning environment is expensive to establish, government and private managements should take necessary steps to provide adequate infrastructure facilities in colleges for web based learning. A proper utilization of available human resources would help improve web based learning. In order to overcome technical limitation, training has to be given to both teachers and learners to create flexible and uninterrupted learning environment. The training of material designers should be especially focused upon. Most of the colleges have not properly utilized the available web resources in their teaching learning strategies. There is only nominal technical support and assistance from technical staff and from government and private managements at the institutional level for web based learning. The author collected sample for the survey of 152 college lecturers was obtained through random sampling.

Objectives

1. To find the effect on learning competency of the students by using Multi media for teaching economics
2. To find the active participation of the teachers in using multi media for teaching economics.
3. To find how the teaching of economics has been efficiently improved using the multimedia.
4. To find the importance of computers and internet in teaching economics.

Methodology

The investigator, for the present study adopts the survey method of research. It is a procedure in which data is systematically collected from a population through some form of direct solicitation such as face to face interview, questionnaire or schedule. The survey is extensive and cross sectional dealing with the relatively large number of cases of a particular time and yielding statistics that are abstracted from particular cases. It is the method of investigation which attempts to describe and interpret what exists at present in the form of conditions, practices, process, trends, effects, attitudes, and beliefs. Using this method the investigator had gathered information's measure the Effect of Multi Media Aids in teaching economics for Higher Secondary Students in Chennai.

Sample

For the present study 155 Higher Secondary Students in Chennai.

Data Collection

Primary data, required for the present research work were collected by conducting direct interviews using questionnaire. All the respondents were given sufficient information about the study. These respondents were provided with the same questionnaires. They were also informed that they have to answer in the same fashion.

Statistical Tools for Analysis

The following tools statistical tools were used for the analysis of data. t-test, one way ANOVA and correlation analysis is used for the present study.

Analysis and Interpretation

Table 1

Six wise distribution of "t" value between the boys and girls of the higher secondary economics students using multimedia resources in their schools

Dimensions	Boys N = 55		Girls N = 100		Calculated value of "t"	Level of significance at 5% level
	Mean	S.D	Mean	S.D		
Working knowledge of computers	79.42	8.17	80.42	8.68	0.71	NS
Knowledge about internet	78.15	9.51	76.88	9.80	0.91	NS
Knowledge using A.V. Aids	79.76	7.48	76.26	10.79	2.37	S
Preparation of computer based study materials	76.40	7.97	74.77	11.04	1.06	NS
Assignment and project	81.75	6.31	78.35	10.18	2.56	S
Interaction with others through web	395.47	28.53	386.5	42.77	1.56	NS

(At5% level of significance, the table value of "t" is 1.96)

It is refereed from the above table that there is a significant difference between boys and of Higher Secondary Students of economics group in there, Knowledge in using A.V. Aids and Assignment and project but there is no significant difference between Male and Female Higher Secondary students of economics group in their Working knowledge of computers, knowledge about internet, Preparation of computer based study materials, interaction with others through web.

Table - 2

Area wise distribution of "t" value between the urban and rural higher secondary economics students using multimedia resources in their schools

Dimensions	Urban N = 55		RuralN = 100		Calculated value of "t"	Level of significance at 5% level
	Mean	S.D	Mean	S.D		
Working knowledge of computers	79.42	8.17	80.42	8.68	0.71	NS
Knowledge about internet	78.15	9.51	76.88	9.80	0.91	NS
Knowledge using A.V. Aids	79.76	7.48	76.26	10.79	2.37	S
Preparation of computer based study materials	76.40	7.97	74.77	11.04	1.06	NS
Assignment and project	81.75	6.31	78.35	10.18	2.56	S
Interaction with others through web	395.47	28.53	386.5	42.77	1.56	NS

(At 5% level of significance, the table value of "t" is 1.96)

It is rcfcrred from the above table that there is no significant difference between urban and rural Higher Secondary Students of economics group in there, Knowledge in using A.V. Aids, Assignment and project, Working knowledge of computers, Knowledge about internet, Preparation of computer based study materials, Interaction with other through web.

Table - 3

"F" value among the boys and girls of Higher Secondary economics Group Students in Using Multimedia resources

Dimensions	df= 2,152			Calculated "f" Value	Remarks at 5% Level
	Source of variation	Sum of squares	M.S.V		
Working knowledge of computers	*Between*	118.75	59.38	0.81	NS
	With in	11110.63	73.10		
Knowledge about internet	*Between*	7.94	3.97	0.04	NS
	With in	14650.81	96.39		
Knowledge in using A.V. Aids	*Between*	23.44	11.72	0.12	NS
	With in	15123.38	99.50		
Preparation of computer study materials	*Between*	155.56	77.78	0.76	NS
	With in	15619.63	102.76		
Assignment and project	*Between*	164.39	82.19	0.98	NS
	With in	12793.88	84.17		
Interaction with others through web	*Between*	216.00	108.00	0.07	NS
	With in	23034.00	1515.39		

(For 2,152 df. At 5% level of significance, the table value of "f" is 3.06)

It is inferred from the above table that there is no significance difference among the boys and girls of Higher Secondary economics group students in using Multimedia resources in the Higher Secondary schools of Chennai.

Table - 4

"F" value among the Rural and Urban Higher Secondary Students of economics Group in Using Multimedia source in Chennai

Dimensions	df= 2,152			Calculated "f" Value	Remarks at 5% Level
	Source of variation	Sum of squares	M.S.V		
Working knowledge of computers	*Between*	39.50	19.75	0.27	NS
	With in	11189.88	73.62		
Knowledge about internet	*Between*	394.39	197.16	2.10	NS
	With in	14264.50	93.85		
Knowledge in using A.V. Aids	*Between*	130.31	65.16	0.66	NS
	With in	15016.50	98.79		
Preparation of computer study materials	*Between*	444.44	222.22	2.20	NS
	With in	153330.75	100.86		
Assignment and project	*Between*	364.69	182.32	2.20	NS
	With in	12593.56	82.85		
Interaction with others through web	*Between*	5628.00	2814.00	1.90	NS
	With in	224924.00	11479.76		

(for 2,152 df.at 5% level of significance, the table value of "f" is 3.06)

It is inferred from the above table that there is no significance difference among the Rural and Urban Higher Secondary students of economics group in using Multimedia resource in the Higher Secondary Schools of Chennai.

Table - 5

"F" value among the Higher Secondary Students of economics Group in Using Multimedia source in Government and Private Higher Secondary Schools in Chennai

Dimensions	df= 2,152			Calculated "f" Value	Remarks at 5% Level
	Source of variation	Sum of squares	M.S.V		
Working knowledge of computers	*Between*	39.50	19.75	0.27	NS
	With in	11189.88	73.62		
Knowledge about internet	*Between*	394.39	197.16	2.10	NS
	With in	14264.50	93.85		
Knowledge in using A.V. Aids	*Between*	130.31	65.16	0.66	NS
	With in	15016.50	98.79		
Preparation of computer study materials	*Between*	444.44	222.22	2.20	NS
	With in	153330.75	100.86		
Assignment and project	*Between*	364.69	182.32	2.20	NS
	With in	12593.56	82.85		
Interaction with others through web	*Between*	5628.00	2814.00	1.90	NS
	With in	224924.00	11479.76		

(For 2,152 df. at 5% level of significance, the table value of " is 3.06)

It is inferred from the above table that there is no significance difference among the Government and Private Higher Secondary students of economics group in using Multimedia resource in the Higher Secondary School of Chennai

Table - 6

The Correlation value between the Male and Female Higher Secondary Students in using multimedia resources in the Higher Secondary Schools of Chennai

Category	?X	?X^2	?Y	?Y^2	?XY	Calculated	Remarks
Boys	683	8595	545	5495	6775	.68	NS
Girls	1199	14757	970	9584	11740	.425	S
Total	1882	23354	1515	15079	18515	.325	S

(Table value of Correlation Co-efficient at 5% level of Significance is 0.161)

It is inferred from the above table that there is no significant relationship between the rural and high secondary economics group boys in using multimedia resources and there is a significant relationship between rural and urban high secondary economics group girls in using multimedia resources.

Findings

There a significant difference among the higher secondary commence group students of boys and girls, higher secondary commence students of government and private schools, higher secondary commence group students of rural and urban schools, in their interest to wards learning commence through multimedia resources in Chennai.

There is significant difference among the higher secondary economics group students in their levels of using multimedia shows moderate knowledge except interaction with others through web and no significant difference in low of using multimedia except interaction with other through web and no significant difference in higher level knowledge of using multimedia.

There is no significant difference among the higher secondary economics group boys in their level of using multimedia shows moderate knowledge and higher level of using multimedia and there is a significant difference low of using multimedia at the area of assignment and project, interaction with others though web.

There is no significant difference among the secondary economics group girls in all the levels of using multimedia resources.

There is no significant difference among the higher secondary economics group students of government school in their level of using multimedia shows moderate knowledge and there is a significant difference in low level of interaction with others though web and shows significant difference in higher level of in knowledge about internet, knowledge in using A.V.aids and in the preparation of computer based study materials.

There is no significant difference among the higher secondary economics group students of private school in their level of using multimedia shows moderate knowledge and higher level knowledge of using multimedia and there is a significant difference in low level of using multimedia at the area of working of computer and in interaction with others though web.

There is no significant difference among the higher secondary economics group of rural school in their level of using multimedia shows moderate knowledge and there is a significant difference in low level of preparation of computer in high level of using multimedia at the is a significant difference in high level of using multimedia at the area of working knowledge of computer and in interaction with others with through web.

There is no significant difference between boys and girls or higher secondary students of economics group in there, knowledge in using A.V aids and assignments and project but there is no significant differences between male and female higher secondary of economics group in their working knowledge of computers, knowledge about internet, preparation of computer based study materials with others thought web.

There is no significant difference between urban and rural higher secondary of economics in there, knowledge in using A.V aids, assignment and project, working knowledge of computer knowledge about internet preparation of computer based study martial interaction with others web.

There is no significant difference among the Male and female higher secondary schools of economics group in using multimedia resource in the higher secondary schools of Chennai.

There is no significance difference among the Rural and urban higher secondary students of economics group in using Multimedia resource in the higher secondary of Chennai.

There is n no significant difference among the Government and private Higher Secondary students of economics group in using Multimedia resource in the higher schools of Chennai.

There is no significant relationship between the Rural and urban high secondary group boys in using multimedia resources and there is a significant relationship between Rural and Urban high secondary economics group girls in using multimedia resources.

1. The research overwhelmingly demonstrates that usages of multimedia will definitely improve the quality of teaching economics in higher secondary classes.
2. The research found that the students are actively involved in learning part if the multimedia is introduced in classroom teaching.
3. The research shows the students are highly motivate towards the subject by using multimedia teaching aids and they are attracted more and improve their understanding and memory power in various economics topics like advertising, banking, etc. While using multimedia resources.
4. It is concluded that there is a positive effect of using multimedia aids in the economics achievement of the students in economics in Chennai.

Conclusion

The present study aims to find out the implications of multimedia in teaching economics with special reference to higher secondary. The researcher framed objectives and hypotheses on the basis of the above context. The research was carried out in 155 samples based randomly. A questionnaire constructed by R was used to collect the relevant data. After collecting the data they were analyzed using statistical tools such as t-test, ANOVA and Correlation analysis. The result concluded that students have average implications of multimedia in teaching at Higher Secondary level.

Reference

1. Beavis C. (2006), popular culture, textual practice and identify and identify: literacy and the new technologies, in the middle years
2. Berry l. And Chapman e, (2006); Effect of Background Information and Audio-visual Presentation Modes on Students' Attention style and enjoyment listening to Unfamiliar Music.
3. Best, (1982); J., Johnson R., Warren W. (2006),a hand book of Education Technology.
4. Blackmork j., Johnson R., Warren W. (2006), A handbook of Education Technology.
5. Bruce B.C (2004); Diversity and critical social engagement: How changing technologies enable new modes of literacy in changing circumstances. IN D.E. Alvermann (E.d), Adolescents and illiteracies in a digital world (pp. 1-18). New York: Peter Lang publication.
6. Coyne, Margaret Ann (2006), Emerging Literacy: Assisting Parents to scaffold the emerging literacy skills of their preschool aged children through the use of electronic story books.
7. Joseph Kacharayll (2006); Educational Technology Year Book, 1998.
8. Lanksherar, C and Knoble, M (2003); New literacies: changing Knowledge and classroom learning. Philadelphia: open University press.
9. Lewis, C and Finders, M. (2004); implied adolescents and implied teachers; A generation gap for new times. D.E Alvermann (Ed.), Adolescents and literacies in adugital world (pp.101-113).New York: peter Lang publishing.

24

Life Skills Coach and Language Trainer

Introduction

In a world of continuous change, few are confident enough to predict the future, yet the need to look ahead and prepare is vital.The objective of the paper is making the Gen Next as an employable generation through innovative educational methods like Blended Learning and thus preparing the generation ready for the Digital Age and era beyond the Digital Age. Though the conventional method of teaching process is useful and achieves its purpose, in the fast moving age the younger generation has to be more technical savvy. The new teaching learning process is the need of the hour and it will make the learners to gain confidence and make them employable to the core, anywhere in the world. Only when there is a rethinking in our approach in learning and education, we can enjoy the complete advantages of the new technologies.

The purpose of education is often considered as a "movement from dark to light", "ultimate change towards betterment "or" preparation for life", but, a content livelihood is the prime focus of education for any individual. Mere knowledge in the respective subject will seldom support one to get his dream job. An aspired livelihood can be achieved only when one is employed better. Employability skills will help one to be placed well. In the current Computer age, every profession, in one way or the other, is interlinked with digital technical knowledge. So, literacy in digital technology, employability skills, and a better livelihood are related to each other. "Tamil Nadu Teachers Education University" in its web page has proudly stated that it is in "pursuit of excellence in Promoting human values for social harmony and to make colleges of education excels through innovative teaching, research and extension activities." Yes, TNTEU University has futuristically foreseen the need of innovative teaching methods and hence emerges this subject of discussion.

The unique word "Employability" should have been coined from two words, Employee's and Ability. Employability, according to Manchester Metropolitan University, is, "the development of skills, abilities and personal attributes that students' capability to secure rewarding and satisfying outcomes in their economic, social and community lives."

Learning Computer as a subject or gaining computer skills through co-curricular or extracurricular learning activities will not help one to attain Digital Fluency. The core method of teaching through Digital technology will for sure help the learners to gain digital literacy. More over Digital technology is not confined to computer alone. It has a vast area to cover, start from children's toy to satellite. So, the very teaching method for the next generation student must be through Digital Technology. Such learning process will instill the digital fluency within the learners in a subtle way.

One among the innovative way of digital learning process is "Blended Learning". It is a very unique and innovative method of learning practice, combining teaching methods both from face to face and online learning. Sometimes learning through face to face method and digital class room, it may not be online, but offline is too, termed as "Blended Learning". It meets all the expectations of 21st century learners in respect to efficiency, digital fluency, self-learning opportunities, optimism, flexibility and personalization of students' learning experience, which makes them employable to the core. It is not of acquiring digital knowledge but learning every subject using and supported by the digital tools. The learners must be able to apply digital tools. Learning can happen through any digital method, visual, audio or textual mode.

Building Innovations

When creativity is thinking up new things, innovation is doing new things. Innovation follows creativity. Innovation's last phase is making invoices, as termed by the trading community. Ideas in paper are turned to be currencies in trade. But in field like education, innovation means much different. The institutions and policy makers aspire to utilise innovative ideas for the uplifting of humanity in all aspects. Considering the growth of the digital technology as well the expectations of the employers the learners of coming generation have to get updated to meet the job market requirements. Today's learners are the tomorrow's, executives, CEOs, labourers, teachers, entrepreneurs, policy makers and more. So, learning methods have to be innovative and creative to imbibe the required technical as well digital skills to the students.

Digital Literacy

In this digital age, our definition of literacy is changing completely. Now a day many jobs require a high level of IT competency and confidence. As such, the concept of Digital Literacy – those capabilities that equip an individual for living, learning and working in our IT-enabled society – is one that needs to be taken seriously by schools, colleges and universities, as well as by employers.

We live in an online and globally connected world. Society has a resulting need for citizens who can thrive in an era of digital information and communication. Those who are digitally literate are more likely to be economically secure, and these skills are especially important in higher education given that graduate jobs will almost invariably involve some level of contact with computers and portable devices. Against this backdrop, there is a clear need for education at all levels to play a part in establishing and developing the skills that the future employees will need.

At the same time, delivering digital literary goes beyond simply teaching the IT skills; a paradigm shift is required to live fully within the modern digital society, from understanding how to communicate ideas effectively in a range of media, to managing digital reputation and history, and understanding how to remain secure and protected throughout the process. Gone is the" Green Revolution" in agriculture which was an outcome of advances in Biotechnology and we are going to have a " Learning Revolution" in education, thanks to new Digital Technology.

Digital literacy gives young people the ability to take advantage of the wealth of new and emerging opportunities associated with digital technologies whilst also remaining alert to the various challenges technology can present.In fact, digital literacy is the 'savvyness' that allows young people to participate meaningfully and safely as digital technology becomes evermore pervasive in society.Schools are to be encouraged to embed the use of ICT in all subject areas of the primary and secondary curricula. Considering how digital literacy supports subject knowledge can help to ensure that technology-use enhances teaching and learning rather than simply becoming an add-on. Indeed, formal education must seek to prepare young people to make sense of the world and to thrive socially, intellectually and economically.

It can be said that digital media is now a central aspect of most people's lives, whatever their age.The skills, knowledge and understanding of digital literacy are therefore becoming indispensible as young people grow up in a society in which digital technology and media play an ever more important role. Digital technology makes the young people creative, and in return, the soceity becomes creative soceity.

Why learning through Digital mode in School Level?

Every third person in an Indian city today is a youth. By 2020, India is set to become the world's youngest country with 64 per cent of its population in the working age group. Quoting a report "The Hindu" newspaper says that the southern and western States will be the first to experience a growth dividend as they account for 63 per cent of all formally trained people. The largest share of youth with formal skills is found in Kerala, followed by Maharashtra, Tamil Nadu, Himachal Pradesh and Gujarat. The report finds that a person in an urban area has a 93 per cent greater chance of acquiring training than someone in a rural area. When the teaching pattern does consist uniform technology like Blended Learning, irrespective of territorial bindings and curriculum methods, the future generation will be more employable and well equipped to take up a career anywhere in the world.

The student population from rural India is in many fold in number than students from urban. They are the people, mostly first generation graduates of the family, who focus on IT and ITES careers. Thanks to MNCs which offer job scope for those students.In county like India, where majority of population live in villages, access to digital gadgets and opportunity to attain digital literacy is denied to every citizen.They dependent on schools and colleges for even to learn basic knowledge in computer. With the very basic skills in technology, they seldom get well paid career. But when the method of teaching itself is based on digital technology with Digital classrooms from the school level, it is easy for the rural students too to become fluent in digital technology.

Normally children arrive schools with basic knowledge of digital technology. It is not exaggerating if it is said that they come with their mobile phone or any other digital gadgets in hand to schools in urban India. When they are taught with black board or any other conventional method of teaching, it is not fair in the part of our educational system. They must be encouraged to enhance the skills they posses when they join the school. We say teacher is one who "Knows the way", "shows the way" and "goes the way". So, teaching all subjects through digital technology, like method of Blended Learning, will be interesting, easy to learn, as well they can attain digital fluency, in a professional manner. The level of motivation will be increased when they are taught through the mode they are familiar with.

Employability and Employable Generation

The term "Employability "can be defined in multiple ways according to the need of the industry, expectations of individuals and society. Employability in the words of Professor Mantz Yorke," is aset of achievements – skills, understandings and personal attributes – that make graduates more likely to gain employment and be successful in their chosen occupations, which benefits themselves, the workforce, the community and the economy".

It is estimated that around 90% of all new graduate jobs in United Kingdom require a high level of digital skills. Though it is the status in UK, it is the global demand. It will not take years for India to get the same scenario. So, the policy makers and educational institutions must focus on creating an Employable Generation rather than focusing on instilling employability skills in the learners.

Current status of the Job Seekers

Surveys on the employability skills of Indian graduates, graduated in any field of study, say, most of the job seekers are not employable in medium and high profile careers. They are not good in communication skills, don't have sufficient digital literacy and other core requirements for a good profile jobs. Neither Indian companies nor MNCs will employ them without a basic training. It is understood more number of trainees are rejected during the training period itself. Such happenings make the rejected hands feel dejected and they think their future is dark. It is the status in all the field of study, like, management, technical and even in teaching profession.

The learners are not the only reason for such adverse scenario but the system we follow too plays major and vital role in this. So, to make our future generation employable we need a system which makes the learner master in all the fields required by the employers.

Blended Learning

"Teaching in the Internet age means we must teach tomorrow's skills today." Jennifer Fleming. "Preparing for future" can be termed as *motto* of Blended Learning. Though there are other new age teaching concepts like Flipped class rooms, Learning without Limits, Cloud Computing , Blended Leaning seems to be more innovative since it not only a blend of technologies but also a perfect blend of Traditional method of class room as well a New Age class room.

Blended learning, where multiple learning environments and activities are combined is a decades' old innovative concept of teaching. But contemporary definitions of blended learning take into account that technology can play more. Current as well futuristic concept of blended learning represents a combination of online and face to face experiences. It is the best of both worlds. Blended learning is a student-centered approach to creating a learning experience whereby the learner interacts with other students, with the instructor, and with content through thoughtful integration of online and face-to-face environments. Sometime Blended Learning consists of face to face instruction and usage of off line Digital tools instead of on line lessons.

In contrast to teacher-centered, rote-learning approaches, blended learning environments provide multiple ways to access content and to demonstrate mastery. As a result, they lend themselves more readily to differentiation of content and process. A blended approach also gives the learner the opportunity to be more responsible for his or her learning, which creates a learning situation that may be more meaningful on an individual level. Because the learner comes to construct knowledge through personal effort, she or he is more likely to demonstrate understanding beyond rote memorization, and to transfer what she or he has learned to new settings.

Blended Learning – An inevitable Teaching Method

India is a country which had more effective and traditional teaching methods like *Gurukula* method. Though it was age old, it has its own value and we respect such methods as they were man making way of teaching. Having such great methods of teaching we need not have to switch over entirely too complete online method of teaching process. Our culture respects *Guru* as father, mother, guide and God. Our *Vedas, Upanishads, Epics* like *Mahabharata and Ramayana*, master pieces like *Thirukural* always speak high and great of Gurus. None other country gives this much respect and high regard to *Guru*, the teacher. Still our education system mostly depends on teachers. We, Indians give more importance to moral and man making education than attaining mass production of graduates. In this back drop, it is difficult to imagine teaching without a teacher or learning without a Guru.

In this digital era, traditional classroom teaching methods are not much effective to achieve current learning standards. Technological approaches alone can't provide students with deep and meaningful learning experience. But the combination of both, say, Blended Learning and face to face teaching can help an individual to attain moral values, command over the subject as well digital fluency. Such an employee with a multiple skills, moral values, digital literacy and adaptability is most wanted by the employers and in coming years, they are the only preferred hands by employers in any field and anywhere in the world. So, for country like ours, Blended Learning could be the most apt mode of teaching, where we have face to face instruction and technology based learning. In this method of learning, the learners will have a personal touch with the teachers as well they are independent in learning. It could be a perfect blend of modern and traditional ways of learning.

Getting blended is vital at this moment. Blended learning is more than electronic textbooks and productivity tools. It means inventing or adopting new learning environments that work better for students as well teachers. It increases opportunities for students to engage with technology such as teacher using digital class rooms, a school computer lab, and computers using digital curriculum in the class rooms are more supportive for the learners to attain digital literacy and to get the dream jobs in future. Clearly there are more opportunities for exploration and growth in the use of blended learning from the school level. Some of this growth may be driven by increasing student demands for more learning process.

Being motivated

Motivation is the driving force for success. The learners have to have a change in their attitude to be taught through a different mode of teaching method, an innovative method. They may feel fish out of water in digital class room and it may be very difficult for them to come out of comfort zone, an accustomed zone of conventional mortar class room learning.

When they are motivated they will readily open their mind for new learning. Yes, mind is like a parachute, it works only when it is open.

Understanding the significance of the learning method

It is in the hands of the teachers to make them to understand the dire need of the change of learning which is going to make them employable. Lot of comparisons can be sited from other countries and cultures to make them to realise the value of the Blended Learning. Even they can be asked to prepare papers supporting the idea. Discussions can be arranged to speak for and against the concept where their eyes can be opened.

Getting accustomed in handling digital tools

It is very vital stage of learning process. Students from rural areas usually will have a pessimistic attitude towards digital tools. It must be taken care that they must not keep aloof in the class rooms and it can be monitored no inferiority complex comes in learners from rural areas. Slowly the digital tools can be introduced to the learners and till they feel free in handling the tools they must be free from core teaching.

Creating awareness of technicalities of the digital tools

Simply using the digital tools will not help the learners to attain expertise in the field. Apart from software knowledge they must have the basic hardware skills too. It will help them to become an all-rounder in his field. So, basic technicalities of the digital tools can be taught to the learners. It is like car drivers knowing the mechanism of the car, which will help them to attend the faults in the machine, complete his journey successfully even after break downs.

Using the digital tools for communication and learning purpose

Once they are motivated and aware of the importance and necessity of the blended learning, accustomed in handling the digital tools and acquire hardware skills, it is right time for them to be introduced to proper and fully fledged learning. The regular subjects will be taught through the blended learning method. Face to face as well online and off line classes will be given. They will gain confident towards the teachers and the new method of learning. Apart from regular subjects they must use the digital tools for communication purpose too.

Acting independently with the digital tools

This is the last phase in Blended Learning. It is an assessment of their learning. Seminars, symposiums, conferences can be conducted in this phase. The learner becomes a teacher now. They can be asked to handle classes for their peer group using the digital tools. Question answer sessions, group discussions on their respective subjects can be arranged in which the Blended Learning pattern can be followed. When they act independently they get confidence in their related subjects as well they feel good and positive in using the digital tools for all purpose.

Conclusion

To conclude, a survey conducted in America can be sited which has found that college students prefer blended learning course over those that are solely face to face or solely online. This is the scenario everywhere in the world. "We need to give people a new set of skills in an explicit way that will make them more marketable for the job market", foresees Cristina Costa. Yes, by providing relevant and authentic learning experiences that offer opportunities to develop and evidence professional practice not only enhances student employability but also more importantly makes good business sense for colleges and universities, for employers and for the economy as a whole.

Normally computers are used as source centre of information and the learners are taught how to browse, send E-mails, know to work in word or excel. But the learners must become fluent with computer so that they can create and express instead passing information. To help the learners to attain Digital Fluency, the mode of teaching must be an innovative one. Among all other technology based teaching methods Blended Learning will be an opt one for our country. When the forth coming age is going to be a Digital Age, the job aspirants must be a computer literate. Any knowledge the learners get learning computer through extracurricular or co-curricular activities will make them aware of computers not expert in it. They can access computer, but they cannot express. They can play for lifelong but cannot make it as bread winner. Shortly, it can be said Blended Learning which is a holistic approach to technology enhanced learning will make the new generation learners employable and we can have an employable generation on the other hand.

References

1. Careers & Employability Service, www.mmu.ac.uk/careers/guides, Manchester Metropolitan University
2. Learning & Employability – Series One – Employability in higher education: what it is what it is not – By Mantz Yorke, publiished by

The Higher Education Academy, Innovation Way, York Science Park, Heslington, York, UK.

3. Blended Learning Implementation Guide. www. blendedlearning-now.com
4. The Hindu, April 17th 2013. Online edition, www.thehindu.com
5. Cristina Costa, Research Technologies Development Officer, Research and Graduate College, University of SalfordEcho360 2012 student survey, "Blended Learning Technology: Connecting with the Online-All-the-Time Student," www.echo360.com/studentsurveys

25

Cloud Computing in Higher Education

Introduction

Cloud computing provides shared resources, software and information through Internet as a PAYGO (Pay-as-you-go) basis. Cloud Computing is a kind of virtualization; thus also known as Virtualization Technology. Cloud Computing and its benefits attracts several other field. Education Systems also interacts with Educational applications for Cloud Computing. Cloud Computing provides several benefits in Educational Systems such as creation of Virtual teaching learning environment, making interacting and speedy smart class room, it also minimizes the time of knowledge collection model preparation and delivery. Cloud Computing and its benefits are used around the world and especially in the Western countries. Due to poverty and underdevelopment; Asian and African and other undeveloped countries are still unable to offer such benefits to teachers, student, administrator, instructor and other stakeholders related to education systems. The challenges and issues are one of the important concerns for strong and healthy educational systems powered by cloud computing and virtualization technique.

Higher Education

Higher education was acknowledged in time as one of the pillars of society development. Through the partnerships between universities, government and industry, researchers and students have proven their contribution to the transformation of society and the entire world economy. The tendency observed during the last few years within the higher education level is the universities' transition to research universities and ongoing update of the IT (Information Technology) infrastructure as foundation for educational activities and Science research.

With the evolution of technology, the number of services which migrate from traditional form to the online form grows as well. For these specific services, an adequate providing form must be found in the online environment, using the proper technologies, guaranteeing the access of large number of users, fast and secure services. Due to this aspect, at the moment universities are confronting with a dramatic increase of costs in higher education, more than the inflation rate and a decrease of universities' budgets, which leads to the pressure of finding some alternative means of reaching their purpose i.e. the education of students and accomplishing the research.

Cloud Computing (CC)

Cloud Computing is a new technology which is an improvement of distributed computing, parallel computing and grid computing. The basic principle of cloud computing is making tasks distributed among large number of computers but not in local computers or remote servers. This is a dynamic model, based on pay-per-use (subscription) or scalable system in which configuration of resources (hardware, platform/services) can be graded to suit the needs of the users for optimum utilization of resources. In simple words, it is a subscription- based or pay-per-use real time service over the internet.The following **National Institute of Standards and Technology (NIST)** definitions are used for deployment models:

Private cloud The cloud infrastructure is operated solely for an organization. It may be managed by the organization or a third party and may exist on premise or off premise.

Community cloud The cloud infrastructure is shared by several organizations and supports a specific community that has shared concerns (e.g., mission, security requirements, policy, and compliance considerations). It may be managed by the organizations or a third party and may exist on premise or off premise.

Public cloud The cloud infrastructure is made available to the general public or a large industry group and is owned by an organization selling cloud services.

Hybrid cloud The cloud infrastructure is a composition of two or more clouds (private, community, or public) that remain unique entities but are bound together by standardized or proprietary technology that enables data and application portability (e.g., cloud bursting for load balancing between clouds).

Characteristics of Cloud Computing

There are many distinguishing features of cloud computing but some important features are.

(a) Versatility
(b) Cost-effectiveness (pay-per-use)
(c) Virtualization
(d) Security
(e) Sustainability
(f) Scalability
(g) User-friendly
(h) Resource Optimisation
(i) Infrastructure and service-level agreements (SLAs)

Types ofCloud Computing

The following is a list of the three main types of services that can be offered by the cloud:

1. Software as a Service (SaaS): The applications, such as e-mail, people use every day.
2. Platform as a Service (PaaS): The operating environment in which applications run.
3. Infrastructure as a Service (IaaS): The on-demand data centers.

Outsourcing some capabilities to the cloud makes the most of what's on-site by freeing time, budget, and people. For example, with SaaS, you can add services, like e-mail, affordably. With PaaS, you can deliver services broadly without having to manage the infrastructure. With IaaS, you get pay-as-you-go data center capacity for adding CPUs, storage, networking, or Web hosting. Take, for example, a typical university with an IT infrastructure that caters for the needs of students, teaching staff and management, research staff and software developers (e.g., Web developers).

Demand for IT services in this environment is directed to the IT Services Department whose job is to:

• provide students and staff with software (e.g., email accounts, operating systems, productivity applications, malware detectors and cleaners, etc.) and hardware (e.g., PCs, Servers, etc.);

• provide researchers and postgraduate students with the required special software and hardware to run experiments that are likely to involve a great deal of processing and computation;

• provide Web developers with the development tools needed to write and host Web applications.

Many aspects of this arrangement can be migrated to the cloud. For example, students, administrative staff and lecturers can be made to use the services of providers of SaaS and IaaS clouds. These services will be ideally accessed through thin clients. Any software launched by these groups of people resides on the servers of the SaaS cloud provider and is accessed online.

A growing number of academic institutions are turning to SaaS for their desktop applications. For example, Madras University uses an e-mail solution hosted in the cloud. Students now have the free collaboration tools they want, people on campus have the tools they need to work together, and administrators are finding it easier and more cost-effective to manage.

SaaS for education: Microsoft Live@edu

Microsoft Live@edu is a program that provides students, staff, faculty, and alumni long-term, primary e-mail addresses and other applications that they can use to collaborate and communicate online—all at no cost to education institutions. Students will be using Microsoft products similar to those used in many workplaces that help to prepare them for jobs after college.

Cloud computing initiatives

There are good number of cloud computing initiatives undertaken by Amazon, Google, Microsoft and others offering various types of cloud computing services for the organizations, businesses, and individuals. IBM Cloud Academy, IEEE Cloud Computing initiatives are offered some services in Education.

IBM Cloud Academy

IBM (International Business Machines) launched the IBM Cloud Academy (2009), a global forum for educators, researchers and information technology (IT) personnel from the education industry to pursue cloud computing initiatives, develop skills and share best practices for reducing operating costs while improving quality and access to education.

IEEE Cloud Computing

The IEEE (Institute of Electrical and Electronics Engineers) Cloud Computing Initiative represents the first, broad-based collaborative endeavor for cloud computing to be offered by a global technical professional organization. Six interdependent activity tracks are included in the IEEE Cloud Computing Initiative: the Web portal; conferences; continuing education courses; publications; standards development; and a test bed to be used in the development of cloud standards and applications as well as for education and research.

Amazon Web Services (AWS)

Amazon is perceived as one of the major players in the business, offering a wide range of prominent cloud computing services such as elastic compute cloud (EC2), simple storage service (S3), simple DB and simple queuing service (SQS). It provides a reliable, scalable, low-cost infrastructure platform in the cloud that powers hundreds of thousands of businesses in countries around the world. Some of the solutions offered by Amazon through cloud computing include application hosting, web hosting, backup and storage, enterprise IT, content delivery, and database.

Google Apps

Google Apps cloud services, a multi-tenant, and internet-scale infrastructure, offers faster access to innovation, superior reliability, and security, and maximum economies of scale as compared to on-premises, hosted and software plus services technologies8. Google Apps is available free for individuals and organizations (limited up to 10 user accounts), educational institutions and US non-profitable organizations and for a price to businesses and organizations.

Microsoft Windows Azure

Microsoft is also investing heavily in this new computing service delivery model and has introduced Azure, as its cloud offering. Azure has three components: Windows Azure (which provides developers with on-demand compute and storage to host, scale, and manage Internet or cloud applications), SQL Azure (which extends the capabilities of Microsoft SQL Server into the cloud as a Web-based distributed relational database) and Azure .Net Services (which include a set of Microsoft-hosted, highly scalable, developer-oriented services that provide key building blocks required by many cloud-based and cloud-aware applications).

Education and the Cloud Computing

Colleges and universities are always on the lookout to upgrade their software and IT hardware in order to attract students and keep pace with the rapid developments in digital technologies. Cloud computing could provide those institutions with the means to achieve those ambitions at prices they can afford. Furthermore, shifting responsibility to external providers for managing some aspects of their software and hardware infrastructures could also result in cost savings with relation to labor, as fewer IT services staff will be needed than before. Cloud Computing is gaining popularity in educational systems, especially in online education and corporate education; E-Learning is gaining popularity through web 2.0 platform of Cloud Computing ; Still in India, higher educational institutes are not moving towards healthy Cloud Computing solutions; Governmental grants, non-availability of software and packages related to educational field are important issues.

1. The online and e-learning systems may gain rapidly with the help of Cloud Computing; the aspects such as online question paper distribution, paper collection, full text book and module delivery is possible with Cloud Computing.
2. Social Computing such as Social 2.0 powered web technologies is also a kind of Cloud Computing; which allows sharing of educational data, text, notes and recorded video without extra support. The challenges of such systems are mainly people awareness, student awareness, teachers and faculty towards sharing and creation of group of learner. Many teachers and students may not aware about IT and Social Networking usages.
3. Creation of smart class room, online and continuing education university education has come to the door step of learner. Here Cloud Computing is used in several cases.
4. More importantly, Cloud Computing based education systems saves cost by centralized IT Infrastructure, rapid transfer, elasticity, flexibility and other benefits in education
5. Cloud computing also promotes some new educational mode such as-corporate learning, industry integrated learning programme; where students get knowledge and classes from online media in his/her office or corporate house. It is helpful for the working students. But for that a mutual understanding between education service provider and corporate agency is essential. The main reason behind this is, space for projection, tools and technological and electricity support and so on.

Advantages of Cloud Computing

1. There is no need to own all infrastructure facilities as cloud computing takes care of it.
2. With the help of Broadband and healthy connection anywhere and anytime services are possible;
3. It provides large amounts of processing power comparable to supercomputer level.
4. It provides an effective and creative service delivery model;
5. Cloud Computing model does not support any long term commitments.
6. Capital expenditure is minimized A convenient tool to engage in the scholarship of teaching and learning.

Cloud Computing Based Education: Challenges and Issues

Many challenges of cloud computing for higher education relate to its relative newness and the underdevelopment of the marketplace for cloud services. For higher education, decisions to adopt cloud computing will be influenced by more than technical and cost considerations.

Information is the lifeblood of higher education, and decisions on how to manage that information can have far-reaching political, social, and economic considerations. Adoption of cloud computing presents many of the same risks and challenges as deciding to use a more traditional outsourcing arrangement. The increased possibility that the service provider or its resources may reside outside of a government's legal or territorial jurisdiction, however, can make some of these concerns more acute. At present, as many universities are trying to update their IT infrastructure and data, but they are facing few challenges which can be solved by cloud computing. The challenges are as follows:

a) **Cost**: choose the subscription or PAYGO plan.
b) **Flexibility**: cloud computing allows to dynamically scale the investment in infrastructures as demand fluctuate.
c) **Accessibility**: making the data and services available publicly without losing the sensitive information
d) **Security**: making data secure.

Conclusion

Cloud computing is a new baby in the computer systems technology emerged owing to the developments in internet and associated technologies. It is in the evolving stage, requires some amount of careful considerations before organizations think about hosting some of their services. E-Learning or online education is need of hour. Today several modes of education have originated with the help of IT and computing. It provides several opportunities; Cloud Computing plays an important role for overall IT infrastructure development. Regular education may also benefit from Cloud Computing. The small room, mobile based education is the wonderful gift of IT and especially Cloud Computing.Universities, Engineering colleges, and other higher educational institutes should go for Cloud Computing and virtualization.Proper funding and planning are essential for healthy Cloud Computing packages. Proper and adequate training programme on Cloud Computing need to be introduced.

Reference

1. Aladwani, Adel M,(2002) "An integrated performance model of information systems projects", *Journal of Management Information Systems*, 19(1).
2. AbdulKalam, APJ (2003) "IT Strategy in Defense Environment", DESIDOC *Bulletin of Information Technology*, 20(1 & 2): 7-12.
3. Bates, M (1990) "Where should the person stop and the information search interface start?' *Information Processing & Management*, 26(5): 575–591.
4. Belkin, N. J., & Robertson, S.E. (1976) "Information science and the phenomena of information." *Journal of the American Society for Information Science*, 27(4):197–204.
5. Denning, P. J., & et al. (1989) Computing as a discipline. *Communication of the ACM*, 32(1),23.
6. Dhawan, Neelam (2011) Cloud computing can counter illiteracy. *Times of India*,
7. Fox, A. (2009) Cloud computing in education. *Berkeley iNews*, https://inews. B erkeley.edu/articles/Spring2009/cloudcomputing
8. Hayes, B. (2008) Cloud computing. *Communications of ACM*, 51(7): 9-11.
9. Scale, Mark-Shane E (2009) Cloud computing and collaboration. *Library Hi Tech News*, 26(9): 10-13.
10. Wikipedia. Cloud computing. http://en.wikipedia.org/ wiki/Cloud computing.

26

Designing Learing Envronment of Tomorrow Foreffective Academic Excellence

Introduction

Education plays a very significant role in developing an individual to his full potential by bringing out his latent talents and nurturing them. The forces of environment begin to influence the growth and development of the individual right from the womb of the mother. A proper and adequate environment is very much necessary for a fruitful learning of the child. In recent years, we have witnessed rapid social and cultural changes, phenomenal advances in communication and information technologies, as well as the introduction of the Internet within schools. These factors have contributed to shape the teaching and operating cultures of schools and created shifts in our expectations of the physical learning environment. They have affected teachers, educators and researchers the world over. These miniature revolutions have given rise to an urgent need for a new generation of facilities to cater for 21st century teaching and learning needs. Good learning environment is one in which staff, students and, parents build safe and peaceful environment where people feel accepted and respected and where learning is the main focus. Therefore a positive learning environment where all students feel comfortable, wanted, valued, accepted, and secure must be created. The use of innovative methods in educational institutions has the potential not only to improve education, but also to empower people, strengthen governance and galvanize the effort to achieve the human development goal for the country. The present paper deals with the effective, appropriate and interactive use of computer – related technologies for designing learning environment of tomorrow which induce and pave ways for academic excellence.

Education plays a very significant role in developing an individual to his full potential by bringing out his latent talents and nurturing them. Education shapes a person. According to Dewey 'Education is a continuous process of experiencing and of revising or non-revising experiences. It is the development of all those capacities in the individual, which enables him to control his environment and fulfill his possibilities'. The forces of environment begin to influence the growth and development of the individual right from the womb of the mother. A proper and adequate environment is very much necessary for a fruitful learning of the child. Especially the school and home should provide the necessary stimulus for learning experience. In recent years, we have witnessed rapid social and cultural changes, phenomenal advances in communication and information technologies, as well as the introduction of the Internet within schools. These factors have contributed to shape the teaching and operating cultures of schools and created shifts in our expectations of the physical learning environment. They have affected teachers, educators and researchers the world over. These miniature revolutions have given rise to an urgent need for a new generation of facilities to cater for 21st century teaching and learning needs. Good learning environment is one in which staff, students and, parents build safe and peaceful environment where people feel accepted and respected and where learning is the main focus. Therefore a learning environment, where all students feel comfortable, wanted, valued, accepted, and secure, must be created. A positive school climate affects everyone associated with the school, be it the students, staff, parents, and the community. Improved school climate is a goal to pursue. Educators need to constant up work towards improving their school climate, culture, and conditions to that students learning is improved. The world could be synchronized with the development of science and technology. Education is the means for all these developments. Education is the essence of every civilization. The use of innovative methods in educational institutions has the potential not only to improve education, but also to empower people, strengthen governance and galvanize the effort to achieve the human development goal for the country.

Conceptual Framework

Learning takes place effectively only when proper and congenial environment is provided for children. Positive learning environment exists when all students feel comfortable, wanted, valued, accepted, and secure in an environment where they trust. Many of the modern learning environments being built today promote and support a range of pedagogies including delivering, applying, creating, communicating and decision-making. Modern learning environments support strengths-based teaching and can offer students and teachers flexibility, openness and access to resources. Providing teachers with an open, flexible learning environment can lead to the development of a robust, continuously improving community of practice.

Learning environment should support multiple perspective or interpretations of reality, knowledge construction, and experience based activities. In the age of globalization the modern computer – related technologies help in changing the learning environment rapidly and make the pedagogy more and more interactive. With the use of computer technology, classroom learning process tends to accelerate day by day. Computer technologies increase the level of teaching and motivate students to provide information in an interesting and innovative way by making teaching more and more effective. The appropriate and effective use of technology facilitates to gain information in depth. The present paper deals with the effective, appropriate and interactive use of computer – related technologies for designing learning environment of tomorrow which induce and pave ways for academic excellence.

Computer – assisted learning provides a huge amount of information to the learners in a short period of time. Learners are reinforced in a powerful way through the medium of discussion in classroom. It helps in stimulating the students to learn through the use of multimedia, provides students different varieties of information, provides more powerful ICT tools for problem solving and learning and allows the students to work at their pace. Every learner should not only be a computer literate but also develop competencies in the effective usage of computers and all the technologies that are related to learning, Age –old method of chalk and talk in classroom should be dead and gone.

Changing the learning process:

In the late '90s' many in the education field and government, as well as in the media and public, recognized a 'digital divide' in which some school districts and classrooms were "wired" and had up-to-date computer technology, while others did not, Accordingly, there were efforts undertaken by government, business and educators to wire classrooms and make computer technology available to a greater number of students and teachers. While many teachers and students are engaging in innovative forms of research and novel projects, there are still many traditional teachers who resist learning new computer skills and do not want to bring computer- based technologies into their classrooms

Teachers have to develop the ability to demonstrate how these technologies can be used for academic purposes and convey the educational advantages of computers and the Internet to their students. This means acquiring and teaching new literacy involving teachers and students in innovative types of research projects, and interacting in novel ways as everyone learns to use new technology and media.

Indeed, to meet the challenges of an always- evolving high-tech society, teachers today need to develop multiple forms of computer and information literacy to help improve education. This means using technology in the classroom to illustrate lesson topics; teaching students how to use the Internet and information technology to research topics; and using technology to enhance education outside the classroom, ideally in the ways that involve students in the learning process.

Teachers might share large learning spaces, rather than traditional classrooms, with children at different levels, learning different things. Classroom design developments include flexible teaching spaces that can be expanded or reduced in size depending on what's being taught and what technology requirements are needed. Some modern options include hexagonal shapes with a shared common centre area, and outdoor areas and decking off each learning space. Sliding glass walls can be used to open up or close down spaces providing both flexibility and an open, bright environment. Specialist equipment within a school can be shared by all, and with the wider community. This could be a fully-fitted industrial kitchen, or a modern science laboratory lined with wall-to-wall glass that allows other students to walk past and observe what's going on. Whole walls can be whiteboard, or white-boards can be movable. Teachers can opt to change the way the class is facing, or break children up into groups.

The key principles of Learning Environment of Tomorrow

Flexibility

Creating flexible spaces that accommodate a wide range of current and future teaching and learning styles is the key. While we cannot anticipate all of the future needs for educational facilities we can know with certainty that they will change. Teaching spaces that can be adapted and support the educational agility of teachers and students will be an environment that can deliver outstanding educational outcomes. We should not get stuck with replicating 'business as usual' solutions when we could have spaces that support innovation and creative learning.

The Learning Community

The modern learning environment can gain significant benefits from being designed for the community it serves. While funding is a one-size-fits-all model, the project team can actually deliver a project that reflects and supports the wider school community. And when a school is designed as a learning community it is a powerful way to engage with students, staff and parents.

Classroom / Learning Studio

A classroom can offer so much more when combined with other spaces such as small seminar or breakout rooms, group learning areas or even external learning decks can offer the opportunity for a wide variety of learning styles. Adjacencies and visibility are so important in making this work well.

Group Learning Areas

Group learning spaces can take over from the corridor for circulation but also create wonderful opportunities for teaching and learning at different scales – from small groups or combined classes. They can also be a powerful physical manifestation of the learning community described above, and surrounded by visible learning studios and small seminar / breakout rooms they support the flexible, agile leaning of the future.

Outdoor Learning Environment

Often the external spaces for the school are an afterthought and yet they represent a fantastic opportunity to create great learning spaces. The key is visibility. The power of passive surveillance through being able to remotely supervise a space through good visibility can transform behaviours and learning outcomes. Careful thought by designers can unlock the potential of the neglected areas in your school grounds, bringing them back into the overall learning environment. School buildings should support and inspire the wonderful learning opportunities that can happen in and around them.

Learning environment of tomorrow must encompass a holistic approach that relates the pedagogy of learning to the physical and virtual spaces in which learning occurs. Each of the following characteristics can pose to design a learning environment of tomorrow:

1. A dynamic transformative learning centre that provides a welcoming, vibrant and culturally inclusive environment
2. A place of awe and enchantment, exploration and curiosity
3. A large, flexible learning space based on fluid design principles
4. A space that includes print, e-resources, and multi-media, and provides access to a range of ICT hardware and software fully supported by robust ICT infrastructure

Functional elements within a learning environment of tomorrow

1. Enable learning to be demonstrated by students participating, reading, watching, publishing, creating, researching, and performing in groups or individually.
2. Have flexible spaces that can be adapted for individual, small or large group use with acoustic considerations. This will allow students to work individually, to reflect, as well as collaborate on projects, and discuss and share ideas.
3. Have interiors designed using modular, flexible, multi-use furniture. Power points will be installed everywhere and offer charging for mobile learning devices.

For augmenting and strengthening the use of innovative strategies in the classrooms of India, we need to work on the following areas:

1. Curricular reforms
2. Faculty development
3. Academic leadership
4. Renewal of Higher Quality standards
5. E-skill development
6. Adopting the under privileged or Rural villages
7. Professional competence.

Conclusion

Academic excellence is one of the most important goals of education. It can be defined as excellence in all disciplines. It encompasses student ability and performance. The effective growth and development, the desirable learning experiences, attitudes and values to be developed in the child depends upon the main factor learning environment. The study demands the designing of learning environment of tomorrow. Further the educational resources and infrastructure needs to be updated in rural schools so that the academic excellence can be uplifted in such schools.

References

1. Dillenbourg, Pierre. "Virtual learning environments" (PDF). EUN Conference 2000: Learning in the new millennium: Building new education strategies for schools
2. Dinesh Kumar, Amit Singh. Computer technology as an interactive teaching system a new trend in education, Edutrack, January 2013, Vol.12, No: 5.
3. *G. Kearsley and B. Shneiderman, 'Engagement theory: A framework for technology-based teaching and learning', Educational Technology,* ***38****, 5 (September-October 1998), pp. 20-23. accessed at*http://home.sprynet.com/~gkearsley/engage.htm on 21 February 2000
4. G.Madhavi, N. Ramnath Kishan. Development of positive learning environment, Edutrack, November 2012, Vol.9, No: 3.
5. Jagannath.K, Dange, Praveen.R. Online learning a new way of education, Edutrack, July 2009, Vol.8, No: 11.
6. *M. J. Stiles, 'Developing Tacit and Codified Knowledge and Subject Culture within a Virtual Learning Environment',* IJEEE, 37, No1 *(January 2000) pp 13-25*
7. Moult, R. R. (2005), Learning to listen: Using ICT to capture pupils' perceptions and help the teacher to respond (PDF), p. 19.
8. Pea & K. Sheingold (Eds.), Mirrors of minds: Patterns of experience in educational computing (pp. 147-177). Norwood, NJ: Ablex Publishing
9. Pea, R. D., & Kurland, D. M. (1987). On the cognitive effects of learning computer programming. In R. D.
10. Puneet,Rahi.Innovations in teaching learning, Edutrack, July 2012, Vol.11, No: 11.
11. Seale, J (2009), A Research Briefing by the Technology Enhanced Learning Phase of the Teaching and Learning Research Programme (PDF).
12. Weller, M. (2007), Virtual Learning Environments: Using, choosing and developing your VLE, London: Routledge.
13. *Modern Learning Environments*, by Mark Osborne *(PDF, 3.1mb)*
14. *www.events.core-ed.org/modern-learning-environments*

27

Designing Learning Environment of Tomorrow

Introduction

Education is the moment to moment experience of the humanity at large. To envisage it, one needs to know the meaning of learning better. Learning depends mainly on three factors, student's interest, teacher's ability and their environment. Increasing the standard of learning means increasing student's interest, diversifying teacher's ability and providing a suitable environment or milieu. Can Innovation, Education and Technology be the Ingredients for a better Society in Generating Employment?

Innovation, Education and Technology

Innovation is a driver of growth and well-being. New technologies, products, services and organizations create jobs and rejuvenate industries – while making others obsolete (out-dated). To reap the gains of innovation, policy makers need to understand, how we innovate the way for change process and what this implies for education and training policies. There is a need for integration of technology in education for innovations and creativity to bloom out of the box. "We've been on the brink (threshold) of radical transformation in education for about 20 years now," says Eylan Ezekiel, digital engagement consultant for *ON School.* The benefits and restrictions of technology and its help in innovation on education are numerous and evident to all of us. But the question that remains us is "how" to do the integration of the same. One strategy can be a step-wise amalgamation of technology with innovation, thus progressively making the learning more productive and 'better'. This can be better said as enhancing the quality of education through increased personalization, precision and introduction of latest Ed-tech knowledge and practices.

Technology with the help of Internet today, gives the perfect personalization and exposure. Thus students can have more interactive sessions and a better environment. Competition is a great motivator and thus broadcasting is one method to bring students with various intelligence levels and combine them for one greater good, ***"Great brains work Miracles"***. This will help in increasing the interests of students all-round the year and making them thinkers, rather than just listeners. Today the task of integrating innovation and education for building a creative society and by the by generating employment-beyond digital age, one has to have more and more facilities and potentialities /nature with prompt methods and means to achieve the same. As discussed, for an improved learning one needs to have better environment/nurture /milieu too.

It is clearly evident that these three major ingredients (Innovation, Education and Technology) are highly needed together for any significant improvement in the learning of children. But the methods to do so, largely depends upon the situation and available resources for the institutions. The benefits and restrictions of technology and its help in innovation on education are numerous and evident to all of us. But the question of hour that remaining us is what about" and "how" that we have to make the 'Designing Learning Environment of Tomorrow'.

The Three Trends in Higher Education

There are three trends on the horizon in higher education. Leading educators shared their **insights and innovative programs** – three dominant themes emerged, 1) The competency based learning, 2) The personalized student learning and 3) The changing role of the instructor. Each presenter shared extensive research in an area of his or her expertise and details of an innovative educational program. That program provides a non-traditional education that defies the status quo. The summary of the trends so designed to provide the readers with a strong practico - practical ideas and ideals for application to their own area of study or work with specialization.

The Competency Based Learning Vs Seat Time

Western Governors University introduced the radical idea of competency based learning in 1997 and was one of the first fully online universitys that did not require classroom attendance; fast forward to 2012 and competency based learning appears to be in the future of higher education. Learning that focuses on measurable outcomes is becoming a reality as technology facilitates self-paced and adaptive learning platforms, and employers lament about the skill- gap that recent college graduates cannot fill. Responsive companies are partnering with education start-ups to create competency learning programs that address the skills needed for 21st century employees.

The Idea of 'Seat Time' is in peril. Key highlights for these are below

1) Employers are coming up with innovative ways to address the skill-gap. Companies including Google and Microsoft have partnered with University to create classes in 3D graphics, appropriate development and more– needed skills that they cannot find even in the recent college graduates (Ripley, 2012).Educomp and TATA Edge are the companies also recruit teachers for software preparations at present.
2) Southern New Hampshire University [SNHU]-The goal of SNHU is to provide affordable quality education, "to reduce costs, increase access and provide transformational experiences for students who have been marginalized by traditional higher education".
3) The colleges are partnering with employers to create programs that not only provide academic preparation but career skills. The New Community Colleges opened its doors with an innovative program designed to link classroom learning to career experiences in the community.
4) Another new university that looks promising a platform to allow students to progress through course work at their own pace. Students learn by spending as little or as much time as needed to master the content. The goal of the schools is to provide affordable education to anyone, anywhere at any time.

Personalized Student Learning

'Learning, your way' is the new motto for numerous higher education institutions across the country, and significant ones too. The University of Central Florida [UCF] that allows students to choose between five learning modalities, customizing their learning based upon their needs. Students expect to be able to learn anytime and anywhere in their chosen institutions, and numerous schools including UCF are responding.

1) **At UCF and University of Wisconsin, Milwaukee (UWM)** students customize their schedule from a choice of many learning modalities. The school's web page features the options for learning, "Flexible and Convenient Online, Evening, Weekend and Hybrid Classes to Accommodate Any Schedule."
2) Research suggests that 'learning is learning' to students regardless of modality. To students, "a course, is a course, modality makes no difference" at all (Cavanaugh, 2012).

Therefore, the colleges will need to address the needs of the life-long learner, not just the college student where schools have traditionally told students when and where they need to go to learn. Students of all ages want to be able to learn anytime and anywhere at times convenient for them. Think of all students as life-long learners, and offer students' choices of learning when, how and where they want.

3. The Changing Role of the Instructor

To focus on this Microsoft issue, **UNESCO** convened a two-day meeting in November 2011 to bring together 30 knowledgeable participants from more than 10 countries to discuss about the accessible technology for students and report on practical solutions for educators. All participants were deeply knowledgeable about accessibility and technology use in schools, including teachers, school administrators and experts from the IT industry and representatives from organizations with a focus on disability issues also.

The professor is no longer the *only* source of knowledge for students. The traditional method of knowledge transfer–the lecture, where the course instructor transfers knowledge [content] to student, is being augmented or replaced by other 'nodes' of information. Nodes are content sources, and might be a video, website, textbook, subject matter expert, or e-resource. Subsequently the teaching paradigm is shifting, students can access content, can learn from a variety of sources (Downes, 2012). The instructor role is thus changing, and in some institutions, the instructor role is being replaced with a mentor **or advisor.** Students in this model tend to take charge of their learning and use mentors, peers and study groups as support mechanisms for their learning goals.

1) University now, "*peer-to-peer learning communities where students share their knowledge and skills, and help each other obtain recognized degrees and credentials*".

2) The program at SNHU (Southern New Hampshire University) about Innovation states that University *"won't have instructors in the traditional sense. Pathways (*program at Innovation) *will employ advisors to help students establish goals and set their learning pace*".

Therefore, higher education still needs experts, and students need role models, leaders and mentors. Acknowledging that students can access content and expertise from a variety of sources which suggests that the course instructor is no less important. Now the instructor's role shifts to one of *guide* or *mentor*, who is influencing, shaping and inspiring students to become educated, life-long learners.

The Time is Now to Move to Competency-Based Teacher Professional Development

At the Recent Education World Forum in London, UNESCO's Director General Irena Bokova, recalled the attention that she announced a new version of the UNESCO ICT (information and communication Technology) Competency Framework for Teachers. This framework identifies key competencies that enable teachers to help prepare a 21st century workforce by using ICT in the classroom. The recent researches show that helping teachers in their challenge of combining ICT with innovative teaching practices that strongly predicts students' acquisition of 21st century skills, the challenge continues to be helping teacher's develop the competencies needed to combine great learning activities with meaningful and relevant use of ICTs.

There are many challenges to Effective Professional Development of ICT integration:

1) Many teachers are aware that they should integrate ICT into their teaching practices, but they are uncertain as to, what that actually it is meant for?
2) The absence of a common internationally recognized standard in the area of ICT integration and the devoid of a training based on those standards that prevents in having a consistent method to assess teacher competency.
3) "One size fits all" training fails to address the needs of individuals. Teachers within the one school itself will have very different needs. While some may have never used a computer, others will be using multiple devices and applications to achieve desired outcomes.
4) Mandatory training which is not at all relevant. But the teacher's self-assessment and their personal planning of their own development, increases the likelihood that what is presented actually

will result in a change in their teaching strategies by diminishing their resistance to training.

5) The ability to have large scale of face-to-face effective professional development to reach all teachers in a country is a frightening and expensive endeavor.

One appreciable response to these challenges is the VERY NEW Partners in Teaching-Learning with Technology Curriculum, now offered via Microsoft IT Academy.Microsoft has worked in partnership with governments, colleges of education and subject matter experts from around the world, to create a curriculum which includes a range of learning scenarios and is associated with the global standards of the UNESCO ICT-CFT (computer facilitation technique) with Technology Literacy Approach.

Rethinking Innovation in Education

The renowned innovative ICT specialized educationist Anthony Salcitosaid that he had the pleasure of attending the Worldwide Innovation Summit for Education (WISE), held in Doha, Qatar recently. This is the third year Microsoft e-summit and it continues to be a very valuable K-20 conversation among the state of education around the world on, "Rethinking Innovation in Education." Here one of the things he (Anthony Salcito) tried to do in his comments was disconnect innovation with technology, because too often it's synonymous for schools...as people think about innovation, they jump too quickly to technology as the solution.

The opportunity to share information and get access to information anywhere, anytime, anyplace, is a game changer that fundamentally will have a huge role in the future. The great teaching that makes sure that the kids are properly motivated to succeed a holistic approach. **Hence Technology can support, enable all of those things, but technology alone is not going to overcome a bad teacher or a bad environment.**

The other issue we have to think about is as it relates to the technology itself, becausc in many cases the technology will evolve to create a new opportunity for learning. Most of what we have done with technology in schools all over the United States and the world has been to automate the passive learning models and modalities. So we have taken classrooms and turned them virtual. We have taken tests and turned them online. We have taken books and created electronic books. While all these transitions are valuable and helpful, they don't provide any transformative experience other than moving from a piece of paper to a digital screen or a phone conversation to a text message. And while the value and efficiencies can support schools and help budgets, but the learning process is not transformed so far.

Then what can make a change? How technology is applied to create much more responsive, reactive and personal learning environments?The answer to these questions is as such;

To create the settings to connect students to quality of content and information that previously was unavailable,

To refine learning to respond predictive to a learner's need based on learning styles, test scores, etc. And when all these aforesaid elements come into play, learning retention increases, test scores potentially increase, and we have more and more of engaged and motivated students with creativity and transformative talents inbuilding a creative society for generating employment in this meta- digital age.

Accept Innovation with Open Arms:

To Teachers

Teachers, you must explore your opportunities. Challenge your administrators to let you try new things. Teaching is all about learning, both for you and the students. Don't feel constrained by your textbooks or curriculum, but rather try to adopt new methods that so what complement them. You know your goals; the path you take to get to your goal is entirely up to you. We have said it before repeatedly and we too will say it again and again: Teaching is an Art.

To the Administrators

Administrators, you should know WHAT**'s** happening now. The only thing certain is, if you are not innovating, you are losing your popularity in no time. You do not necessarily need to pioneer change, but do not be the force that holds your teachers back. You have hired great people and allowed them to set goals. Now let them go out and are great. If they come to you with new tools and ideas, and a burning look in their eye, certainly they are onto something. Do not take hold of every innovation insight, but listen and work with your teachers to move forward.

Bservation

It is so correctly observed by Mr.Christensen that your best think is not layering technology on top of your current educational practices, but instead spinning off a few classes where technology is the primary driver of education. This is where true innovation can occur, and you can test the success on a small sample of audience and then extend it then and there.

Conclusion

That is why; this present inter-national Conference very rightly focuses its attention on building innovations for developing creative society and generating employability as it envisages that innovation is an indispensable one in the present day world. Like that creativity is the essence of human life that has made the progress ever since the inception of human beings in the world from Stone Age to Digital age. The time is now so reaped to think beyond digital age/meta-digital age.

Thus this meta-digital age has seen tremendous changes in the field of Education to have the high-tech classrooms. Teachers with software knowledge have become acquired the essential qualifications. The new kind of job demands the teachers to become the digital content developers, effective consumers, efficient disseminators for promoting meta- digital aged ultra-model creative society with E- content and digital learning materials, men, methods, modes, manners and modalities that may suit the ever-enshrining single global humanity with an ardent spirit and fervor in respecting the oneness of humanity.

References

1. The report of the redical idea of competency based learning, Western Governors University1997.
2. **2.** Cavanaugh, the Directions of UCF(Univercity of Centrral Florida) and UWM(University of Wisconsin, Milwaukee) on the Modality of learning Corses,2012.
3. The report of Downes, on the teaching Paradigm shift from instructor to mentor or Advisor, 2012.
4. Report of the Microsoft IT Academy, the global standards of Unesco ICT – CFI, Technology Literary Approach, 20145.
5. Technology and Education, Mind springs Enrichment Centre, 2012
6. Anthony Salcito, A turning Point for Education? - Trends to watch in 2012.
7. Anthony Salcito,JP Sa Couto and Critical Links at CES, 2012.
8. Anthony Salcito, Navigating the World via Bing and Microsoft Translator, 2012.
9. Anthony Salcito, Microsoft Technology preserving Local languages and Cultures. 2012.
10. Anthony Salcito, Join the new Partners in Learning Network Today and start spreading Ideas to improve Worldwide, 2012.

28

Effectiveness of Multimedia Programme in Perceiving Human Anatomy

Introduction

Research work is being continuously done in the field of science and also in the related teaching methods and materials. In order to keep pace with the development of science, the need for new instructional strategies was greatly felt. One such innovative teaching strategy, called multimedia programme, has been chosen and studied by the investigator in this research work. Upgrading Biology curriculum by introducing Human anatomy demands a change in the instructional strategy. The need for developing an instructional strategy for teaching Human anatomy and physiology is very important to make the teachers and students aware of the scientific principles that govern the advances being made in medicine. The functions of the internal organs of human body can be easily explained through a multimedia programme. This also saves the use of expensive chemicals and sophisticated instruments which are beyond the reach of higher secondary schools. In schools, the required equipment to explain the human anatomy is not available. In this situation, the working mechanism of internal organs can be explained by a multimedia programme, which when used as an instructional strategy will make the task of learning human anatomy easier, effective and less expensive. The present study aims to find out the effectiveness of multimedia programme in perceiving human anatomy among higher secondary students in Tindivanam. A samples of 100 higher secondary students selected randomly were studied. A questionnaire method of survey was used to find out the effectiveness of multimedia programme in perceiving human anatomy. The data were collected by using questionnaire as an instrument. Primary data were collected by conducting direct structured interview using questionnaire. All the respondents were asked the same questions in the same fashion and they were informed the purpose of study. Mean, SD, and t-test analysis was applied to test the hypotheses. The findings and observations are the result and outcome of the interpretations made during the study of analysis. The result found that majority of the higher secondary students satisfied about multimedia programme.

In view of growing importance of science education, old concepts of science teaching have therefore, rather become completely outmoded and an entirely new ethos and approach to science curriculum have come into existence. Moreover, unprecedented development of scientific research, new discoveries, and new methods of investigation, in the early twentieth century, has created a need and urge to examine and reorganize science teaching programmes at all levels in schools. Institutions are functioning in an era of rapidly emerging new technologies. Some of them, like information and communications technology, have fuelled a veritable explosion of rising expectations everywhere. When such is the pace of developmental processes, it becomes fairly imperative on the part of the students not only to possess sound knowledge and understanding of fundamental concepts, but also to understand and appreciate the ramifications of various developments in the field of science and technology, especially in the context of their future career. The situation underscores the significance of research in science education and it is time for the educationists to evolve a proper and appropriate strategy for teaching science.

At the Higher Secondary level, the science subject is divided into Physics, Chemistry, Botany, and Zoology according to Tamil Nadu State Board syllabus. Zoology deals with the life history, distribution, structure, reproduction, and importance of animals including Homosapiens, the human beings. 'Human anatomy' is one of the units of the Zoology subject. Human anatomy is the branch of anatomy devoted to the structure of the human body. In general the study of human anatomy helps the students to do their higher studies in Medicine, Physiotherapy, Nursing, Degree courses like B.Sc., Zoology, and Microbiology etc. Apart from acquiring the technical knowledge, it is necessary for human beings to know and control their own systems of their body for healthy life. Hence the investigator has selected the unit "human anatomy" to teach through multimedia programme for the higher secondary students in the present investigation.

An instructional or teaching strategy refers to a pattern of teaching act that serves to attain certain goals and to guard against others. An instructional strategy is a purposefully-conceived and determined plan of action. It also occupies a central position in formal education. Instructional strategies aim at establishing relationship between teaching inputs and learning outputs, mainly in terms of realizing the learning outcomes. Instructional strategies include teaching methods, approaches and techniques.

Methods of instruction may be teacher-centered such as Historical method, Biographical method, Lecture method, Lecture-demonstration method or pupil-centered method which includes group methods such as project method, discussion, seminar and workshop. The pupil-centered methods also include individual methods such as programmed instruction, Computer Aided Instruction, Instructional Modules and Multimedia packages.

Review of Literature

Chang, Kuo-En et al. (2008) studied**the effects of learning support in simulation-based physics learning.** The results of the study revealed that the outcome for learning about the basic characteristics of an optical lens was significantly better for simulation-based learning than for laboratory learning.

Djeassilane (2008) investigated the effect of computer aided instruction (CAI) in enhancing the academic achievement of higher secondary students in commerce. The findings of the study showed that the computer aided instruction was effective in helping the students of the experimental group to perform better in the post-test. It proved the effectiveness of the computer aided instruction in commerce developed by the investigator. And also it was found that the experimental students had more favourable attitude towards computer assisted instruction.

Garnett, Hackling and Oliver (2009) developed an interactive multimedia package to improve students' understanding of the particulate basis of chemical reaction, and their ability to interpret chemical equations and solve problems based on equations. The study showed that Interactive multimedia provided learners with access to a rich information source and appropriate activities to promote learning and understanding.

Junaidu, Sahalu (2009) studied effectiveness of multimedia in learning & teaching data structures online. This paper explores and reports on the importance of creating multimedia-rich course content and the important role that animations can play in creating a successful online learning experience. Results indicated that students consistently perform much better in questions requiring application of material taught in carefully animated algorithms. These results should carry over to other educational environments.

Liao, Yuen-kuang C., Chang, Huei-wen and Chen, Yu-wen (2009) compared the effects of computer applications (i.e., computer-assisted instruction, computer simulations, and Web-based learning) versus traditional instruction on elementary school students' achievement in Taiwan. The results suggest that computer application instruction is more effective than traditional instruction for elementary school students in Taiwan.

O'Day, Danton (2010) studied on "using animations to teach biology: past & future research on the attributes that underlie pedagogically sound animations". Multiple technical resources (commonly referred to as multimedia) are currently used by many instructors to communicate difficult topics and concepts to their students in meaningful ways. Various sources have shown that animations are more effective than static sequential images. This study evaluated how animations can be and have been used as effective teaching and learning tools in biology and what more needs to be done to understand their true value.

Ozmen, Haluk (2010) studied on "The influence of CAI on students' conceptual understanding of chemical Bonding and attitude towards chemistry: A case for Turkey". The results of this study suggested that teaching-learning of topics in chemistry related to chemical bonding can be improved by the use of computer-assisted teaching materials.

Ponraj and Nellaiyapen (2010) investigated the effectiveness of CAI in teaching Zoology. The major finding of the study showed that the experimental group performed better than the Control group in the post-test. The results of the study revealed that experimental method of teaching is more effective than the traditional method of teaching the topic 'Nucleus' in Zoology.

Pryor, Caroline and Bitter, Gary (2010) used multimedia to teach in-service teachers and studied its impacts on learning, application, and retention. The study found that the video modeling in the module was effective in helping teachers learn, and discourse strategies were learned, applied, and retained.

Rotbain, Marbach-Ad and Stavy (2011) used a computer animation to teach high school molecular biology. The achievements of the experimental group were compared with those of a control group. Analysis of the post-test showed that the mean score of the experimental group was significantly higher than the mean score of the control group.

Venkataraman (2011) prepared software packages (CAI) for XI standard physics and studied the effectiveness of it's among selected modes of CAI in physics in relation to learners' personality. The results of the study showed that the CAI is effective with different modes. Computer Assisted Instruction shows significant difference in the achievement of different instructional objectives. Further Computer Assisted Instruction enhances the retention of the learnt content.

Vernadakis et al. (2012) examined the effect of multimedia computer-assisted instruction (MCAI), traditional instruction (TI), and combined instruction (CI) methods on learning the skill of shooting in basketball. Additionally, a comparison of the students' attitudes towards the MCAI and TI methods was made. Students took pre-, post-, and retention written test covering techniques and rules of the games. Post-test results indicated no significant differences between the groups concerning the written test. Nevertheless, the attitude test scores of the CI group were more favourable to MCAI method than the TI method. Retention test results showed that groups retained the knowledge acquisition. However, the combined method of instruction tended to be the most effective for cognitive learning.

Victor, Adeosun Olufemi (2012) investigated the relative effects of three multi-media instructional packages on Nigerian students' achievement in social studies. The purpose was to determine which of the combinations of videotape recording presentation, pictures and the chalk and talk method; the combination of audiotape recording presentation, pictures and the chalk and talk method and the combination of pictures and the chalk and talk method. The study revealed that the combination of pictures and the chalk and talk method was most effective among the packages tested in the learning of social studies.

Objectives

1. To develop a Multimedia Programme for the unit of Human anatomy

from XI standard Zoology subject in order to teach the higher secondary students.

2. To find out the effectiveness of Multimedia Programme in teaching Human anatomy among higher secondary students.

Methodology

The methodology adopted for the study is explained in detail. The sampling technique, size of the sample, variables of the study, description of the tool used and administration of tool are elaborated.

Sample

A samples of 100 higher secondary students in selected randomly were studied in Tindivanam Town.

Data Collection

The present study aims at developing and using Multimedia programme for perceiving human anatomy for higher secondary students to enable them to understand the concepts very easily through individualized instructional technique. It is maintained that the Multimedia programme may reduce monotony in the classroom by bringing out real life situations and motivate them for self-study and provides opportunities for individual pace and ability.

The study intends to develop a multimedia programme for human anatomy for XI standard Zoology subject prescribed by Tamil Nadu State Board Syllabus and find out the effectiveness of the Multimedia programme through experimentation in perceiving human anatomy among the higher secondary students. The study provides scope for the development and use of many Multimedia programmes in the concerned discipline as well as other disciplines for the benefit of learners of different categories. Hence the multimedia programme can be used as an individualized instructional technique for the students of different categories in the science subjects as well as other subjects.

Analysis and Interpretation

Performance of control group students between the pre test and post test in human anatomy

The Mean, Standard Deviation and Co-efficient of Variation were computed for the control group students in their performance in human anatomy between the pre test and post test.

Table 1

Distribution of Mean, Standard Deviation and Co-efficient of Variation on the performance of control group students between the pre test and post test in human anatomy

Group	N	Mean	S.D	CV
Pre test	100	42.69	13.60	31.86
Post test	100	52.46	13.28	25.31

The Co-efficient of Variation of the pre test and post test for the control group students was found to be 31.86 and 25.31, which reveals that the control group students are more consistent in their performance in human anatomy in the post test than the pre test. It reveals that the control group students have improved in their performance in human anatomy in the post test than the pre test.

To find out the significance of the difference between the control and experimental group students in their performance in human anatomy in the pre test, the 't' test was used.

Table 2

Distribution of 't' value between the control and experimental group students in their performance in human anatomy in the pre test

Group	N	Mean	S.D	't' value	Level of Significant
Control	100	42.69	13.60	0.17	p>0.05
Experimental	100	43.31	12.59		

There is no significant difference between the control and experimental group students in their performance in human anatomy in the pre test.

The obtained 't' value 0.17 is not statistically significant since it is less than the table 't' value 1.96 for 50 df at 0.05 level of significance. Hence the null hypothesis is accepted. It shows that there is no significant difference between the control and experimental group students in their performance in human anatomy in the pre test. It is therefore concluded that both control and experimental group students have the same level of performance in human anatomy in the pre test.

To find out the significance of the difference between the control and experimental group students in their performance in human anatomy in the post test, the 't' test was used.

Table 3

Distribution of 't' value between the control and experimental group students in their performance in human anatomy in the post test

Group	N	Mean	S.D	't' value	Level of Significant
Control	100	52.46	13.28	14.38	$p<0.05$
Experimental	100	92.81	5.31		

There is no significant difference between the control and experimental group students in their performance in human anatomy in the post test.

The obtained 't' value 14.38 is statistically significant since it is greater than the table 't' value 1.96 for 50 df at 0.05 level of significance. Hence the null hypothesis is rejected. It shows that there is significant difference between the control and experimental group students in their performance in human anatomy in the post test. It is therefore concluded that the experimental group students performed significantly better in human anatomy than that of control group students in the post test.

To find out the significance of the difference between the pre and post test mean scores of control group students in the performance in human anatomy, the 't' was used.

Table 4

Distribution of 't' value for the pre and post test mean scores of control group students in the performance in human anatomy

Group	N	Mean	S.D	't' value	Level of Significant
Pre test	100	42.69	13.60	2.62	$p<0.05$
Post test	100	52.46	13.28		

There is no significant difference between the pre and post test mean scores of control group students in the performance in human anatomy.

The obtained 't' value 2.62 is statistically significant since it is greater than the table 't' value 1.96 for 50 df at 0.05 level of significance. Hence the null hypothesis is rejected. It shows that there is significant difference between the pre and post test mean scores of control group students in the performance in human anatomy. It is therefore concluded that the control group students have improved in their performance in human anatomy in the post test.

Suggestions

The present study aims at developing and using Multimedia programme for perceiving human anatomy for higher secondary students to enable them to understand the concepts very easily through individualized instructional technique. It is maintained that the Multimedia programme may reduce monotony in the classroom by bringing out real life situations and motivate them for self-study and provides opportunities for individual pace and ability.

Conclusion

The study intends to develop a multimedia programme for human anatomy for XI standard Zoology subject prescribed by Tamil Nadu State Board Syllabus and find out the effectiveness of the Multimedia programme through experimentation in perceiving human anatomy among the higher secondary students. The study provides scope for the development and use of many Multimedia programmes in the concerned discipline as well as other disciplines for the benefit of learners of different categories. Hence the multimedia programme can be used as an individualized instructional technique for the students of different categories in the science subjects as well as other subjects.

The present study reveals that the experiment group students who used multimedia programme performed significantly better than that of the control group students who did not use, which implies that the multimedia programme has tremendous impact upon the performance in human anatomy than the students learning through traditional method. This proves the effectiveness of the multimedia programme in human anatomy developed by the investigator.

The present study reveals that the performance of the control and experimental group students in the post test is significantly higher than the pre test. But the performance of the experimental group students in the post test is more significantly higher than the post test performance of control group students. Thus, it proves the supremacy of the multimedia programme over traditional method.

References

1. Chang, Kuo-En; Chen, Yu-Lung; Lin, He-Yan; Sung, Yao-Ting (2008).

Effects of learning support in simulation-based physics learning. Computers & Education, 51(4): 1486-1498..

2. Djeassilane, N. (2008). Effect of computer aided instruction (CAI) in enhancing the academic achievement of higher secondary students in commerce. Unpublished Doctoral Dissertation, Alagappa University, Karaikudi.
3. Garnett, P., Hackling, M., & Oliver, R. (2009). Designing interactive multimedia materials to support concept development in beginning chemistry classes.
4. Junaidu, Sahalu (2009). Effectiveness of multimedia in learning & teaching data structures online. Turkish Online Journal of Distance Education-TOJDE, 9(4), Article 7. Retrieved March.
5. Liao, Yuen-kuang C., Chang, Huei-wen & Chen, Yu-wen (2009). Effects of Computer Applications on Elementary School Students' Achievement: A Meta-Analysis of Students in Taiwan. Computers in the Schools, 24(3-4): 43-64. Retrieved.
6. O'Day, Danton H. (2010). Using animations to teach biology: past & future research on the attributes that underlie pedagogically sound animations. The American Biology Teacher, 70(5):274-278. Retrieved March 20.
7. Ozmen, Haluk (2010). The influence of Computer-Assisted Instruction on students' conceptual understanding of chemical Bonding and Attitude toward chemistry: A case for Turkey. Computers and Education, 51(1): 423-438. Retrieved March.
8. Ponraj, P., & Nellaiyapen, N. O. (2010). CAI in teaching Zoology. Research and Reflections on Education, 6(2): 18-21.
9. Pryor, Caroline R., & Bitter, Gary G. (2010). Using multimedia to teach in-service teachers: Impacts on learning, application, and retention. Computers in Human Behavior, 24 (6): 2668-2681. Retrieved March.
10. **Rotbain, Y., Marbach-Ad, G., & Stavy, R. (2011). Using a computer animation to teach high school molecular biology. Journal of Science Education and Technology, 17(1): 49 - 58.** Retrieved March.
11. Venkataraman, S. (2011). Relative effectiveness among selected modes of CAI in physics in relation to learner's personality. Unpublished Doctoral Dissertation, Annamalai University. Chidambaram.
12. Vernadakis, N., Zetou, E., Tsitskari, E., Giannousi, M., & Kioumourtzoglou, E. (2012). Student attitude and learning outcomes of multimedia computer-assisted versus traditional

instruction in basketball. Education and Information Technologies, 13(3): 167-183.

13. Victor, Adeosun Olufemi (2012). Relative effects of three Multi-Media Instructional Packages on Nigerian student's achievement in Social Studies. Pakistan Journal of Social Sciences, 5 (5): 415 - 420. Retrieved March.

29

The Role of Virtual Classroom in Enhancing Teaching and Learning

Introduction

With the ever-increasing popularity and accessibility of the Internet, it is only natural that the educational community should want to make use of this tremendous resource. Use of the Internet and Web are leading to significant changes in educational models. As this use of Internet is increasing, a traditional classroom has shifted to E-Learning. Thus, E-Learning can be defined an approach to facilitate and enhance learning by means of personal computers, multimedia components and the Internet. The growing popularity of E-Learning has introduced new terms to education, as Virtual Classroom, where student will be present with his professor and fellow learners in a classroom. They will not be present physically in the classroom but connected to the classroom via Internet. This new facet of life highly increases students of acquiring technological skills as they are exposed to the tools used for web-based learning, computer-based learning typically provided by Internet. This is extremely valuable since computers are becoming prevalent for future student. The present paper emphasizes on the role of virtual classroom in enhancing teaching and learning process.

With the advent of the Internet there has been much talk about how learning can now be delivered at a distance. With no need for individuals necessarily to attend face-to face courses. It is suggested that the Internet has the potential to open up learning to a wider audience by allowing a person to have greater flexibility regarding where, when and how they learn. This concept is often referred to in education as the *virtual classroom*, *virtual university* or *virtual learning environment*. A *virtual classroom* enables to bring learners from around the world together online in highly interactive virtual classes while greatly reducing the travel, time and expense of on-site teaching/training programs. It can be used as a solution for live delivery and interaction that addresses the entire process of creating and managing the teaching-learning process. It facilitates instructor and student in teaching-learning events, such as a seminar, online discussion or a live training for teachers or administrator in the school. In a traditional classroom, professor, students and fellow learners are present, similarly, the same set of participants are present in a virtual classroom. They can talk with each other alike the traditional classroom via chat. Similarly presenter uses whiteboard, gives notes/resources and gives presentation as given in traditional one. Thus, virtual classroom can be visualized as a classroom where a lecture or session is conducted using Internet. As this use of Internet is increasing, a traditional classroom has shifted to E-Learning. While advancements in communication tools were easily adapted to learning methods, it was the introduction of the personal computer and the development of the Internet that would create the most radical transformation in higher education.

Virtual classroom

Virtual classroom is a computer medicated communication system. The need of gathering at one place for communication in traditional classroom is been overcome by virtual classroom, the main advantages of virtual classroom is that due to shrinking distance communication is improved. The architecture of virtual classroom is in *three* phase which include the normal instructor to classroom setup, classroom behind firewall setup and instructor to group of geographically dispersed student. The term virtual means a simulation of the real thing, *Virtual Classroom is a simulated classroom via Internet, which provides a convenient communication environment for distance learners just like traditional face-to-face classroom.* A virtual classroom allows learners to attend a class from anywhere in the world and aims to provide a learning experience that is similar to a real classroom. In a college setup, lectures are scheduled, students arrive on time; find their teachers, fellow learners, a blackboard or whiteboard, LCD projector, optionally a television screen with videos. Likewise, a Virtual

Classroom is a scheduled, online, teacher-led training session where teachers and learners interact together using computers linked to a network such as the Internet. They will not be present physically in the classroom but connected to the classroom via Internet. Virtual classroom aims to simulate the experience of attending a class over the web. So everyone is able to see other participant virtually. *A virtual classroom is an advanced learning environment, created using internet, computers, supplicated video conferencing devices, in which either teacher is not physically present (for remote learning)or students are not present (distance education)in the classroom.*Virtual Classroom learning is an evolving way of learning where the learner attends LIVE lectures remotely on his/her computer terminal, given by the subject matter experts or instructors at other end, using Internet as the medium between the learner and instructor. As lectures are given LIVE on internet, the student gets to have the opportunity of asking his/her queries to the instructor at any instant. Most of the distance learning degree and training courses heavily rely on the concept of ***'Virtual Classroom'.*** As the learner is no more required to attend the lectures/ sessions in person, this new method of learning helps keeping the lecture costs much lower than conventional classroom teaching without compromising on the quality of learning. This makes Distance learning much affordable compared to regular training courses. Virtual classroom is very multipurpose technology or platform which can be used for Webinars, Tuition, One-to-one training and tuition, mentoring, Interviews, Team meetings, Project meetings, demonstrations, staff or students meetings, Technical support, student service, On-line user communities. A virtual classroom enables to bring learners from around the world together online in highly interactive virtual classes while greatly reducing the travel, time, and expense of on-site teaching/training programs. It can be used as a solution for live delivery and interaction that addresses the entire process of creating and managing our teaching-learning process. In Virtual classroom commonly we find the tools like *Projector, LCDs, Server Machine, Video conferencing System and its accessories, High-Definition Multimedia Visualizer, Interactive Whiteboard or Touch Panel, Digital Canvas, High-Definition Cameras etc.* Thus, virtual classroom can be visualized as a classroom where a lecture or session is conducted using Internet. Rather than being built of steel and concrete, the Virtual Classroom consists of a set of group communication and work ***"spaces"*** and facilities that are constructed in software. Thus it is a ***"virtual facility"*** for interaction among members of class, rather than a physical space.

Objective of Virtual Classroom

The following are the objectives of virtual classroom:

1. To **support live on-line classes** for distance learning and remote education.
2. To **pool academic resources thereby** improving access to advanced educational experiences
3. To **improve the quality and effectiveness of education** by collaborative learning and teaching process.
4. To **hold and participate** in the meetings, webinars, Conferences/ Symposium /Workshop, interviews, etc. through video conferencing.
5. To **increase and improve** the accessibility of educational resources to the **persons with disabilities**

Different Users of Virtual Classroom

There are different classes of users of virtual classroom based on the roles that they play. When presenter enters in virtual classroom, he has different work to do than participant. Depending on the user type, virtual classroom takes different form for each user. These forms can be categorized depending on the user's role. These roles are as follows:

Facilities provided by presenter interface to Faculty

1. **Register new users:**Presenter as an administrator has to register new users that will be attending the session.
2. **Create a session:** Presenter has to decide the session time, users that will be invited for the session. While creating a session, he can specify the time and users of the particular session.
3. **Cancel a user registration**:If any registered user does not want to attend the session, presenter cancels his registration.
4. **Conduct Online presentation:**As a presenter, he conducts the session for participants. During presentation he performs various activities in the classroom. He can load the presentation slide that will be displayed to participants.
5. **Share Resources:**Presenter can add various resources to the session. It may be a file or just a simple web page link that participant can download at their end.
6. **Conduct Poll:**He can create a poll for participants. Also he can chat with participants.
7. **Explain concepts using Whiteboard:**He can use whiteboard to explain some of the topic, which may not be able to explain via

presentations, or to solve any particular doubt asked by the participant.

Facilities provided by participant interface to students

1. **View online presentation:**When a participant joins the session, they can view the presentation (PowerPoint presentation slides or it may also include the snap of the whiteboard), which are conducted by the presenter in the virtual classroom.
2. **Public/Private Chat:**The participants can have a conversation with the fellow participants publicly or privately via the chat feature available in the interface, the chat allows the participant to send the instant messages to the participants who are also attending the session. Participants can also send private messages to any of the participant but he is not allowed to send private messages to the presenter but can do so by using the hands up facility.
3. **Raise Hands:**Whenever any participant will have any doubt, then he can tell that to presenter by using the hands up facility available in the user interface of the participant, using this feature the participant can interact with the presenter via the private chat.
4. **Give Response to the polls:**The participants can answer the polls that are submitted by the presenter by using the "Submit Response" facility provided in the interface. The poll can be of type objective or it may be of Yes/No type. If the particular poll is public then participants can see response for that particular poll, else it will be kept hidden from the participant. The only presenter is able to see the response for private poll.
5. **Download Resources:**The resources that are been shared by the presenter can be downloaded by the participants at their machine. The resources can be the files which may include course material, e-book's etc, or it may be also web links which presenter may want the participants should refer.

Mode of Virtual Classroom Session

The presenter can create the session in the beginning & will conduct online presentation in the session. The participants can attend this session using the name of the session and view the presentation made by the presenter. In the session of the classroom, various functionalities that will be performed by the users are as follows:

1. **Agenda:**The presenter creates the agenda in the beginning of the session. This agenda specifies an outline of the session. The

participants can only view the agenda in their main window. The agenda will give him the idea about the topics that will be covered in the session.

2. **Presentation Area:**In the presenter interface, the presentation area allows presenter to upload the presentation file. It also allows him to navigate between the slides in the participant window; the presentation area will display the slide that the presenter is explaining.
3. **Whiteboard:**The presenter will be able to write, draw and highlight any particular area on the whiteboard. The white board will be consists of various components such as various shapes, lines, eraser, pointer, etc, using which he will be able explain the particular topic to the participants. The participants can view the whiteboard in their interface, but they will not be allowed to use it (they will not be allowed to make any changes to whiteboard). The changes made by the presenter on the whiteboard will be displayed to the participants.
4. **Shared Resources & Web links:**The presenter can share their resources using the load resources facility that will be present in the presenter interface. The resources will be files of type (doc, rtf, pdf) or web links (URL). The participants can download these shared resources on their machines, also they can refer the given web links using their web browser.
5. **Poll:**The presenter can ask the participant any question by using the poll functionality that will be of the objective or yes/no type question. The response of the poll will be public or private. If the response of any particular poll is private then the response will not be shown to the participants, only presenter will be able to see the response. The response will be shown in the vertical bar chart format. The participant will be able to submit his response to the poll submitted by presenter. Also, he can view the responses of the polls for which presenter has allowed permission to see the response by participants. The private responses will not be shown to the participants
6. **Chat:**The presenter will use the chat functionality to send text messages to the participants. He can send a message to particular participant or to all participants. The participants will be able to send text messages to each other. But, he will not be able to send message to presenter directly. He can do it by using the hands-up facility.
7. **Hands-up:** The presenter interface will consist of hands-up list, which will display the names of the participants, which has raised

their hands. Hands-up by participant indicates he has some doubt or question to be discussed with presenter. Participant will use the hands-up facility if he wants to ask some question or want to talk with presenter. He can use this facility to initiate the conversation with the presenter. After the participant uses the hands up facility, presenter will allow him to have a private chat with him.

8. **Participant list:**In the presenter interface, there will be the list of participants, which will consist of the names of the participants that will be attending the session. If the presenter has to eject any particular participant, then he can use the eject facility that will be available in presenter interface. In the participant interface, the list of participants will only show the names of the fellow participants that are attending the session.

Advantages of Virtual Classroom

Following are the advantages of Virtual classroom over traditional classroom model:

1. **Removal of geographical barriers (Anywhere learning) :**A virtual classroom allows learners and teachers to attend a single live training session from any place in the world, provided they have a computer and Internet connection.
2. **Sessions can be recorded:**A virtual classroom has a facility to record the session so learners or teachers can replay it afterwards. Teachers can get an opportunity to review their own or their colleagues' performance. The entire classroom session can be recorded in video format and stored in library for future reference. This feature is extremely useful, especially for absent students, who can review the recordings later and understand the concepts elaborated by the professors. Moreover, the students can also refer to the recordings for revision purpose, at their convenience.
3. **Quicker to organize:**Training can be organized more quickly than traditional classroom-based training. Classrooms and projectors do not need to be reserved; materials do not need to be distributed. The sessions are easier to schedule or reschedule since attendees will not be traveling to the venue of the session.
4. **Synchronous Learning:**In this type of learning process, students and professors connect and interact with each other in real time. This is indeed a very significant process where students get answers to their queries & questions then and there. Interaction with professors and peers makes the learning process interesting and enriching for students.

5. **Live Audio-Video Support:**Audio and video support both contribute towards the e-learning process in virtual classroom. Various tools are available for text-based chat- verbal interaction through audio conferencing and sharing of one's own video through web-camera. Professors can share their audio and video, thus establishing one-to-one relation with students. Moreover, the students asking questions can share their videos with the fellow students as well.
6. **White Board:**It is an alternative to the traditional blackboard method, used as a tool for drawing graphics or diagrams in virtual classroom. It comes handy when professor wants to visually explain any abstract concept.
7. **Sharing of Learning Resources and/or Desktop Screen:**The resource sharing feature in virtual classroom allows professors to share varied content in different formats with the students in real time while delivering lectures on various course topics. This resource sharing feature supports sharing of various file formats – MS-Word/ Excel/ PowerPoint, PDF files, flash presentations, flash videos etc. While teaching, the professors can exhibit all the operations from the desk, by sharing a particular application or the entire desktop. This resource sharing feature is extremely useful for sharing various course materials like topic notes, subject diagrams or graphs, explanatory videos etc. With this type of supportive and informative course material, learning becomes interesting and gives an interactive experience.
8. **Classroom Control by Professors & Active Student Participation** : In virtual classroom when professors deliver lectures to the students while explaining or elaborating concepts, ideally one sided process of communication is followed, and students are not permitted to talk/ express themselves at the same time in order to avoid chaotic situations. Though all the participants from the virtual classroom are connected through audio and/or video conference, the participation rights are controlled by the professors. During the lectures, in case the students come across a particular doubt or query, while the professors are explaining, the students can set their status to "raise hand" which indicates that the student has a question which needs to be addressed by the professor. However, only one student can ask question at a time, in order to avoid confusion as well as commotion and to maintain focus and clarity on queries asked. Since the professors have the control rights, they can respond to the question or else disable the status of "raise hand" and take the question at the end of the session.

9. **Multi-Level Fallback Mechanism for Class Continuation:**Virtual classroom is a web-based tool which is solely dependent on internet connectivity. If in the remotest possibilities, participants get disconnected from virtual classroom, there are various alternatives to keep the class active. The technical team operates the fallback mechanism. If the internet is intact, then with the pre-configured ***Skype***accounts of all participants, a common Skype call is initiated to connect all participants to further carry on with the class. In case all the participants lose internet connectivity then the successive portion of the class is conducted through telephone.
10. **Live Tech Support:**With this feature, technical support representatives of the institutes or corporate organizations will be able to provide text based chat and live tech support to their users.
11. **Offers any time Access:** Offer live classes, office hours, and group discussions at times that are convenient for instructors and students, not just when the physical facilities are available.
12. **Ensures Comprehension: Ensure** students understand their lessons by asking for immediate feedback, answering questions, and giving in-depth verbal explanations of complex material.
13. **Electronic whiteboard and polls, quizzes, and surveys:** A best practice of live instructions to regularly offer interactive exercises. By offering whiteboard exercises and asking polling questions, students will remain highly engaged.
14. **Flexible content area:** A variety of content types can be viewed such as PowerPoint, Word, Excel, HTML, WebPages, images, movie clips, PDF, Flash etc.
15. **Access to persons with disabilities:**Just because a student has a disability doesn't mean they shouldn't be able to attend live on-line class. Live and archived classes can be close-captioned for the **hearing impaired** persons while also reaching out to the **visually impaired persons** by offering numerous key board short cut keys, hotkeys and compatibility with most screen readers. These accessibility features will ensure this technology is inclusive to all.
16. **Create Community:** Create a sense of community among students and instructors who might not otherwise interact with one another.
17. **Public & private text chat:**Some students are more comfortable writing than speaking, and our chat messaging allows the shy student to communicate textually so they can participate with their more talkative classmates.
18. **For Participants**

1. Offers the combined advantages of face-to-face interaction and distance learning.

2. Enables working professionals who would like to acquire new skills and/or enhance their knowledge in their respective functions to do so without taking a career break.
3. Offers those who missed obtaining a degree the chance to get one now from premier colleges without having to take leave from work or travel out of their hometown.
4. Minimizes disruption to work as classes are conducted on weekends or at convenient timings during weekdays

19. **For Institutes :**

a) Increases the institute's reach to a vast and geographically dispersed pool of potential students across globe.
b) Enables institutes to meet the demand for quality education, given the heavily skewed demand-supply ratio of students and educational institutes.
c) Facilitates access to a network of Virtual Classrooms across different cities.
d) Enables seamless delivery of lectures and supports display of PowerPoint/Audio/ Video/Animation presentations and usage of whiteboard.

Disadvantages of Virtual Classroom

Though it gives lots of advantages, it has some pitfalls also. *Following section describes some limitations of virtual classroom.*

1. **Teachers and students need to become familiar with the tools** :Teachers and students are familiar with the workings of a traditional classroom, that is, they understand the concepts of hand raising, the whiteboard, assignments, and so forth. With a virtual classroom, all attendees must become familiar with the way the virtual classroom works before virtual classroom based training starts.
2. **Time dependency for Live Sessions:**Attending virtual classroom training is restricted to a certain scheduled time.
3. **Infrastructure for the participants:** Personal Computer (PC) needs to be prepared Virtual classroom sessions need to be scheduled, teachers need to be invited, and participants' PCs need to be prepared.
4. **Technical Limitations:**Technical issues such as bandwidth speed of the connection or power failure may create problem while presentation is going on.

Conclusion

The emergence of Virtual Classroom is arguably one of the most powerful tools available to the growing need for education. Virtual Classroom education is rapidly increasing and becoming as a viable alternative for traditional classrooms. A virtual classroom enables to bring learners from around the world together online in highly interactive virtual classes while greatly reducing the travel, time, and expense of on-site teaching/training programs. It can be used as a solution for live delivery and interaction that addresses the entire process of creating and managing our teaching-learning process. In the end, we can assume that the concept of ***'Virtual Classroom'*** is truly the way towards ***'Global learning'*** on web.

Reference

1. Aggarwal J.C. (1999), *Essential of Education Technology*, Vikas Publishers Pvt. Ltd., New Delhi.
2. Gupta Vikas (2004), *Comdex Computer Course kit*, Dreamtech, 19-A, Ansari Road, Daryganj, New Delhi-110002.
3. Jagannath Mohanty(1992), *Education Technology*, Deep and Deep Publication, F -159, Rajouri Garder, New Delhi-110027.
4. Mangal S. K. (2000), *Advanced Educational Technology,* Prentice – Hall of India Pvt. Ltd. New Delhi.
5. Meena Kumari Goswami (2008), *Educational Technology*, Asian Book Pvt. Ltd, New Delhi.
6. Microsoft Corporation-India (2003), *Partners in Learning*, Microsoft Corporation (India), Pvt. Ltd, 9th Floor, DLF Cyber Greens, Gurgaon-02.
7. NCTE (2009), *Organizing Teaching Learning Resources in Teacher Education Institution*, NCTE, New Delhi.
8. UNESCO (2012),*Information and Communication Technologies in Education: A curriculum for schools and Programme of Teacher Development,* www.unesco.org, Accessed from website.
9. Vanaja. M. (2009), *Educational Technology*, Neelkamal Publication Pvt. Ltd, Hyderabad.

30

Awareness on Digital Techniques Applying in Classroom Teaching

Introduction

Education is the foundation stone of a Nation's intellectual power which steps its power profile. Thus, it is rightly said that it depends upon the quality of its Teachers. The destiny of India is being shaped in its classrooms. In class room Teaching, Digital Technology provides the opportunity to go beyond the class room boundaries to the outside world and events. Hence the Government is very keen in implementing the scheme of Teaching through computer in Government schools. When the Government is very much interested in the computer Teaching, It is essential that the Teachers must be well aware of the potentiality of the computer Technology. Hence the Investigators were interest to know the level of the Awareness on Digital Technology of Teacher Educators. It is a survey Research. The Investigators developed the opinion scale contains 40 statements with different dimensions such as Computer in Teaching Learning, Power point Presentation and Internet. Four points scale ranges from Strongly Agree, Agree, Strongly Disagree and Disagree was used. Developed Opinionnarie was administered to 100 Teacher Educators who are working in various Colleges of Education in Perambalur and Trichy Districts. Gender, Locality and Subject they studied were taken as the variables. The collected data was using Statistical Analysis like Mean, SD and't' test which have revealed the varied results.

Modernization is generally regarded as a process of change of traditional society into a society based on technology. As Teaching has entered the Digital age over the last several years, Technology in the Classroom is an area that all Teachers and Students are Embracing. For Teachers who have taught many years before this can be a challenging one. There are many Computer lesson plans, CDs, DVDs, audio e -books and videos available that will help in the transition. Digital Technology in the Classroom involves a lot of time and focus in its infancy, but with the Computer Lesson plans mentioned, it will develop into a fun and creative learning experience for Students and new and exciting challenges for Teachers. The incorporation of Digital technology in the education sector is important to meet the challenges presented by new trends, especially with the Global Communication of Knowledge. It is essential that the Students become familiar with the concept and use of Computer Technology in order to equip them for future job market. Similarly, the teacher can achieve better quality in Teaching Methodology.

Rationale of the Study

Computer plays key role in Education. Learning through Computer is an interesting affair. Now–a-days Digital Technology in Education has become the essential part of the system. In fact Teacher must well aware of the potentiality of the Digital Technology. Government is very much interested in introducing Computer Technology in Class Room instruction in Teacher Education. Hence the Investigator was interested to know the level of Awareness on Digital techniques applying in classroom teaching for present generation among Teacher Educators. **STATEMENT OF THE PROBLEM**

The important key words used in this problem were i) **Awareness:** Alertness, New Idea.

ii) **Digital Technology**: The Technology which is used to change the method of Class Room Teaching with the help of Electronic machines and Computer, iii) **Teacher Educators** Teachers who are working in the Colleges of Education.

Overview of the Study Already Done

Askin Asan(2003) studied on "Computer Technology Awareness by Elementary School Teachers: A Case Study from Turkey" and found that many Teachers were not computer users. At the same time Wheatley, (2003) also studied on increasing computer use in early childhood Teacher Education. The study was found that Teachers lacked a functional Computer Literacy Foundation to new Technology and skills. Nickish and

Reinhard (1992) in their study "Teacher Anxiety toward Computer Technology" found that Urban Teachers are used Computer often than Rural Teachers. Sengamalam @ Vanathi (2013) Studied on Awareness one learning among M.Ed scholars under Bharathidasan University, found that the awareness of scholars whose major subject is Science was found to be superior to the scholars with Arts as major subject.

Objectives of the Study

The objectives of the study were i)to measure the level of Awareness on Digital Technology among Teacher Educators. ii) To measure the level of significant difference on the Awareness on Digital Technology among Male and Female, Rural and Urban, Science and Arts group Teacher Educators.

Method and Materials

It is the Normative Survey method. Investigator constructed a Tool Awareness on Digital Techniques applying in Classroom Teaching for present generation among Teacher Educators.That consists of 40 statements with different dimensions such as Computer in Teaching Learning, Power point Presentation and Internet, which have four point scale such a Strongly Agree, Agree, Disagree and Strongly Disagree. After the Development of the Questionnaire, the Investigator distributed it to Teacher Educators for validation. Their valuable ideas were taken care. Then the questionnaire was given to 10 Teacher Educators by Test - Retest method. The obtained r value 0.84 reveals that the tool is reliable one.Investigators randomly selected 100 Teacher Educators from various Colleges of Education in Perambalur and Trichy Districts.

Analysis

The collected data was analysed by using different statistical technique like Mean, SD and 't' test. The results are given in the following Tables

Table: 1

Significant Difference on the Mean Scores of Male and Female Teacher Educators

S.No	Dimension	Gender	Mean	SD	t test	Remarks
1.	**Total**	MaleFemale	64.363.0	0.740.92	**7.38**	**S**
2.	**CTL**	MaleFemale	60.5461.62	1.191.41	1.48	NS
3.	**PPT**	MaleFemale	65.0461.24	3.890.98	**6.43**	**S**
4.	**INT**	MaleFemale	71.0769.58	1.923.35	**2.38**	**S**

CTL – Computer in Teaching Learning **PPT** – Power Point Presentation

INT Internet **NS** - Not Significant **S** - Significant

From the above Table it is noted that the 't' values are significantly difference at 5% level of the Teacher Educators for Total, PPT(Power Point Presentation) and INT(Internet) . Total, PPT (Power Point Presentation) and INT (Internet) the Mean score of Male Teacher Educators are higher than the Female Teacher Educators. In CTL(Computer in Teaching Learning) there is no significant difference at 5 % level of the Teacher Educators.

Table: 2

Significant Difference on the Mean Scores of Rural and Urban Teacher Educators

S.No	Dimension	Locality	Mean	SD	t test	Remarks
1.	**Total**	Rural	64.7	0.837	**5.46**	**S**
	Urban	63.07	0.823			
2.	**CTL**	Rural	60.74	1.61	1.69	NS
	Urban	63.18	0.989			
3.	**PPT**	Rural	62.90	0.78	1.06	NS
	Urban	63.07	0.65			
4.	**INT**	Rural	74.53	1.72	**3.62**	**S**
	Urban	70.93	1.68			

From the above Table, the calculated 't' values are reveal that there is no significant difference at 5% level for the dimensions CTL and PPT. But there exists significant difference at 5% level with respect to Total and INT. In the Total and INT the Mean score of the Rural Teacher Educators are higher having higher awareness on Digital Technology than the Urban Teacher Educators.

Table : 3

Significant Difference on the Mean Scores of Science and Arts Teacher Educators

S.No	Dimension	Subject	Mean	SD	t test	Remarks
1.	**Total**	Science	63.83	0.929	1.21	NS
	Arts	64.31	0.779			
2.	**CTL**	Science	62.43	1.06	**4.79**	**S**
	Arts	61.28	1.11			
3.	**PPT**	Science	63.02	4.22	**3.27**	**S**
	Arts	60.34	0.934			
4.	**INT**	Science	71.94	1.19	**6.03**	**S**
	Arts	73.38	1.02			

The Mean scores and the calculated 't ' values from the above table shows that there is significant difference in all the mean score of CTL, PPT and INT at 5% level except Total. It can be understood that the level Awareness on Digital Technology among Teacher Educators are good in CTL , PPT and INT.

Results and Discussion

The salient findings of the study are i) All the Teacher Educators are having good Awareness on Digitaol Technology. ii) The Mean score of Male Teacher Educators are higher than the Female Teacher Educators towards Awareness on Digital Technology with respect to the dimensions such as Total, PPT and INT. iii) With regards to Locality, the Mean score of Rural Teacher Educators are higher than the Urban Teacher Educators towards Awareness on Digital Technology in Total and INT. iv) The Mean scores of Teacher Educators with respect to Science Subject are higher in CTL, PPT and Arts Teacher Educators are higher in INT.

The result shows that Gender, Locality and Subject of Teacher Educators were not the influencing factor in determining Awareness on Digital Technology. While considering the Gender, Male Teachers are having higher Awareness on Digital Technology than the Female Teachers. This is because Male Teacher Educators may have more time to work in the Computer but the Female Teachers have the commitment to look after their family. By this way Rural Teachers are having Good Awareness on Digital Technology than the Urban Teachers. This is due to the fact that Rural Teachers may show more interest to know about the new things. As well as Science Group Teacher Educators are show more awareness than Art Group Teacher Educators. It may be due to their subject knowledge.

Recommendations for Policy Makings

The result of this study shows that the Teacher Educators are having Good awareness on Digital Technology. Hence the usage of Computer must be increased to develop their practical knowledge. They are having more involvement in using Digital Technology in their class room Teaching. Effective teaching to promote better learning, proper orientation training Programme must be provided them to develop their knowledge in Digital Technology. The Government must ensure proper training to Teacher Educators to maintain Computers and Electronic things. Educational Authorities should create, improve and sustain the Awareness of Teacher Educators about Computer Knowledge. Teacher Educators should be encouraged by Administrators to use the stand alone Computer Applications in their Teachings. Using Internet application should be given special concentration, because, it empowers and enhance creativity. Digital Technology acts as a catalyst to support change in Teacher Pedagogy.

Conclusion

The Good Awareness on Computer Technology among Primary and Middle School Teachers will show the Conducing Climate towards Educational Technology. The Instruction through Computer has been making wonders in the Class Room Activities. Hence Teachers must have Awareness on Computer Technology to get success and enjoy their Professions.

Reference

1. BEST,J.W,(2003). *Research in Education,* Prentice – Hall of India (P) Ltd., New Delhi.
2. LOKESH KOUL.(2005). *Methodology of Educational Research,* Vikas Publishing House (P) Ltd, New Delhi.
3. SINGH.Y.K,(2005). *Instructional Technology In Education,* P. P. H Publishing.
4. Corporation, New Delhi-110002.
5. SAREEN.N, (2005). *Information and Communication Technology,* Anmol Publication Pvt.Ltd, New Delhi-110002.

31

Blended Learning- A New Horizon of Holistic Education

Introduction

The education sector, where student-centric learning is the core aspects to take into consideration, is highly influenced by technology. There are two forms of affective learning methodologies, i.e., face to face learning methodologies and online learning methodologies. While each of these two modes of instruction has its advantages and disadvantages, the need would be for a method that will combine the positive features of both, and would provide both the educational institution and the student with competitive and learning advantages respectively. This need is being satisfied with the emergency of a new wave of learning called "hybrid or blended learning". Blended learning can make use of the powerful internet technology, and at the same time, provide the elements lacking in web based instructions such as engagement and social contact. Blended learning within a flexible-learning framework offers a unique opportunity to fully integrate pedagogy and technology with teaching and learning. It should also provide a wide choice to learners as per their self-regulatory perception. It is essential to provide a good support and training model and should keep the cultural components also in mind. A blend which make the right balance between innovation and mass utility as well as which bridge the digital divided will be the successful blended learning model.

Blended learning which is also called hybrid learning is a blend of both class room or face to face learning and online learning (Garrisen and Kanaka, 2004). It is commonly known classroom instruction, learning takes place inside the classroom, where students gather in a physical place (the classroom), listen to lectures, hand in homework assignments and take scheduled examinations. Blended learning offers more choices to benefit educators and learners than either classroom based or web based learning alone (Singh, 2003). According to him blended learning can make use of the powerful internet technology, and at the same time, provide the elements lacking in web based instructions such as engagement and social contact. Blended learning can improve student retention in higher education.

Blended learning includes face to face learning, E-learning and self-paced instructions. It is the learning which offers learners the opportunities "to be both together and apart".

Face to face +E-learning (synchronous or asynchronous conversation) =Blended learning

Thus blended learning courses are:

1. Not traditional "distance education" courses,
2. Not entirely online
3. Not simply traditional classes with a Web site
4. Online time replaces some classroom time,
5. Not just transferring information to the Web
6. Involves an extensive course redesign
7. Many different formats and schedules are possible

Dimensions of Blended Learning

The dimensions of blended learning are Pedagogical, Technological, Interface Design, Evaluation, Management, Resource Support, Ethical and Institutional Dimensions.

Promises of Blended Learning

Among the electronically instructional strategies blended learning is fast picking up with the following benefits.

1. It addresses the different learning styles, methods of information delivery to reinforced lessons
2. It offers improved pedagogy as it increases the level of active learning strategies peer to learning strategies and learning centered strategies.

3. Boundless information in the world wide web can be accessed instantly; social interaction is relatively more in blended learning then e-learning
4. For self-motivated adult learners it offers the benefits of self-regulatory learning in case of revision.
5. Designing the blended learning modules is not a costly affair too.

Elements of Blended Learning

As per the learners demand and expected learning out comes the blended learning experience is designed by the experts. Bersin and Associates (2004) have identified the following elements related to blended learning.

1. Instructors led/ lecture/training.
2. Webinars
3. Web-based courseware
4. Simulations
5. CD-ROM based courseware
6. Internet delivered videos
7. Offline videos
8. Electronic performance support system
9. Rapid e-learning courseware
10. Collaboration system(chat room, discussion board)
11. Video conference
12. Conference calls
13. Job aids
14. Work books
15. Books
16. On the job exercise

Variants of Blended Learning Models

The various structural and functional variants of blended learning models are

1. Program flow blend
2. Core -spoke blends
3. Concentric blends
4. Branching blends
5. Enabling
6. Enhancing
7. Transforms

8. Knowledge driven
9. Skill driven
10. Attitude driven
11. Competency driven

Kinds of Blending/ Components of Blend Learning

1. Blend learning environment
2. Blending instructional strategies
3. Blending instructional media

Blending in Teaching Learning Process

Although blended learning environment differs from place to place, there are some similarities among them. The commonly used models of blended learning are:

Rotation Model: In this type of blending, students are rotated within a given course, on a fixed schedule between learning modalities, at least one of which is an online learing and other modalities might include activities such as small group instruction, projects, individual tutoring etc.

Flipped Model: in this model within a given course students are rotated on a fixed schedule between face to face teachers guided practice in school and online delivery of content and instruction of same subject from a remote location after school.

Flex Model: It is amodel in whichcontent and instructions are delivered primarily by the internet and the teacher–of–record is available, students move on an individually customized schedule among modalities.

Self-Blend Model: In this, students choose to take one or more courses entirely online to supplement their traditional courses. Students self-blend some individual online courses with courses at campus with face to face teachers.

Enriched Virtual Model: It involves a whole school experience in which within each course, students divide their time between attending the traditional class and learning remotely using online delivery of content and instruction.

Teachers' Role in Blended Classroom

Role of Teachers in Blended Classroom is

- Help to guide students

- Manage their activities.
- Direct their learning.
- Help develop their skills.

Teachers are essential in the success of the classroom

Advantages of Blended Learning

There are some obvious advantages to the use of digital media for content delivery

1. Students have greater time flexibility, freedom, and convenience by working part of the time online from home due to decreased commuting and parking hassles.
2. Students are likely to interact more with the instructor and fellow students since there are numerous opportunities to do so both in class and online.
3. Students have access to unlimited up-to-date resources available via the Web.
4. Students often develop or enhance skills in time management, critical thinking, and problem solving.
5. Students enjoy increased success as measured by fewer course withdrawals and somewhat higher grades.
6. Students can participate more in class discussions since they can choose environment — online or face-to-face — in which they feel more comfortable.
7. Students have more time to reflect and refer to relevant course and other research materials when working and writing online than when responding in class.
8. Students typically have 24/7 access to online course materials.
9. Students usually receive more feedback, and more frequent feedback, from their instructors.
10. Students can acquire useful skills from using the Internet and computer technology.

Challenges Ahead

6. Negative attitude towards new technology among the instructors and learners.
7. Cost of many on-line components is high
8. Teachers and learners should be made accustomed with modalities
9. Lot of e-content in various topics should be developed
10. Bandwidth needed for the fast access of internet should be improved

11. Server with better capacity needed for congestion free learning
12. Developing adequate technological and human resources
13. Developing adequate contingency plan in case of technical problem

Conclusion

The success of blend largely depends on the right mix of the elements it posses. A good blend should provide optimum role of live interaction. It should also provide a wide choice to learners as per their self-regulatory perception. It is essential to provide a good support and training model and should keep the cultural components also in mind. A blend which make the right balance between innovation and mass utility as well as which bridge the digital divided will be the successful blended learning model. So blended learning may be considered as "the right mix of various media to maximize learning experience with minimum utility of resources to ensure optimum realization of educational objectives, by making the perfect blend of information technology and instructional technology.

Reference

1. Atken, J (2006) *Education and assessment; update on changes*. Accountancy Ireland Vol. 38, 1
2. Singh. H(2003) *Building effective blended learning programs.* Educational Technology (43), 51-54.
3. http://www.uwsa.edu/ttt/articles/grantam2htm
4. Mohana sundaram,K and Siva kumar, A (2010). B.L; *A new Horizon*,University News.Vol.47, No.50.pg14-17
5. Bersin,J (2004) *The blended learning book: Best practices, proven methodologies, and lessons learned* San Francisco: Pfeiffer.
6. Kurtus, R (2004) *Blended learning* http://www.school-for-champions.com/elearning/blended.htm
7. Valiathan; P (2002) *"Blended learning models"*, ASTD Learning Circuits,2002 http://www.learning circuits.org2002/june 2002/ elearn.htm.retrieved on April21.
8. Warrier,B.S(2006)*"The perfect blended learning"* www. thehindu. com/thehindu/edii 2006/05/08/stories/2006050800250700.htm.

32

Blended Learning

Introduction

Blended learning can be thought of as a pedagogical approach that combines the effectiveness and socialization opportunities of class room with the technologically advanced active learning possibilities of the online environment. Research has shown that high level of student and instructor satisfaction can be produced in the fully online environment. But both faculty and students lament the loss of face-to-face interaction.

Blended learning models comprise of the following elements like learning through information, learning through interaction, learning through collaboration and learning through classroom experiences mixed in varied proportions according to an organization's requirements. Dziuban, Hartman and Moskal (2004) in a research brief for EDUCAUSE titled "Blended Learning" noted "Blended learning should be viewed as a pedagogical approach that combined the effectiveness and socialization opportunities of the classroom with the technologically enhanced active learning possibilities of the online environment, rather than a ratio of delivery modalities.

In recent years, ICT has paved the way for accelerating the paradigm shift through providing more flexible ways of learning. The students can do self-learning using enormous potentials of Internet and providing them with several online exercises. The main focus should be on learning rather than on technology.. Blending of face-to-face instruction with various types of non-classroom technology mediated delivery has been practiced within the academy for more than four decades. A good blend would provide optimum role of live interaction. It is essential to provide a good support and training model and should keep the cultural components in mind. It is the responsibility of authorities to provide necessary learning support in providing access to online learning so that out students become 'blended learners' with self-regulatory authentic learning experience.

Blended learning can be thought of as a pedagogical approach that combines the effectiveness and socialization opportunities of class room with the technologically advanced active learning possibilities of the online environment. Blended learning models comprise of the following elements like learning through information, learning through interaction, learning through collaboration and learning through classroom experiences mixed in varied proportions according to an organization's requirements.

What is Blended Learning

Blended Learning means many things to many people, even within our relatively small online learning community. It is referred to as both blended and hybrid learning, with little or no difference in the meaning of the terms among most educators. In general terms, blended learning combines online delivery of educational content with the best features of classroom interaction and live instruction to personalize learning, allow thoughtful reflection, and differentiate instruction from student-to-student across a diverse group of learners. Definitions of blended learning range from some so broad that practically any learning experience that integrates some use of educational technology might qualify, to others that focus on a specific percentage combination of online curriculum and instruction in a face-to-face setting. A few of the many definitions of blended learning include:

1. The integration of face-to-face and online learning to help enhance the classroom experience and extend learning through the innovative use of information and communications technology. Blended strategies enhance student engagement and learning through online activities to the course curriculum, and improve effectiveness and efficiencies by reduction lecture time.
2. A course that blends online and face-to-face delivery. Substantial proportion of the content is delivered online, typically uses online

discussions, and typically has some face-to-face meaning. "The sloan Consortium defines blended courses as having between 30 percent and 79 percent of their content delivered online, with the remaining portion of the course content delivered by face-to-face instruction or other non-web-based methods, such as paper textbooks.

3. The combination of multiple approaches to learning. Blended learning can be accomplished through the use of 'blended' virtual and physical resources.

Dziuban, Hartman and Moskal (2004) in a research brief for EDUCAUSE titled "Blended Learning" noted "Blended learning should be viewed as a pedagogical approach that combined the effectiveness and socialization opportunities of the classroom with the technologically enhanced active learning possibilities of the online environment, rather than a ratio of delivery modalities. Blended learning redesign the instructional model with the following characteristics.

1. A shift from lecture to student centered instruction in which students become active and interactive learners.
2. Increases in interaction between student-instructor, student-student, student-content, and student-outside resources;
3. Integrated formative and summative assessment mechanisms for students and instructor.

Blended learning consists of two features

1. It is a planned combination of online learning and Face-to-face (F2F) instruction using a variety of learning resources.

2. It is an educational format that integrates online learning techniques including online delivery of materials through web pages, discussion boards, and e-mail with traditional teaching.

Ingredients of Blended Learning

1. Live Events:

Synchronous, teacher-led learning environment in which all learners participate at the same time. It can be in real classroom or can be virtual.

2. Self-paced learning:

Recorded live events, Internet based or CD ROM based, which helps the learner to learn at his own pace.

3. Collaboration:

It implies a more dynamic communication and interaction among many learners that brings about knowledge sharing.

4. Assessment:

It is both live and online measure of learner's knowledge to determine prior knowledge as well as to measure learning transfer.

5. Performance Support:

These are reference materials that enhance learning, retention and transfer. It may be printable references, downloaded multimedia learning objects, documentations etc.

Smart Classrooms

Smart Classrooms are technology enhanced classrooms that foster opportunities for teaching and learning by integrating learning technology, such as computers, specialized software, and audience response technology, networking, and audio/visual capabilities. The smart class-rooms demand learning initiative that assists educators to make ICT integral to learning. The strategy is about engaging the digital generation, improving individualized learning opportunities, sparking innovation in learning, enhancing teachers' digital pedagogy and getting the best from schools ICT investment.

Smart Classrooms Vis-à-vis Blended Learning

Smart classroom uses following elements, mixed in varied proportions according to an organization's requirements of blended learning:

Learning Through Information

Material based information is the first coherent step towards starting a learning program. Web based material can now be handed to the learners, thanks to e-learning techniques, which can render the learning program easy to deliver and fasters to implement. Making the information accessible all the time will give learners the liberty of scrolling through the content at their own convenience, which, in turn, will enhance understanding and enthusiasm.

Learning Through Interaction

The learner instructor, learner-content, learner-learner, and learner-infrastructure interactions become all the more important in a blended-learning environment. Web can assist all the above mentioned forms of interaction, which together, help retain the knowledge that is acquired through information. Web simulations of real life situations allow learners to apply their knowledge practically, without the possibility of them affecting your business directly.

Learning Through Collaboration

Collaborative learning includes peer-to-peer discussions, conference calls, chat, team rooms and instant messaging. Technology has enhanced the concept of collaboration manifold, where learners, even though geographically remote, can communicate in real time. The collaborative environment also heightens the chances of collaboration between e-learners and subject matter experts (SMEs).

Learning Through Classroom Interactions

Conventional, tested and, by far, one of the most effective approaches to learning, classrooms are the best places to personally connect to peers and instructors. No technology can replace the advantages of this approach, which is exactly why no e-learning or blended-learning model will skip this element for any reason. But, as one would like to believe, blended learning has never attempted to replace classroom-based learning.

Potential Constituents of a Blended Learning Approach:

The notion of blending is nothing new. Good classroom teachers have always blended their methods – reading, writing, lecture, discussion, practice and projects, to name just a few, are all part of an effective blend.

Virtual Fieldtrips:

Blended learning Virtual Fieldtrips can be used in any number of ways to serve a variety of educational goals. Using blended learning through the virtual fieldtrip is a wonderful opportunity. The virtual fieldtrip experience is an excellent model of a teaching strategy that was not possible before the advent of computers in the classroom.

Blogs:

Blog is a term coined for the combination of two words, web and log. As part of a blended-learning project, it is an asynchronous form of online discussion. A blog is a publicly accessible website which contains a journal or diary of sorts. Anyone can initiate a blog either as a part of another website or personal web page or a blog can stand alone.

Blogs offer a forum for many people to state their opinions or comment on others opinions. Blogs could provide a great medium to enhance student writing through the use of technology.

A good blend would provide optimum role of live interaction. It is essential to provide a good support and training model and should keep the cultural components in mind. A successful blend would strike the right balance between innovations and mass utility. Some of the basic factors which should be considered in identifying the blend are:

1. Course instructional goals
2. Student profile
3. Hours of learning/training
4. Teacher experience and teaching style
5. Cultural dimensions
6. Resource availability
7. Budgetary requirement for training implementation

What Kind of Learners we Require?

1. Demonstrate creativity and intellectual curiosity resulting in enjoyment, fun and resilience.
2. Exhibit a sense of self-confidence and enjoyment
3. Are self-directed and can work independently, collaboratively and cooperatively to learn and to develop products of use with themselves and others.
4. Display innovation and entrepreneurship.
5. Continually develop communication and collaboration skills.
6. Communicate globally through e-learning spaces.
7. Are able to research effectively and have information fluency.
8. Have developed digital literacy and understand technology operations and concepts.
9. Have developed digital proficiency to work effectively in 21st century environments.
10. Understand digital citizenship and work on issues and challenges that are real and relevant, that make a difference to them and to others.
11. Demonstrate accountability and adaptability.
12. Have developed skills to design, create, share and publish.
13. Build critical and systems thinking enabling problem identification, formulation and solution, and decision making.
14. Use ICT purposefully to engage in real research
15. Explore new ideas and tools in authentic contexts.

What Kind of Teachers we Require?

1. Demonstrate an on-going commitment to professional knowledge,

professional practice, professional relationships and professional values.

2. Have understanding of the transformative role of ICT for 21st Century curriculum design/interpretation, pedagogy and student learning.
3. Make conscious decisions about student learning based on an understanding of digital learners.
4. Are lifelong learners who are willing to take risks, fail and explore areas outside his or her expertise?
5. Employ a variety of methodologies, current learning theories and practices.
6. Constantly collaborate with colleagues and practicing professionals in order to consolidate understanding and to share and reflect on their learning, wonderings and discoveries.

Challenges

The challenges in a blended-learning environment can be looked in two different perspectives learners' perspective and teacher perspective. In focusing on the learner perspective, there is a need to consider the learning style and perceptual skills and abilities of students while designing blended-learning strategy. Learner's proficiency in using ICT is also important in a blended-learning environment. Therefore determining the skills and the ways students acquire and construct knowledge online is very important while designing blended-learning strategy.

One of the major challenges the teachers faces while designing a blended-learning strategy is to determine the balance between online and face-to-face instruction. There is a need of great expertise on the part of the teacher to design the strategy by considering both the educational provisions of the institute and the learner's needs in a blended-learning environment.

Conclusion

A good blend would provide optimum role of live interaction. It is essential to provide a good support and training model and should keep the cultural components in mind. A successful blend would strike the right balance between innovations and mass utility. It is the responsibility of authorities to provide necessary learning support in providing access to online learning so that out students become 'blended learners' with self-regulatory authentic learning experience.

33

Hyper Diversed Teacher and Digital Skills

Introduction

Social media have risen to prominence in recent years, beginning first with sites like Classmates in the mid-1990s, followed by Friendster in 2003. The most significant growth of social media has occurred since 2004 when Facebook.com was introduced. Today there are over 550 million Facebook users alone, along with millions more using sites such as Twitter, MySpace, Plaxo, LinkedIn and others. While early adopters of these sites were digital natives (i.e., those born and/or raised in the internet era), all age groups are now embracing these sites. At present there is a gap between campus pedagogy and social media usage among students and faculty. Teaching community need to be skilled digitally. This paper works to examine that chasm, and to draw some conclusions as to why it may be time to incorporate this technology into our classrooms.

Need for the Study

Social media sites such as Face book and Twitter have come to dominate internet usage in recent years. Face book alone has over 550 million users as of fall 2010, while Twitter claims over 100 million users. While academia was fairly quick to adopt online education models in the 1990s, it has thus far not yet embraced social media portals as a way to deliver course content and engage students. This may be due to uncertainties regarding student perceptions about social media, its purposes, and its applications. Teacher Educators and Student teachers always find it easier to use the already made teaching aids for teaching practice for preparation of lessons and in their theory learning and submission of assignments .in such situation the modern technology i.e. internet is challenging them to be more innovative , explorative and modern in their teaching and learning experiences . Teaching faculty is challenged by the digitalworld to be in pursuit of skills development.

Background of the Study

The researcher is involved in the educational institution which is in the forefront to promote quality of pedagogy. The experience of the researcher has often been frustrating with lack of digital climate .Since the Tamil nadu Teachers Education University has created a platform for such pondering this study found its way out to reach out to the professional mob to leverage the educational system through virtualization of the academia. The HD (Hyper Diversified) Classroom is the need of the hour. Just as the digital divide vanished over time (males once dominated all computer and internet usage), it is possible that similar usage divides will also disappear. Online college courses, for example, have broad-based appeal, and even traditional campus-based courses often have high computer usage expectations. Given that social media are now part of the cultural fabric, it is necessary to explore if and how social media might find their place in academia. Therefore the researcher undertook this study.

Sample for the Study

300 Samples Comprising Teacher Educators and Student Teachers (100 Teacher Educators and 200 Student Teachers)

Objectives of the Study

1. To construct a tool to find out the level of hyper diversification among teacher educators and student teachers
2. To realize the importance of hyper diversification and developing digital skills among teacher educators and student teachers.
3. To find out whether any difference exists among teacher educators and student teachers in their hyper diversification and digital skills in terms of the following variables:

1. Locality
2. Residence
3. Status(teacher/student)
4. Educational qualification(UG/PG)
5. Browsing habit

Hypotheses of the Study

1. The level of hyper diversification among teacher educators and student teachers is high.
2. There is a significant difference among teacher educators and student teachers in their hyper diversification and digital skills in terms of the following variables:
6. Locality
7. Residence
8. Status(teacher/student)
9. Educational qualification(UG/PG)
10. Browsing habit

Methodology

In order to carry out the study the researcher used the following statistical

Techniques: MEAN, STANDARD DEVIATION and 't' test

Mean

Mean was calculated by the formula

$\overline{X} = \frac{\Sigma X}{N}$ Where X = Score, N = Total Number of the scores.

Standard Deviation:

Stadard deviation was calculated by the following formula

$$\sigma = \frac{\sqrt{(X - \overline{X})^2}}{N}$$

Where $\overline{X}$ = Mean

X = Individual score

N = Total Number of the scores

Test of significant difference ('t' test)

Since the groups were large independent samples, the 't' test was applied through the statistical package by using the following formula:

$$t \quad \frac{M_1 \quad M_2}{\sqrt{\frac{\sigma_1^2}{N_1} \quad \frac{\sigma_2^2}{N_2}}}$$

Where M_1- denotes mean of group 1

M_2- denotes mean of group 2

$\acute{o}_1$- denotes standard deviation of group 1

$\acute{o}_2$- denotes standard deviation of group 2

N_1- denotes total number of respondents in group 1

N_2- denotes total number of respondents in group 2

Hypothesis 1:

The level of hyper diversification and digital skills among teacher educators and student teachers is high.

Table 1 showing the analysis of hyper diversification and digital skills among teacher

educators and student teachers.

Entire Sample	N	Mean	S.D
Hyper Diversification	300	109.1	2.79
Digital Skills	300	24.21	3.40

The above table 1 shows that the mean and standard deviation on hyper diversification of the entire sample of teacher educators and student teachers' scores are 109.1 and 2.79 respectively. As 109.1 is higher than the mid-value of 64.1 (maximum score 129), it is concluded that the teacher educators and student teachers have a high level of hyper diversification. The mean and standard deviation on digital skills of the entire sample of teacher educators and student teachers' scores are 24.21 and 3.40 respectively. As 24.21 is higher than the mid-value of15 (maximum score 30), it is concluded that the teacher educators and student teachers have a high level of hyper diversification and digital skills.

HYPOTHESIS 2(a):

There is a significant difference among teacher educators and student teachers in their hyper diversification and digital skills in terms of Locality.

The details of the results of the't' test in the level of hyper diversification and digital skills among teacher educators and student teachers based on Locality is given in table no.2.

Table- 2 Difference in the level of hyper diversification and digital skills based on Locality

Variables	Sub variables	N	Mean	SD	' t' value	Level of Significance	Result
Locality	Urban	160	21.31	3.12	**1.13**	**0.05**	**NS**
	Rural	140	23.52	2.86			

It is evident from table no.2 that the calculated't' value 1.13 is less than the table value 1.96 at 0.05 level. This shows that there is no significant difference among teacher educators and student teachers in their hyper diversification and digital skills in terms of Locality.

Hence, there is no significant difference between the samples (teacher educators and student teachers) that live in Urban and Rural areas in their hyper deiversification and digital skills.

Hypothesis 2(b)

There is a significant difference among teacher educators and student teachers in their hyper diversification and digital skills in terms of Residence.

The details of the results of the 't' test in the level of hyper diversification and digital skills among teacher educators and student teachers based on Residence is given in table no.3.

Table- 3 Difference in the level of hyper diversification and digital skills based on Residence

Variables	Sub variables	N	Mean	SD	' t' value	Level of Significance	Result
Residence	Hostel	130	22.42	3.40	**1.049**	**0.05**	**NS**
	Home	170	25.63	4.60			

It is evident from table no.3 that the calculated 't' value 1.049 is less than the table value 1.96 at 0.05 level. This shows that there is no significant difference among teacher educators and student teachers in their hyper diversification and digital skills in terms of Residence.

Hence, there is no significant difference between the samples (teacher educators and student teachers) who reside at hostel and at home in their hyper deiversification and digital skills.

Hypothesis (2c)

There is a significant difference among teacher educators and student teachers in their hyper diversification and digital skills in terms of Status (teacher educator/student teacher).

The details of the results of the 't' test in the level of hyper diversification and digital skills among teacher educators and student teachers based on Status((teacher educator/student teacher) is given in table no.4.

Table- 4 Difference in the level of hyper diversification and digital skills based on Status (teacher educator/student teacher)

Variables	Sub variables	N	Mean	SD	't' value	Level of Significance	Result
	Teacher Educators	100	20.24	3.983	**1.61**	**0.05**	**NS**
STATUS	Student Teachers	200	22.57	3.793			

It is evident from table no.4 that the calculated 't' value 1.61 is less than the table value 1.96 at 0.05 level. This shows that there is no significant difference among teacher educators and student teachers in their hyper diversification and digital skills in terms of Status.

Hence, there is no significant difference between the samples (teacher educators and student teachers) in Status in their hyper deiversification and digital skills.

Hypothesis 2(d)

There is a significant difference among teacher educators and student teachers in their hyper diversification and digital skills in terms of Educational Qualification (UG/PG).

The details of the results of the 't' test in the level of hyper diversification and digital skills among teacher educators and student teachers based on Educational Qualification(UG/PG) is given in table no.5.

Table – 5 Difference in the level of hyper diversification and digital skills based on Educational Qualification(UG/PG)

Variables	Sub Variables	N	Mean	SD	't' value	Level of Significance	Result
Educational Qualification	UG	100	22.35	3.902	**1.21**	**0.05**	**NS**
	PG	200	21.50	3.340			

It is evident from table no.5 that the calculated 't' value 1.21 is less than the table value 1.96 at 0.05 level. This shows that there is no significant difference among teacher educators and student teachers in their hyper diversification and digital skills in terms of Educational Qualification (UG/PG).

Hence, there is no significant difference among teacher educators and student teachers in their hyper diversification and digital skills in terms of Educational Qualification (UG/PG).

HYPOTHESIS 2(e)

There is a significant difference among teacher educators and student teachers in their hyper diversification and digital skills in terms of Browsing habit.

The details of the results of the 't' test in the level of hyper diversification and digital skills among teacher educators and student teachers based on browsing habit is given in table no.6

Table – 6 Difference in the level of hyper diversification and digital skills based on Browsing Habit

Variable	Sub variables	N	Mean	SD	't' value	Level of Significance	Result
Browsing Habit	Frequently	120	17.73	3.679	**5.820**	**0.05**	**S**
	Rarely	180	19.28	3.431			

It is evident from table no.6 that the calculated 't' value 5.820 is higher than the table value 1.96 at 0.05 level. This shows that there is a significant difference among teacher educators and student teachers in their hyper diversification and digital skills in terms of Browsing habit.Hence, there is a significant difference among teacher educators and student teachers in their hyper diversification and digital skills in terms of Browsing habit.

Hypotheses Verification

1. The level of hyper diversification among teacher educators and student teachers is high- **Accepted**
2. There is a significant difference among teacher educators and student teachers in their hyper diversification and digital skills in terms of Locality - **Rejected**
3. There is a significant difference among teacher educators and student teachers in their hyper diversification and digital skills in terms of Residence - **Rejected**
4. There is a significant difference among teacher educators and student teachers in their hyper diversification and digital skills in terms of Status(teacher/student) - **Rejected**
5. There is a significant difference among teacher educators and student teachers in their hyper diversification and digital skills in terms of educational qualification(UG/PG) - **Rejected**
6. There is a significant difference among teacher educators and student teachers in their hyper diversification and digital skills in terms of Browsing habit - **Accepted**

Educational Implications

1. The result of the study leads to encourage Teacher Educators Student teachers to be hyper diversified and digitally skilled.
2. The usage of virtual world can be enhanced in colleges to develop skills and build capacity as part of professional life.

   Therefore Teacher Educators and Student Teachers can:
3. create and edit digital audios
4. use Social bookmarking to share resources with and between learners
5. use blogs and wikis to create online platforms for students
6. Exploit digital images for classroom use
7. Use video content to engage students
8. Use info graphics to visually stimulate students
9. Use Social networking sites to connect with colleagues and grow professionally
10. Create and deliver asynchronous presentations and training sessions
11. Compile a digital e-portfolio for their own development
12. Have a knowledge about online security
13. be able to detect plagiarized works in students assignments
14. Create screen capture videos and tutorials
15. Curate web content for classroom learning

16. Use and provide students with task management tools to organize their work and plan their learning
17. Use polling software to create a real-time survey in class
18. Understand issues related to copyright and fair use of online materials
19. Exploit computer games for pedagogical purposes
20. Use digital assessment tools to create quizzes
21. Use of collaborative tools for text construction and editing
22. Find and evaluate authentic web based content
23. Identify online resources that are safe for students browsing
24. Use digital tools for time management purposes
25. Learn about the different ways to use YouTube in your classroom
26. Use note taking tools to share interesting content with your students
27. Annotate web pages and highlight parts of text to share with your class
28. Use of online graphic organizers and printable
29. Use of online sticky notes to capture interesting idea
30. Use of screen casting tools to create and share tutorials
31. Exploit group text messaging tools for collaborative project work
32. Conduct an effective search query with the minimum time possible
33. Conduct A Research Paper Using Digital Tools
34. Use file sharing tools to share docs and files with students online
35. Reduce Infrastructure Costs Through Consolidation
36. Virtualize the Most Demanding Workloads
37. Virtualize for High Availability
38. Improve Security and Reliability with Microkernel zed Hypervisor
39. Protect Important Data Using Live Backup
40. Minimize Downtime with Quick Migration
41. Delegate Virtual Machine Management
42. Reduce Support Time with Integrated Management
43. Save Time and Money with a More Flexible Test Environment
44. Take Advantage of Broad Compatibility
45. Reduce Support Time with Integrated Management
46. Save Time and Money with a More Flexible Test Environment
47. Take Advantage of Broad Compatibility
48. Exploit Facebook,Youtube,Flickr and Social networking Sites(SNS) for sharing eduinformation
49. Use Smartphones, iphones, tablets as educational resources.
50. Accomplish content delivery and student engagement by creating and maintaining a Fan Page, at no cost to anyone involved, and

completely away from the limitations of course management systems such as Blackboard, Angel and Web CT.

Bibliography

1. Baird, D., Fisher, M. (2005). Neomillennial user experience strategies: Utilizing social networking media to support "always on" learning styles. Journal of Educational Technology Systems. 34 (1) 5 - 32.
2. Bimber, B. (2000). Measuring the gender gap on the Internet. Social Sciences Quarterly, 81 (3):25-32.
3. Broos, A. (2005). Gender and information and communication technologies (ICT) anxiety: Male self-assurance and female hesitation. Cyber psychology &Behavior (1):21-31.
4. Dennis, A.R., Kinney, S.T., & Hung, Y.T.C. (1999) Gender differences in the effects of media richness.Small Group Research. 30 (4): 405-437.
5. Dillon, D. (2001). E-books: The University of Texas Experience. Library Hi Tech. 19 (4) 350-62.
6. Gefen, D. & Straub, D. W. (1997) Gender differences in the perception and use of email: an extension to the technology acceptance model. MIS Quarterly 4: 389-400.
7. Horowitz, R. & Mohum, A. (1998). His and Hers: Gender Consumption & Technology. University of Virginia Press.
8. Jackson L.A., Ervin, K.S., Gardner, P.D. & Schmitt,N. (2001). Gender and the internet: women communicating and men searching.
9. Lenhart, M. (2010). Teens and Social Media, An Overview. Pew Internet and American Life Project.
10. Summerfield, M., Mandel, C., Kantor, P. (1999). Online books at Columbia: Early findings on use, satisfaction, and effect. Technology and Scholarly Communication. Berkley; University of California Press 282-308.
11. Wilska, A. (2003). Mobile use as part of young people's consumption styles.

34

Learning with Cloud Computing Technology

Introduction

'Swami Vivekananda voice education is the process of bringing out the potential that is latent is every human being India's educational system is the most ancient in the world's history teaching and learning is as old as human race'. Education is closely bound with the intellectual, economic, cultural, emotional and social life of the community. Education is one of the important instruments for improving the quality of people, society nation and it also helps in meeting challenges of fast developments in the world. Innovation in education is a means to enhance quality in education.

Innovations societies at large will make the fortune innovative centric teaching learning process need to be promoted in schools, colleges, institutions and universities. Education is a challenging academic discipline, learning with cloud computing is become a dominant model in information technology (IT) Field these days, this paper focuses on integrating and enhancing the learning using cloud computing technique.

Cloud computing has refers to the applications delivered as services over the internet and the hard ware and system software located in the data centers that provide the services. Cloud computing in an internet-based technology through which information stored in servers and provided as a service on-demand to clients. This technology has made the software more attractive as a services and shaped various industries

Many students would likely cite a desire to learn. Students assume that, because they have read their text and memorized facts, they have learned something. Definition of 'learn' in a dictionary step, Step1. To acquire knowledge of a subject or skill through education or experience, Step2. To gain information about somebody or something. Step3. To memorize something. This definition is not particularly insightful, although it reminds us that the word can be used to describe the acquisition of both knowledge and skill, and that acquisition can be by a variety of means. Including education experience, or memorization.

Effects of educational Technology with multiples Intelligence

1. Educational technology has a significant positive impact on achievement in all subjects' area, across all levels of school and in regular classroom as well as those for special-needs students.
2. Educational Technology has positive effects on student attitudes.
3. Technology makes instruction more student-centered, encourages co-operative learning and stimulated increased teacher/ student interaction.
4. Positive changes in the learning environments evolve over time and do not occur quickly.
5. Educational games which challenge fine motor coordination while developing logical thinking skills and mastery over abstraction.

Learning

Learning is modifying the existing knowledge behavior skill etc., this can be achieved through continuous process and the change that and individual exhibit in relatively permanent. Psychologists explain many theories when an individual acquire difference patterns in behavior.

1. Conditioning learning theory
2. Cognitive learning theory
3. Social learning theory

Conditioning learning theory

Pavlov (1927) Pavlov conducted an experiment with a dog by providing it with piece of meat bone and by introducing bell sound to test its stimulus and response. Behavior can be learned by repetitive association between a stimulus and response. This is law of exercise.

B.F. Skinner (1938) operant conditioning learning theory: It is a type of conditioning in which desired voluntary behavior leads to a reward or prevents a punishment. This theory status that behavior is voluntary and it is determined maintained and controlled by its consequences.

Cognitive Learning theory: Edward c. Tolman (1948) an American psychologist stress the importance of perception problem solving and insight. Tolman found that learning in corporate relationship between cognitive environmental cues and expectation.

Social learning theory: this theory proposed by Albert (1977). Individual can learn through observation and direct experience.In common the above three theories states that learning is done by observation, response and stimulus though which an individual reacts.

We have two type of learning one is horizontal learning and other one is vertical learning. Horizontal learning is eye view over a concept. But vertical learning is deep study is not done in totality but focuses on specific topics. Integrating IT advanced techniques in all fields will enhance their proficiency. An individual can attain proficiency only by continuous learning.Cloud computing is an emerging process in IT Industries. The process is carried out over internet integrating cloud computing and vertical learning can bring tremendous change in knowledge.

Different kinds of thinking and learning

In cognitive theory and education have used Bloom's (1956) taxonomic of learning. Bloom and colleagues identified three learning domains.The cognitive domains involve thinking of all sorts. The affective domain includes feelings, emotions, attitude, values and motivations.

The psychomotor domain of learning includes physical movement, coordination, motor, and sensory-skills. When a learning experience has a profound effect on a student, it can result in a greater sense of caring for the subject, for them, other or learning in general. Greater caring can lead to new interests, energy for learning, or a change in values. 'To learn how to learn' this includes learning how to diagnose one's own need for learning and how to be a self-learner. Then type of learning enables students to continue learning with greater effectiveness and is a particularly important skill with the recent explosion of knowledge and technology.

Cloud Computing

Cloud storage is a network-based service which does not exist physically rather it's a virtualiesed pool of networking for sharing data over network. Cloud computing is mostly hosted by third parties and its limits the user to work with given configuration and storage. Hence individual can create their own cloud. Own cloud is a free, open-sources and powerful web application for data synchronization file sharing and remote storage of files. It is written in java script languages.

Uses

Vertical Integrated teaching and learning makes teaching learning process fruitful and is carried out by creating own cloud install own cloud storage in Linux, create cloud database.

1. Students or learner are allowed to access the cloud to upgrade their knowledge that shapes an individual. Students can access their account any time anywhere depending on their conveniences.
2. Individuals are provided with username and password. Even user can undelete the accidentally deleted data's from trash.
3. Uploading Videos, images in the cloud excites their interest and thinking process of the learners.

Conclusion

Technology is a tool for teachers to deliver knowledge and a tool for students the acquire it in the best and most efficient way. It will create different atmosphere in education program. Students will acquire knowledge and new way of learning by using technological resources. As education is a wide sector in today world, integrating it with IT techniques will enhance nation's development towards ICT and individual to be an optimistic learner' Education plays on important role in growth of a nation and hence a developed India by 2020 can be achieved.

Bibliography

1. AACU,2002, Greater Expectations: A New Vision for Learning as a Nation Goes to College: National panel Report, American Association of Colleges and Universities, Washington,DC62p.
2. Atkinson,R.L Atkinson R.C Smith, E.E and Bem D.J., 1993, Introduction to Psychology, Harcourt Brace Jovanovich, Fort Worth, TX, 11 th edition
3. Cuesta College, 2004, Characteristics of a Successful Student: Cuesta College. Available at:http://academic. Cuesta.edu/accasupp/as/201.HTM.

4. Johnson, D.W., Johnson, R.T., and Smith, K., 1991,Active Learning: Cooperation in the College Classroom Interaction Book Company,Edina,MN.
5. Krathwohl, D.R.Bloom, B.S, and Masia,B.B., 1964, Taxonomy of Educational objectives. The classification of Educational Goals, Handbook II: Affective Domain. David McKay Company,Inc
6. Teaching Goals Inventory,2004, Available form: http://www.uiowa.edu/-centeach/tgi/.
7. Williams,John,H., 1993, clarifying grade expectations. The Teaching Professor, August/September

35

Learning without Limits for Creating an Innovative Society

Introduction

'The 11th Plan Guidelines (2007 – 2012) on Lifelong Learning and Extension speak of continuous up-gradation of skills to be a critical development issue. This, in turn, will ensure the production of man-power resources of the kind and number required by society. There have been innumerable lifelong learning programs implemented by governmental and non-governmental organizations, as also various universities right across the country for the past three decades. The massive number of non-literates (3.14 million) and neo-literates (110 million), has been estimated by the National Literacy Mission.

The formulation of the 11th Plan brought in the Lifelong Education and Awareness Program (LEAP) by expanding the scope of its earlier avatar – the Continuing Education Program. The socio-economic changes that are taking place both within and outside the country, as also discussions at the global level, have been the cause of bringing in LEAP. The present scenario represents a knowledge based competitive economy which is technology driven and so the learning landscape is undergoing imminent changes in the country.

Growth Factor

The economic survey (2006 – 2007)[2] has recorded an average growth rate of 9.2% per annum. There has also been tremendous expansion in the Information Communication Technology (ICT) and taking into consideration the process of rapid globalization, there has come a need for changes in job skills and the work-force is expected to keep on learning and updating skills to survive global competition. The 61st Round of the National Sample Survey (2004 – 2005) also stresses on the need for periodic skill up-gradation to compete in the globalised economy.

UGC Measures

In order to equip the labor force with relevant skills, it is imperative that a variety of learning and training opportunities are created. It is in this area that India's university system has a vital role to play. The University Grants Commission (UGC) have brought in a number of measures such as post-literacy programs, continuing education, population education, refresher courses and a variety of extension and field outreach activities. The UGC has also encouraged the universities with adequate funding to institutionalize these programs by setting up specific departments with core faculty, who in turn, would undertake teaching and research. The according of maximum priority to lifelong learning or in other words learning without limits is to help meet the demands of the emerging knowledge society and to help create a conducive atmosphere for creating an innovative society.

The Census Report (2011)[4] shows that half of India's population is within their quarter century of existence. While the enrolment ratio in higher education institutions is held to be 20% in advanced and certain developing countries, it is a sad reality that the gross enrolment in higher education institutions in India is only 10%. It is only the universities that can prepare the student to be a lifelong learner effectively. The youth of the country need to sustain their knowledge level skills at an international benchmark criterion.

Learning Avenues

The concept of lifelong learning or unlimited learning bespeaks the need for learning avenues that can be traversed even while one is engaged in fruitful employment. The years spent within the portals of a higher education institution will definitely have advantageous inputs on a person's psychic. But, when the economic status of an individual and family constraints impel the acceptance of employment, this sincere and hardworking citizen of the country should not be left in the lurch having academic doors slammed in their faces for want of regular study.

Distance Education

This is where the strength of flexibility of time, duration of learning as also choice of subjects comes into play. Self – learning, learning through the distance education mode, correspondence education, online education and also other modes of equipping oneself with knowledge have become a reality in the present day. There is no embargo on a student earning and learning simultaneously.

To be Aware and Beware

A student in the present day whether pursuing studies in the regular formal stream or the distance education non-formal stream, needs to take into consideration the following:

a) **Purpose of Study**

A student should be fully aware of the purpose for which he/she is studying. If a student is working in a bank, studying courses that will aid him/her progress further on in the promotional avenue will be most helpful. Concentrating on subjects like banking services, CAIIB, chartered accountancy, financial management as also courses on technology would help further their promotional prospects. If such a person is going to concentrate on a course in philosophy, anthropology, classical languages etc., such a procedure maybe a soul satisfying action, i.e. acquiring knowledge for knowledge sake but will not help in improving the individual's quality of life or standard of living. The student should beware the lure of various courses which may help them pass time but would not be of intrinsic value in their careers.

b) **Affordability**

A person wanting to pursue a particular course/subject should take into consideration his/her financial position. A student should also analyze the various financial avenues open to them such as scholarships, stipends, grants and loans. At every stage care should be taken to understand the ramifications of consequences in pursuing a particular course. There are many instances where students have committed themselves to serve the organization giving the scholarship/stipend etc. for a certain period of time and not being able to comply. When taking a loan scholarship one should scrutinize the rate of interest and the period of repayment in order to ensure that they are capable of proper and easy repayment. In this regard, care should also be taken to ensure that the course of study pursued will certainly pay dividends for rising the standard of one's living.

c) **Choice of Subject / Field of Study**

Knowledge for knowledge sake is a commendable proposition. In the present day of whirlwind economy and super-fast competition, one needs to surge forward both academically and economically. Selecting a subject/field of study therefore has to necessarily impinge on the fact of how fast such an endeavor will help the student ascend the economic ladder. Even when one is settled in a secure job one needs to update knowledge and come by certification to be authorized to practice their profession at any given level. A basic degree in medicine will ensure a job in a hospital with fixed timings and a regular pay cheque. If one wants to go beyond the basic level of medicine and become a specialist/expert one needs to update their knowledge by pursuing further degrees and courses. This is so for every profession in the organized, as well as, the unorganized sectors. Whyte (1989), has stressed that lifelong learners including persons with academic or professional credentials tend to find higher paying occupations leaving monetary, cultural and entrepreneurial impressions on communities.

d) **Metacognition**

This is thinking about the process of knowing and refers to a higher order thinking which involves active control over the cognitive processes engaged in learning. Knowledge is the awareness of one's own thought processes and learning styles and knowledge strategies involve using this awareness for different learning tasks. Exercising control and self-regulating one's thought processes helps one not only to keep track of his/her thinking processes but also for evaluating them.

Conclusion

Lifelong learning that leads to the creation of an innovative society is not only a lifelong process but is flexible, diverse and available at all times and in different places. Crossing sectors of space and segments of society, lifelong learning promotes the acquirement of knowledge beyond traditional schooling and throughout one's adult life. In accordance with Delors' (1996), Four Pillars of Education for the Teacher, one needs to know which is mastering learning tools rather than the mere acquisition of knowledge;

one needs to do, which is equipping people for the types of work needed now and in the future, which includes innovation and adaptation; one needs to live together and with others peacefully resolving conflict, discovering other people's cultures, fostering community capability and individual competence and capacity with economic resilience and social inclusion and finally one needs to be with education contributing to a person's complete development of body, mind, intelligence, sensitivity, aesthetic appreciation and spirituality. These components can be underpinned by the label learning to learn lifelong to create an innovative society that will "strive, to seek, to find and not to yield".

References

1. NLM – Literacy Facts At A Glance, 2007.
2. National Sample Survey, 61st Round, 2004 – 2005.
3. Whyte, Cassandra B.; Student Affairs – The Future; Journal of College Student Personnel; Vol. 30, No.1, 1989.
4. Livingr, A.; Metacognition: An Overview; 1997.
5. Delors, J.; Learning: The Treasure Within; Report to UNESSCO of the International Commission on Education for the 21st Century; UNESSCO, 1996.
6. Tennyson, Alfred Lord; Ulysses; MacMillan & Co., 1963.

36

Implementation of Cloud Computing in Education

Introduction

Innovation is necessary to ride the inevitable tide of change and one such hot recent area of research in Information Technology (IT) is cloud computing. Cloud computing is a distributed computing technology offering required software and hardware through Internet. It also provides storage, computational platform and infrastructure which are demanded by the user according to their requirement. Due to the growing need of infrastructure educational institutes, organizations have to spend a large amount on their infrastructure to fulfill the needs and demands of the users. Cloud computing is a next generation platform that allows institutions and organizations with a dynamic pools of resource and to reduce cost through improved utilization.

In the present scenario, many education institutions are facing the problems with the growing need of IT and infrastructure. Cloud computing which is an emerging technology and which relies on existing technology such as Internet, virtualization, grid computing etc. can be a solution to such problems by providing required infrastructure, software and storage. In this paper a basic research has been carried out to show how cloud computing can be introduced in the education to improve teaching, agility and have a cost-effective infrastructure which can bring a revolution in the field of education. It also tries to bring out its benefits and limitations.

The concept of cloud computing dates back to 1960, when John McCarthy opined that "computation may someday be organized as a public utility". The term 'cloud computing' is confusion to many people as the term can be used to mean almost anything. 'Cloud' is used as a metaphor for Internet and its main objective is customization and user defined experience. In other words cloud computing provides shared resources, software and information through Internet as a PAYGO (Pay-as-you-go) basis. In the recent years, where educational institutes, universities, industries are giving their full contribution in transforming the society and entire world economy. Various researches are carried out to update the present IT infrastructure especially in the area of education.

Cloud computing can be a welcomed optioned in the universities and educational institutes for higher studies. It gives a better choice and flexibility to the IT departments by building multipurpose computational infrastructure once and then Manuscript received. Uses it for several purposes for several times. Amazon, Google have already started providing their facilities for large business group. With the help of cloud computing the platform and application the user uses can be on-campus or off-campus or combination of both depending on the institutions need. Due to the evolution of cloud computing number of services have migrated from the traditional system to the online form. At present, as many universities are trying to update their IT infrastructure and data, but they are facing few challenges.

Defining the cloud

Broadly, the cloud can be described as on-demand computing, for anyone with a network connection. Access to applications and data anywhere, anytime, from any device is the potential outcome. The consumer-level cloud is a good starting point for this – sites like Flickr and Face book act as digital repositories for data and we can access this data from any internet-enabled device, from our iPhones to our desktop computers. In the case of Flickr and the like, storage of our digital images is, from the consumer point of view, somewhere in the cloud. We don't need to know where specifically, we just need our Flickr login credentials and a web connection. We can see this model as evident in web-based email too.

The starting point (the bottom layer) is the physical hardware – the servers in data centers, whether owned by a firm or university for internal use or by the likes of Amazon or Google for public access. The next layer is virtualization. Virtualization allows a single physical server to run many independent virtual servers and is a necessary part of gaining the efficiencies (built on economies of scale) that cloud computing can offer those running the data centers. Automating the allocation of computing resources amongst the virtual servers and tracking user (customer) resource use requires a management layer. As Naone (2009a) highlights, this allows "true pay-as-you-go" billing which is part of the appeal of the cloud for users.

The cloud, however, doesn't stop here. The provision of software (services) to end-users mediated by the web is what has come to be known as Software as a Service (resulting in the rather clumsy acronym SaaS). This builds a further layer – the software running in the cloud and being accessed by users through their browser or other web-compliant tool. Firms like Salesforce.com have successfully built their business model entirely around providing web-based software, with the users' data storage and the processing of that data taking place in the cloud, rather than on the clients' own servers or their local machines.

Services of Cloud

With an aim of reducing the expenditure of the universities for IT infrastructure and the complexity faced by universities and institutions, the traditional installed software on the campus computers are now replaced by cloud computing. With the power of cloud, today higher education can gain significant flexibility and agility and can migrate the sensitive data into remote and world wide data center ' the cloud' itself. To use the cloud services the universities and the institutions has to first define their requirements and has to take a special attention for the privacy and critical issues.

There are several cloud services as follows

1. Software as a Service (**SaaS**): the application service provider is hosting the application which runs and interacts through web browser, hosted desktop or remote client. It eliminates the need to install and run the application on customer own computer and simplifying maintenance and support.
2. Infrastructure as a Service (**IaaS**): can be used to satisfy the infrastructure needs of the students, faculties or researcher globally

or locally with some specific hardware configuration for a specific task.

3. Platform as a Service (**PaaS**): certain providers are opening up application platforms to permit customer's to build their own application without the cost and complexity of buying and managing the underlying hardware and software layers.
4. Computing as a Service (**CaaS**): providers offer access Implementation of Cloud Computing in Education – A Revolution.

Cloud Architecture for Education

Due to the higher accessibility, availability and efficiency of cloud services many universities, businesses are trying to make use of these services. Today's cloud computing providers are offering higher education, the opportunity to substitute their data and information in the 'cloud' for universities with existing data centers, servers and application replacing these traditional campus machines. Developing a cloud architecture for education can be distinct according to the purpose and infrastructure of the institution and can be challenging. The universities has to follow all the rules and regulation of the state and country for developing a cloud for education as many countries are very strict in cross broader transfer of information. Once the university establishes where their data will reside and gives the measure of data security an agreement called SLA (Service Level Agreement) can be made with the cloud service provider.

The SLA is a document which can ensure educational cloud users regarding the services provided by the cloud. It tries to identify the users need and simplifies complex issues and creates a relationship between the user and the service provider. It helps to specify the privacy, consistency and integrity. Privacy is one of the important factors which have to be taken care for cloud computing, as the service provider may require some personal information which is related to the data on what the user is trying to store in the cloud. So the universities should be very careful before disclosing the data and it should not lose the integrity of educational data.

There are many solutions that can ensure the security and protection of sensitive data in the cloud. These are;

1. Mask or de-identify of the data
2. Firewalls
3. Encryption and decryption
4. Authorization identity management.

Institutes can develop their own cloud called as 'private cloud' by making use of their existing Resources or multiple universities can come together and can develop a hybrid cloud called as 'educational cloud', in which they can share all the resources from the various universities. Private cloud makes use of the local network whereas the educational cloud makes use of public network to access the services provided by the cloud. Both private and educational cloud which is developed for education has to specify the services provided by them. Following table shows the differences between private and educational cloud.

Benefits and Limitations of Cloud Computing

Due to the recent development in IT technologies, infrastructure and continuous upgrades in software and hardware has put a great deal of pressure on the budgets and expenses of universities and educational institutes. Cloud computing development provides many universities with an opportunity to take advantage of new IT technologies at an affordable cost. Allows the lecturer to get their work done in their web browsers rather storing and carrying it on the hard drive.

Its gives the TEN benefits

1. **Flexibility**
   The second a company needs more bandwidth than usual, a cloud-based service can instantly meet the demand because of the vast capacity of the service's remote servers. In fact, this flexibility is so crucial that 65% of respondents to an InformationWeek survey said "the ability to quickly meet business demands" was an important reason to move to cloud computing.
2. **Disaster recovery**
   When companies start relying on cloud-based services, they no longer need complex disaster recovery plans. Cloud computing providers take care of most issues, and they do it faster. Aberdeen that businesses which used the cloud were able to resolve issues in an average of 2.1 hours, nearly four times faster than businesses that didn't use the cloud (8 hours). The same study found that mid-sized businesses had the best recovery times of all, taking almost half the time of larger companies to recover.
3. **Automatic software updates**
   In 2010, UK companies spent 18 working days per month managing on-site security alone. But cloud computing suppliers do the server maintenance – Including security updates –themselves, Freeing up their customers' time and resources for other tasks.

4. Cap-Ex Free

Cloud computing services are typically pay as you go, so there's no need for capital expenditure at all. And because cloud computing is much faster to deploy, businesses have minimal project start-up costs and predictable ongoing operating expenses.

5. Increased collaboration

Cloud computing increases collaboration by allowing all employees wherever they are – to sync up and work on documents and shared apps simultaneously, and follow colleagues and records to receive critical updates in real time. A survey by Frost & Sullivan found that companies which invested in collaboration technology had a 400% return on investment.

6. Work from anywhere

As long as employees have internet access, they can work from anywhere. This flexibility positively affects knowledge workers' work-life balance and productivity. One study found that 42% of working adults would give up some of their salary if they could telecommute, and on average they would take a 6% pay cut.

7. Document control

According to one study, "73% of knowledge workers collaborate with people in different time zones and regions at least monthly". Cloud computing keeps all the files in one central location, and everyone works off of one central copy. Employees can even chat to each other whilst making changes together. This whole process makes collaboration stronger, which increases efficiency and improves a company's bottom line.

8. Security

Some 800,000 laptops are lost each year in airports alone. This can have some serious monetary implications, but when everything is stored in the cloud, data can still be accessed no matter what happens to a machine.

9. Competitiveness

The cloud grants SMEs access to enterprise-class technology. It also allows smaller businesses to act faster than big, established competitors. A study on disaster recovery eventually concluded that companies that didn't use the cloud had to rely on tape backup methods and complicated procedures to recover – slow, laborious things which cloud users simply don't use, allowing David to once again out-manoeuvre Goliath.

10. Environmentally Friendly

Businesses using cloud computing only use the server space they need, which decreases their carbon footprint. Using the cloud results in at least 30% less energy consumption and carbon emissions than using on-site servers. And again, SMEs get the most benefit: for small companies, the cut in energy use and carbon emissions is likely to be 90%.

Limitations

Cloud computing has the potential for improving the efficiency, cost and convenience for the universities and educational sectors, but it has few limitations such as;

1. Not all application run on cloud
2. Risk related to data protection and security and its integrity
3. Organizational support
4. Dissemination politics, intellectual property
5. Security and protection of sensitive data
6. Maturity of solutions
7. Lack of confidence
8. Standard adherence & Speed and lack of Internet can affect work methods

Conclusion

Cloud computing is an emerging computing paradigm and next generation platform that can provide tremendous value of information of any size. The shift towards cloud computing would enable the universities and educational institutions to save money and take benefit of the developing technology. Both private and educational cloud can provide the necessary computational facility on demand of the user without any expense and can create a common platform for sharing the various resources from the various institutions. In spite, of limitations of cloud computing and keeping in mind the present scenario of economic crisis many universities, educational intuitions, organizations etc are trying to adopt cloud computing as a solution to the developing technologies and try to reduce their expenses. The main objective of the paper was to identify the essentials of cloud computing which can be considered as a new dawn to the higher education and has the full potential to make a 'revolution' in the field of education.

Reference

1. J. L. Nicholson. Cloud Computing: Top Issues for Higher Education.
2. A. S. Dutta, Use of Cloud Computing in Education.

3. B. R. Kandukuri, V. R. Paturi, and A. Rakshit, "Cloud Security," in proceedings of the 2009 IEEE International Conference on Services. Computing, Washington, DC, USA, 2009, IEEE Computer Society, pp. 517-520.
4. R. N. Katz, The Tower and the Cloud: Higher Education in the age of cloud computing, 2008.
5. T. Ercan, "Effective Use of Cloud Computing in Educational Institutions," Procedia Social and Behavioral Science, vol. 2, pp 938-942, 2010.

37

New ways of Tomorrow Learning and Teachingenvironment

Introduction

There is general agreement as we approach the next century and next millennium that our society is changing into a knowledge and information society. The world is constantly evolving now at a faster pace than ever before, creating the challenge for individuals and organizations to deal with changes and for schools and universities to prepare people for changes. There is trend indicating that the amount of people working with knowledge and refinement of data and information is increasing. More and more of the laborers can be categorized as knowledge workers, hence knowledge workers is a group of workers who is growing in size and importance. Scientists, stockbrokers and journalists are examples of knowledge workers of today. The fact is that many tasks traditionally performed in physical environments are now done in virtual (electronic) environments, or they have been altered to fit to the new premises of emerging physical-virtual environments.

Knowledge work

"The manual worker is yesterday. The basic capital resource, the fundamental investment, but also the cost centre for a developed economy is knowledge worker who puts to work what he has learned in systematic education, that is, concepts, ideas and theories, rather than the man who puts to work manual skill or muscle. History also indicates the existence of such metaphors, where the users have more control over the working situation, as in the case with craftsmanship a knowledge worker metaphor.

Pedagogical Issues

What kind of pedagogical framework has the ability to cope with the educational requirements that arise from this increasingly important group of laborers? A point of departure for this paper is a view on learning based on the following definition: "Learning is an active, constructive, cognitive and social process where the learner strategically manages available cognitive, physical, and social resources to create new knowledge by interacting with information in the environment and integrating it with information already stored in memory".

Furthermore, we assume that learning can be characterized by the following features:

Learning is embedded

Learning will take place in a situation we learn out in the real world where the knowledge and skills are needed to solve problems. "We must, therefore, attempt to use the intelligence in the learning environments to reflect and support the learner's or user's active creation or co-production, in situ, of idiosyncratic, hidden models and concepts, whose textures are developed between the learner/user and the situating activity in which the technology is embedded."

Learning is a constructive process

As indicated by the fact that learning is embedded, we should view learning as a constructive process rather than a passive absorption of facts and rules. The view that the learner should acquire the expert's knowledge does not necessarily acknowledge this constructive perspective. Knowledge and skills are gained and regained over and over in an on-going process between the learner and situations in which the knowledge and skills are required. The central notion is that understanding and learning are active, constructive, generative processes such as assimilation, augmentation, and self-reorganization.

Knowledge is very much a question of understanding phenomena

The area of pedagogy traditionally takes a positivistic and quantitative view on knowledge. Phenomenography in contrast takes quite different view knowledge is understandings of phenomena, and learning is viewed as a process where these understandings are changed; this is a central principle. Other important characteristics are the analysis of the outcome of the learning process in qualitative terms, the move of focus from the "teacher-side" to the "learner-side" of the learning situation and the view on learning as a generative process, which is constantly going on.

The kind of motivation, and the kind of relevance of the topic, is two important factors that affect the level of processing. Internal motivation factors and internal relevance lead to a depth-directed level of processing which in turn implicates a better understanding or higher level of outcome. These relationships are almost functional.

Active learning is good for the quality of the outcome

A deep-directed level of processing is characterized by an active way of processing the material active reading. Beside internal and external factors of relevance, the researchers have found the vicarious relevance important. Active reading has at least four components:

1. **Explore;** The ability to study the topic partly in the course material and partly by searching for material that is relevant in the learner's personal context.
2. **Form;**adding notes, making references to other relevant material, by changing the structure of the texts, change the text to fit the learner's understanding and previous knowledge, and more.
3. **Analyses;** The ability to analyze the topic and or the intended meaning of the text, ask oneself processing questions, working with the structure of the text, or by analyzing how one and other learners have worked or processed the material.
4. **Administrate;** The ability to keep track of the exploring, forming and analyzing activities by administrating references, recording how one have worked with the text, which questions one has asked oneself, etc.

New ways of Learning and Teaching

In order to better prepare for lifelong learning activities, learners must be exposed to learning activities that require them to take on and develop many of the responsibilities normally afforded to educators. To achieve this requires moving away from a view of learning that is controlled outside the individual by a teacher, trainer, instructional designer, or subject matter expert to a view of learning that is internally controlled by the individual.

As mentioned above, IT plays an important role in the working situation for the knowledge worker of tomorrow. How and why should we use information technology in learning environments? These are two relevant questions to ask in this context. In this section we discuss these two questions putting our main focus on the "how question", although the "why question" is first briefly discussed. We believe it is important to give a historic perspective on the use of IT for the design learning environments in order to identify how and why to use modern IT in many educational settings.

Why

Traditionally there are three major motives behind the use of IT for learning: economical and efficiency motives have traditionally played a big role, and also the possibility to bridge distances in time and space. It is necessary to extend the concept of distances to also include distances between the ways of study or learning and distances between documents. We believe that an elimination of distances in learning environments, for instance, by forcing learners to study at the same location and time, and use the same material and study it in the same manner mainly have negative effects for learners' situation. Consequently IT plays a very important role for the learning situation of tomorrow, and must be viewed as a natural part of the learning environment.

How

Skinner, Pavlov, and Piaget all played important roles as founders of theories of learning. Skinner's and Pavlov's ideas about the way we learn things, based on the stimulus-response concept, were one source of inspiration for programmed learning or programmed instruction. Those theories have been used as the foundation for the design of the first generation of computer-based learning environments. Using this pedagogical model a huge industry of learning grew up during the early.

The First generation of ILE

Computer Assisted Instruction systems (CAI) are a kind of interactive learning environment based on programmed learning, which became common in the period from the mid of the 60s to the early 70s. Still, many projects are based on behaviouristic ideas. This seems strange since these ideas and all what they stand for have been almost completely rejected in traditional classroom learning environments. At the same time, there is a very simple explanation: two of the major advantages with programmed learning are the possibility of self-administration of a course and the simplicity of implementing a computer-based learning environment with a behaviouristic control mechanism, see Figure 2. Therefore, it is not hard to see the possibilities to make it serve as a basis for computer-based learning environments.

The Second Generation of ILE

Even if one can get positive results with regard to learning in these learning environments, there is much one can do to speed up the process of learning. One of the major drawbacks of these learning environments is the lack of individualization. The learning situation is one-to-one, but all learners are still running through the course in the same order. Below, we present three examples of ideas that have been exploited in attempts to improve performance:

1. multiple paths through the curriculum;
2. present the material in different ways;
3. analyze the errors that the learners do.

Knowledge of the domain the expert model

1. Knowledge of the learner (the student model)
2. Knowledge of teaching strategies (tutor)

The Third Generation of ILE

The ITS approach has many good results to show, although it has also been criticized for a long period. Much of the criticism has concerned the possibilities to trace learners' state of knowledge.. Cognitive tools are artifacts that amplify, support, and unburden the user. They have the possibility to affect the task, and the user's state of knowledge. In some sense they amplify and unburden the user in the same manner that the winch amplifies our ability to lift things (heavy things), a backpack unburdens the carrier, and the hammer supports nailing. The cognitive tools approach has its pedagogic base constructivist ideas of knowledge and learning, where the learners consider as active knowledge constructors.

Learner centered design

Not many of the approaches used for the design of ILEs are able to meet the demands and requirements of tomorrow's learning situations. In these situations the integration of physical and virtual work as well as theoretical and practical work is very natural.

1. **Growth:** At the core of education is the growth of the learner; promoting the development of expertise must be the primary goal of educational software. Rather than just support "doing" tasks, software designed for learners must support "learning while doing."
2. **Diversity:** Developmental differences, cultural differences, and gender differences play a major role in the suitability of materials for learners. To be usable by all learners, a range of software tools that address these differences must be available.
3. **Motivation:** In contrast to software developed for professionals, the student's initial interest and continuing engagement cannot be taken for granted.

IT-augmented

In fact, we have to take future information technology into consideration because it will have a major influence on the conditions for future knowledge work and learning. Information access everywhere, through new 'physical' devices with computational power, will contribute to bridge the gap between the physical and virtual worlds. New tools will so close to our cognition and perception that they almost become part of our personalities. These new computerised environments will complement and eventually replace the desktop PC as provider of cognitive tools. All these aspects will cause a new knowledge reorganisation that should not be ignored.

The way we use Computers

Using IT for learning has a long tradition but we need new ways of doing it Mainly because many of the traditional approaches of involving IT in learning situations do not meet the requirements of future more dynamic physical-virtual learning environments. A futuristic learning environment should include elements where learners can put the topic into a context and relate it to things, situations, and events that are relevant to them — promote active learning. One such element for instance, could be an open hypertext environment; open meaning that there are possibilities to search for information external to the course material, possibilities like those offered by the World-Wide-Web. It would also be open in a wider meaning, letting the learner view how other people (learners and teachers) have worked with the topic. Learning in such environment demands much support from the system, in order to help the learners to manage the new kind of learning situation. This support could be of the kind of: to establish goals, to manage goals, to manage the in-stream of information, searching for relevant information, etc.

Conclusion

To be able to meet the challenges for the design of tomorrow's learning environments we propose a pedagogical framework based on knowledge work approach to learning. This framework has its base in five cornerstones: Knowledge work tasks are those that most likely many people will be doing in the future. There is continuous knowledge reorganization in the society partly caused by the use of new technologies. People in the future will become more and more IT-augmented. The use of computers for learning purposes is still in its infancy.

References

1. Broberg, A. (1997) Cognitive Tools for Learning. Licentiate thesis. Umeå University, report UMINF 97.18.
2. Cochinaux, P & de Woot P. (1995). Moving Towards a Learning Society. A CRE-ERT Report on European Education.
3. Drucker, P. F. (1973). Management: Tasks, Responsibility and Practices. New York: Harper & Row.
4. Drucker, P. (1993). The Post Capitalist Society, Editorial Sudamericana.
5. Gentner, D., & Nielsen, J. (1997). The Anti-Mac Interface. In Communications of the ACM, August 1997/Vol. 39, No 8, pp70-82.
6. Hoyles, C., & Noss, R. (Eds.). (1992). Learning Mathematics and logo. London: The MIT Press.
7. Kidd, A. (1994). The Mark are on the Knowledge Worker," presented at The Human Factors in Computing Systems (CHI'94), Boston.

38

Tablet Computers in Education

Introduction

Tablet Computers are quickly emerging as a powerful Learning tool in higher education. The unique functionality of the Tablet Computer allows teachers to create lecture materials for their classes using digital format that can be distributed to students for later review. A tablet enhanced learning environment is an environment where single or multiple tablets are implemented to enhance student learning. Though a universally agreed-upon definition is currently lacking, there is some agreement that a tablet is a computer is a personal computer whose primary input device is a screen or a convertible notebook computer whose screen can be used as an input device.

The Tablet Computer is the next innovative device to hit the educational technology sector. Its design and handwriting functionality, challenges the way faculty and students integrate tablet computers into their teaching and learning process. Tablets are becoming increasingly common tools in schools. There's a wealth of options available, a range of web apps or apps designed for different operating systems and so many choices for teachers and students to make that it is sometimes useful to know the range of ways that they are making a difference across a range of different subject areas. Though this range can't be exhaustive or final, given the early stages of widespread adoption, it will provide a starting point for those aiming to use these tools to enhance learning through appropriate and effective use of the technologies available.

Tablet Computers in Education

Pedagogy is related to how teachers teach, and the strategies they use in their work. The impact of tablets on pedagogy has been a central focus of the Tablets for School. The success of tablets depends on the school's approach to learning, and the extent to which the tablets are integrated into this approach. Schools that link technology use to pedagogy, and set clear goals for use, are more likely to see positive effects.

Learning should never be technology led. This is an important statement, and one that is often forgotten. Focus should be placed on how the technology can be used to aid learning. There are a number of advantages to using this type of technology with students, one of which is the additional engagement that the touch interaction with the content brings. There is a clear educational advantage to be gained from better engagement, including increased stimulation, decreased 'time to learn' and enhanced knowledge retention. Additionally, tablet technology offers a change to the traditional use of ICT such as fixed computers or Laptops, allowing for additional usage scenarios and inclusion in learning activities not previously associated with ICT.

Tablet Computers in Teaching and Learning

Mobile learning involves the use of tablet computer technology, either alone or in combination with other information and communication technology (ICT), to enable learning anytime and anywhere. Learning can unfold in a variety of ways: people can use mobile devices to access educational resources, connect with others, and create content, both inside and outside classrooms. Mobile learning also encompasses efforts to support broad educational goals such as effective administration of school systems through the use of tablet computer devices.

Tablet computers provide a unique opportunity to create a truly portable learning experience. Lightweight with a long battery life, they offer possibilities not previously seen with other 'mobile' computing solutions. This lends itself to better use of technology within teaching. For example, quick access to reference material during a lesson, previously difficult to achieve with existing ICT, can bring key advantages and enhance learning. Using tablets in less typical scenarios, such as field trips, workshops or physical education lessons offers opportunities for research, evidence gathering and presentation. Brining devices such as these into the classroom and everyday life for students is in itself a learning experience. Couple this with the resources a tablet computer can deliver, such as text and reference books, audio and video resources, internet research, document preparation and review, and specific eLearning applications and activities and you have a truly versatile learning tool.

The increasing prevalence of digital technology in academia requires that teachers and students become more comfortable using technology to facilitate instruction and learning. This digital transformation has the potential to change the ways that teachers instruct, how students learn and how course material is delivered.

The Tablet PC is also quite handy for faculty use outside of the classroom. When preparing lecture material such as figures and diagrams, we were often able to draw and create these items more quickly. The Tablet PC has also been quite useful for note-taking at conferences, department meetings, research meetings, and committee meetings. Finally, the Tablet PC has promising potential for use as a distance education tool. All content can be managed through one tablet device: audio lecture, handwritten material, prepared electronic slides, and live software demonstrations. Several software programs allow such content to be streamed live for use with synchronous distance courses, or archived for asynchronous courses.

Face to Face Instruction

Tablets can effectively enhance instruction in a traditional classroom setting in various ways. Using a tablet, an instructor can construct and deconstruct notes and diagrams starting with a blank screen or using a skeleton outline of a topic. Given this ability, instructors can model how to solve problems and create materials through the course of a lesson. This allows the instructor to be better able to respond to feedback from students during a lesson so that he/she can 'change courses' or explain a topic in more detail should it be necessary. Tablets are advantageous when compared to black or whiteboards in that they allow the instructor to face the class. Furthermore, tablets are wireless devices and, providing that the connection to a projector is also wireless, the instructor is able to wander about the environment rather than stay at the front of the class. This affords instructors proximity to their students which, in turn, allows for better classroom management and interaction with students.

Digital ink annotations can be saved directly onto the original document and uploaded onto a webpage or Learning Management System to allow students access. In doing this, students can concentrate more on the instruction in class than on taking notes. Tablets are computers and, as such, allow instructors to incorporate and display a variety of multimedia and presentations. Again, the major advantage that tablets afford is that the instructor can write on these multimedia (including video, simulations and models) and presentations to enhance their effectiveness as learning objects.

Blended Environments

In a blended learning environment, students are able to not only access information from instructors but also actively participate in the construction of knowledge. When tablets are used by students in blended learning environments, new opportunities for collaboration and creative problem solving emerge. Teachers in this environment can switch from the role of instructor and distributor of information to facilitator. Interaction between instructors and students can increase because instructors spend less time teaching.

Students can use time to collaboratively solve problems and socially negotiate what they have learned. A tablet allows students to collaborate in new and meaningful ways. For example, students can access learning materials online and then co-create a concept map to represent their knowledge using software called Puzzle view.

Distance / Online Education

One of the primary benefits of using tablets in an online course environment is that students can receive more personalized notes and feedback from their instructors. Instructors can mark digital assignments using a tablet, and the ink annotations can be saved and sent back to the student on the original document. Because instructors can mark directly where they want to on the document, students ultimately get more specific and useful feedback on their assignments.

Another advantage that tablets afford is the ability to hold interactive virtual office hours. Using programs such as illuminate, instructors can conduct synchronous office hours and, in doing so, use their tablet to sketch or otherwise mark-up documents to support their explanations to students. The major use of the Tablet PC in this course was to replace the blackboard with the tablet. The machine was connected to a projector.

The use of the tablet, as an educational tool can have several benefits. These advantages include:

1. Being highly portable (easy to use in classroom, fieldtrips)
2. Consolidation of learning material into one device (textbooks, notes etc.)
3. No compatibility or technological issues since the same type of device is used
4. Quick access to the Internet
5. A convenient alternative to the laptop or desktop
6. Useful tool during group work and brainstorming activities (information stored in a drop box)

Conclusions

This paper has described how the Tablet PC can be used as an effective tool for grading, preparing lectures, and delivering classroom presentations. It provides a simple way to integrate live, handwritten material with slides and figures prepared in advance. Lectures can be easily captured for viewing at a later time. Rather than save the lecture as a static document, our work explored methods for capturing lectures into Flash movie files so that audio and gestures could be recorded. Students reported very positive feedback about the approach. In the future we intend to explore uses of the Tablet PC for distance delivery and collaborative applications where all students in a classroom are working on Tablet PC's.

References

1. Clark, C. (2004) Notre Dame Tablet PC Initiative. Retrieved from http://www.nd.edu/learning/tabletpc/
2. Lowe, P. (2004) Bentley College students evaluate Tablet PCs. Retrieved from http://www.hp.com/hpinfo/newsroom/feature stories/2004/04bentley.html
3. Mock, K. (2003) The Development of a CS Course for Distance Delivery. The Journal of Computing Sciences in Colleges, 19 (2), p. 30-38.
4. Wachsmuth, B. (2003) SHU Tablet PC Project. Retrieved from http://www.cs.shu.edu/tabletpc/

39

The Process of Blended Learning

Introduction

Blended Learning is about effectively integrating ICTs into course design to enhance the teaching and learning experiences for student and teachers by enabling them to engage in ways that would not normally be available in their usual environment, whether it is primarily face-to-face. Blended Learning technologies are as follows;

1. Broaden the space and opportunities available for learning;
2. Support course management activities;
3. Support the provision of information and resource to students;
4. Engage and motivate students through interactivity and collaboration;

The learning and teaching activities need to be meaningful and relevant for the student learning. "Too often the opportunities and advantages of the use of technology in the learning process are poorly exploited".

Characteristics of Blended learning

H-learning means that learning requires students to meet for face to face classes while providing much of the learning content and interaction online via delivery software and instructional tools. The main characteristics of H-learning can be concluded as:

1. Mixed Mode: H-learning combines the socialization, group learning and hands-on opportunities of the classroom (face to face) with the learning possibilities of the online environment (U-learning).
2. Student Cantered: Learning shifts from lecture to student-cantered instruction.
3. Communications Important: The key element behind a hybrid learning environment is the scope and nature of the communication channels provided to support learners.
4. Access flexibility: Blending is used to provide a balance between flexible learning options and knowledge access.
5. Cost-effectiveness: Hybrid learning provides an opportunity for reaching a large, globally dispersed audience in a short period of time with consistent, semi-personal content delivery.

The process of Blended learning:

Designing for Blended learning process requires a systematic approach:

Planning

Planning the first stage of the design process. At this point you should think about a number of critical considerations before jumping in to designing the blended learning components of your course.Planning is developing a new course:

1. We suggest you first take a look at some general curriculum and course design guidelines.
2. It will be important to have course aims and learning objectives set before considering blended learning opportunities for your course.
3. Once you have a set of course aims and objectives you can then start to consider ways in which you might integrate blended learning in the design of the course.

Implementing

Even a well-designed blended learning element can fail, or at least suffer significant drawbacks, if time and consideration is not given to a range of issues associated with the implementation of blended learning in a course.

Course orientation

When student are required to study online, even for part of a course, creating an opportunity for students and staff to come together as a group is an important first step in building a successful learning and teaching experience.So consider designing formal course sense orientation program components that includes the following:

Purpose- Begin building a common sense of purpose for the blended learning components of the course.

Expectations-set clear expectations for students right from the beginning. Use consistent and transparent communication regarding these expectations to help students understand the blended learning process.

Guidelines-provide guidelines and tips on how to use the particular tools that you are integrating into the course well in advance.

Evaluating

As with any course, obtaining feedback about various aspects of the course experience is a crucial part of the course design process, as well as being important to your own ongoing professional development in curriculum design and teaching.

Evaluating in the blended learning environment entails the same basic elements of a course, however; because of "blend" and the use of technology, these will present an additional range of issues to gather data about. Herrington et al (2001) propose a model of evaluation for online learning and teaching which based is around the three main areas:

1. Pedagogies-the learning activities which underpin the unit;
2. Resources-the content and information which are provided for the learners;
3. Delivery strategies-issues associated with the ways in which the course is delivered to the learners.

Improving

Blended learning can increase access and flexibility for learners, increase level of active learning, and achieve better student experiences and outcomes. For teaching staff, Blended learning can improve teaching and class management practices.

Benefits of Blended Learning

1. **Enhanced learning:**Students usually receive more feedback, and more frequent feedback, from their instructors. Students can acquire useful skills from using the Internet and computer technology. (Live instructor presence, technological enhancements) Students have more time to reflect and refer to relevant course and other research

materials when working and writing online than when responding in class.

2. **Support for student collaboration:**Real-time real-space interactivity and asynchronous online interactions, synchronous online interactions
3. **Course accessibility:**Students have access to unlimited up-to-date resources available via the Web. Live signing in live courses, transcription of audio and video, labelling of images with alt text online.
4. **Learner convenience:**Students have greater time flexibility, freedom, and convenience by working part of the time online. Time flexibility without full-term scheduling, asynchronicity (non-real-time learning), the repeatability of some automated learning, and the ease of accessing course materials
5. **Rich learner assessment:** Automated assessments, live instructor-led assessments, peer assessments live or via the online classroom.
6. **24/7 Accesses:** Students often develop or enhance skills in time management, critical thinking, and problem solving. Students typically have 24/7 access to online course materials.
7. **Multi-use / Dual use resources:** Course contents may often be used in both contexts (F2F and online)

Many students say that they learn more in a hybrid course, because they can use outside resources more easily than in a traditional course, but they still have face-to-face access to the instructor and the other students in the course. Almost all students who take hybrid courses appreciate the convenience and flexibility to adapt to individual work and family schedules.

Conclusion

Blended learning as the principle means of addressing the use of Information and Communication Technologies (ICT) to enhance its learning and teaching activities. Improving the blended learning experience for both staff and students. Designing for the teaching and learning activities need to be clearly linked in time and content. The blended learning is more efficient of teaching and styles of learning. Blended learning to provide opportunities for the use of technology in both staff and students.

Reference

1. Getting started with Blended learning (2007)- http://www.griffith.edu.au

2. http://en.wikipeatia.org/wiki/Blended learning.
3. http://www.blendedlearning now.com/
4. http://coe.sdsu.edu/eet/Articals/blended learning/index.htm.
5. http://www.e-learningguru.com/w papers/blended-bersin.doc.
6. http://www.knewton.com/blended learning/

40

Generating Employability Skills for Digital Age Students

Introduction

Many jobs now require a high level of IT competency and confidence. Digital literacy – IT and online communication skills – is necessary for living, learning and working. Colleges, universities and employers need to prioritize digital literacy. In our online and globally connected world individuals who are digitally literate are more likely to be economically secure. IT and online communication skills are especially important in higher education, as graduate jobs will almost certainly involve working via computers and portable devices. There is a clear need for education at all levels to help establish and develop the skills future employees will need. Universities and colleges have a responsibility to develop students into individuals who can thrive in an era of digital information and communication – those who are digitally literate are more likely to be economically secure and these skills are especially important in higher education given that graduate white collar jobs are almost entirely performed on computers and portable devices. But it's not just about *employability* – increasingly digital literacy is vital for learning itself. Digital tools such as virtual learning environments, e-portfolios and social networking software for peer mentoring are now common within further and higher education and students without the skills to navigate them risk suffering an inferior student experience at best, and being left completely behind at worst. It goes beyond IT skills; a complete culture change is required to live fully within the modern digital society, from understanding how to communicate ideas effectively in a range of media to managing digital reputation and history.

"We are living in a new economy—powered by technology, fueled by information, and driven by knowledge and the influence of technology will go beyond new equipment and faster communications, as work and skills will be redefined and reorganized". The key in engaging the digital generation is for educators to apply the right technology at the right time. Using technology advances, teachers can present lessons in ways best suited to the cognitive styles of their students. For example, the use of video, audio, and text can mutually reinforce concepts and enable students to engage the same ideas in multiple ways. However, accomplishing this means that educators must view technology not as "the enemy" but as a key tool to motivate and engage students. By addressing students at this level, schools can overcome problems with "emotional truancy," where students show up for class but essentially tune out the lesson.

Employability

A set of achievements, - skills, understandings and personal attributes – that make graduates more likely to gain employment and be successful in their chosen occupations, which benefits themselves, the workforce, the community and the economy is known as employability.

Digital Age

1. The digital age, also called the information age, is defined as the time period starting in the 1970s with the introduction of the personal computer with subsequent technology introduced providing the ability to transfer information freely and quickly.
2. The time period in which we live now where Internet and email are available is an example of the digital age.

21st Century Skills

Department of Commerce reports that "workers who use a computer at work can earn 17 to22 percent more than other workers" (Economics and Statistics Administration, 2002, p. 49). These same analysts note that rapid change and increased competition require that workers use their "soft skills" (e.g., interpersonal, management, and problem-solving skills) to adapt quickly to changing technologies and organizational structures. The CEO Forum (2001) advises that "students require higher levels of education to succeed in the new knowledge-based economy".

Paths to Successful Education

Teachers are typically not digital natives; the key to success isn't to simply add technology to the classroom. Instead, the focus needs to be on enabling teachers to integrate the tools into their curricula, so they are comfortable letting their students use them. Both K-12 and higher education will evolve along four paths to help ensure that current and future generations are engaged in the classroom and have developed the proper skills to succeed in the global economy.

Customized: Educational institutions will need to offer personalized instruction to accommodate different learning styles and tailor courses and services to meet the individual needs of students, faculty, and staff.

Collaborative: The level of collaboration between students and faculty will continue to grow, and faculty will increasingly become facilitators who help co-create knowledge. Students and faculty will work in face-to-face and virtual teams worldwide to tackle complex and sophisticated projects, and bring together different perspectives and skills.

Creative: By integrating the technology that students use, admire, and aspire to, education institutions will appeal to digital natives, driving innovation and enthusiasm and setting students on a path to success.

Distributed: Students will increasingly be attending institutions virtually, making knowledge more accessible and available to a greater number of people.

Changing Behaviours and Emerging Benefits

While the pace of technological change appears to be rapid, it can take time to develop appropriate and effective responses. Technology offers flexible blended learning opportunities that work around employers' needs and can simulate real-life situations when financial, logistical or ethical reasons make these real-life experiences difficult to provide.Developing and implementing the use of appropriate technologies and processes to enable higher-education-level learning services to meet the needs of learners in the workplace, and of their employers.

Exploring Emerging Practice

1. Support openness and collaboration among colleges and universities by sharing effective practice.

2. Highlight opportunities to transform practice, uncovering some of the benefits and challenges as well as signposting information that are useful to know.
3. Stimulate debate that may help to propagate new ideas.
4. Working in partnership with students – how students are being engaged as agents of change and collaborators in their own learning.
5. Developing students' employability potential – how institutions are using technology to provide relevant and authentic learning experiences to enhance student employability and develop professional practice.
6. Preparing for the future – how colleges and universities are looking ahead and developing the skills, knowledge and cultural environment that will help to build the future.

Emerging Practice Technologies Among Students

1. Improved preparation for practical laboratory work Video cameras
2. Enhanced relevance of module learning to overall course Laptop
3. Increased student enjoyment, engagement and motivation Web server
4. Vidiscript open source software
5. Reflective practice through peer review mechanisms embedded in social media Video conversion software
6. Range of student-developed materials to support revision
7. Integration of technology across Business School, leading to higher student engagement

Emerging Practice on the Part of Teachers

8. Enhanced interactivity in lectures
9. Improved lecture attendance
10. Support for students, particularly international students, during transition period
11. Collaborative development between students and staff, and between peers
12. Development of desirable employability skills (research, business and personal) for students
13. Student-owned mobile devices
14. Enhanced student engagement and motivation
15. Increased levels of attainment
16. Student advocacy leading to improved communication between staff and students

17. Support for staff in use of social media
18. Development of inclusive pedagogies
19. Developing professional practice
20. Augmentation to real-life working
21. Support for revision with detailed formative assessment feedback
22. Collaboration between academic specialists and learning technologists
23. Developing active and engaging problem-based learning experiences
24. Enhancing access to multimedia resources
25. External collaboration with other universities
26. Internal collaboration between academic staff and learning technologists

Conclusion

"The technology and the learning are developing together, and that co-evolution of learning and technology is really important for us to understand and to develop employability skills." In higher education we have to create a better learning environment for all learners, wherever and however they study. By enhancing the overall educational experience by improving flexibility and creativity and by encouraging comprehensive and diverse personal high quality learning, teaching and research will generate employability beyond digital age.

References

1. www.jisc.ac.uk/elearningprogramme Emerging Practice in a Digital Age
2. .http://www.heacademy.ac.uk/assets/documents/employability/pedagogy for employability update 2012.pdf
3. http://www.businessdictionary.com/definition/employability-skills.html#ixzz305IECjAv

41

Cloud Computing

Introduction

Computer-based multimedia could include several forms of media-audio, text, graphics, and video or film. With computer-based training, the role of both the student and the instructor change. Students become more involved in their own learning, and instructors may no longer occupy a center-stage position in a typical classroom setting. Something similar is happening today in the world of computing. Data and programs are being swept up from desktop PCs and corporate server rooms and installed in "the compute cloud". In general, there is shift in the geography of computation. What is cloud computing exactly? As a beginning here is a definition "An emerging computer paradigm where data and services reside in massively scalable datacenters in the cloud and can be accessed from any connected devices over the internet". Like other definitions of topics like these, an understanding of the term cloud computing requires an understanding of various other terms which are closely related to this. While there is a lack of precise scientific definitions for many of these terms, general definitions can be given.

Cloud computing is an emerging paradigm in the computer industry where the computing is moved to a cloud of computers. It has become one of the buzz words of the industry. The core concept of cloud computing is, quite simply, that the vast computing resources that we need will reside somewhere out there in the cloud of computers and we'll connect to them and use them as and when needed.

Computing can be described as any activity of using and/or developing computer hardware and software. It includes everything that sits in the bottom layer, i.e. everything from raw compute power to storage capabilities. Cloud computing ties together all these entities and delivers them as a single integrated entity under its own sophisticated management. Cloud is a term used as a metaphor for the wide area networks (like internet) or any such large networked environment. It came partly from the cloud-like symbol used to represent the complexities of the networks in the schematic diagrams.

Cloud Computing

Cloud Computing is the internet-based storage for files, applications, and infrastructure. One could say cloud computing has been around for many years, but now a company may buy or rent space for their daily operations.

The cost savings in implementing a cloud system is substantial and the pricing for use of cloud computing can easily be scaled up or down as determined by necessity.

A definition for cloud computing can be given as an emerging computer paradigm where data and services reside in massively scalable data centers in the cloud and can be accessed from any connected devices over the internet. Cloud computing is a way of providing various services on virtual machines allocated on top of a large physical machine pool which resides in the cloud. Cloud computing comes into focus only when we think about what IT has always wanted – a way to increase capacity or add different capabilities to the current setting on the fly without investing in new infrastructure, training new personnel or licensing new software. Here 'on the fly' and 'without investing or training' becomes the keywords in the current situation. But cloud computing offers a better solution. We have lots of compute power and storage capabilities residing in the distributed environment of the cloud. What cloud computing does is to harness the capabilities of these resources and make available these resources as a single entity which can be changed to meet the current needs of the user. The basis of cloud computing is to create a set of virtual servers on the available vast resource pool and give it to the clients. Any web enabled device can be used to access the resources through the virtual servers.

Based on the computing needs of the client, the infrastructure allotted to the client can be scaled up or down. From a business point of view, cloud computing is a method to address the scalability and availability concerns for large scale applications which involves lesser overhead. Since the resource allocated to the client can be varied based on the needs of the client and can be done without any fuss, the overhead is very low. One of the key concepts of cloud computing is that processing of 1000 times the data need not be 1000 times harder. As and when the amount of data increases, the cloud computing services can be used to manage the load effectively and make the processing tasks easier. In the era of enterprise servers and personal computers, hardware was the commodity as the main criteria for the processing capabilities depended on the hardware configuration of the server. But with the advent of cloud computing, the commodity has changed to cycles and bytes - i.e. in cloud computing services, the users are charged based on the number of cycles of execution performed or the number of bytes transferred.

Characteristics of Cloud Computing

Multi-tenancy

With cloud computing, any application supports multi-tenancy - that is multiple tenants at the same instant of time. The system allows several customers to share the infrastructure allotted to them without any of them being aware of the sharing. This is done by virtualizing the servers on the available machine pool and then allotting the servers to multiple users.

Service-oriented

Cloud computing systems are all service oriented - i.e. the systems are such that they are created out of other discrete services. Many such Cloud Computing discrete services which are independent of each other are combined together to form this service. This allows re-use of the different services that are available and that are being created.

Virtualized

The applications in cloud computing are fully decoupled from the underlying hardware. The cloud computing environment is a fully virtualized environment.

Flexible

Another feature of the cloud computing services is that they are flexible. They can be used to serve a large variety of workload types - varying from small loads of a small consumer application to veryheavy loads of a commercial application.

Need for Cloud Computing

What could we do with 1000 times more data and CPU power? One simple question,that's all it took the interviewers to bewilder the confident job applicants at Google. This is a question of relevance because the amount of data that an application handles is increasing day by day and so is the CPU power that one can harness. There are many answers to this question. With this much CPU power, we could scale our businesses to 1000 times more users. Right now we are gathering statistics about every user using an application. With such CPU power at hand, we could monitor every single user click and every user interaction such that we can gather all the statistics about the user. We could improve the recommendation systems of users. We could model better price plan choices. With this CPU power we could simulate the case where we have say 1, 00,000 users in the system without any glitches. There are lots of other things we could do with so much CPU power and data capabilities. But what is keeping us back.

Uses of Cloud Computing

1. Rapid Service
2. Secure Service
3. Satisfying User Experience
4. Lower Costs
5. Multi-User Access
6. Development Platform
7. Infinite Storage

Speed

Use cloud computing to innovate fast. Quickly build cloud applications. Tap into pay-for-use global cloud infrastructure.

Empowerment

Give users the software they need. Free developers to focus on apps. Enable IT to become a service provider.

Economics

Save time with self-service cloud. Buy just what you need. Get to market faster. Shift CAPEX to OPEX. Increase utilisation.

Cloud Computing in the Real World

Time Machine

Times machine is a New York Times project in which one can read any issue from Volume 1, Number 1 of The New York Daily Times, on September 18, 1851 through to The New York Times of December 30, 1922. They made it such that one can choose a date in history and flip electronically through the pages, displayed with their original look and feel. Here's what they did. They scanned all their public domain articles from 1851 to 1992 into TIFF files.

Conclusion

Cloud computing is a powerful new abstraction for large scale data processing systems which is scalable, reliable and available. In cloud computing, there are large self-managed server pools available which reduces the overhead and eliminates management headache. Cloud computing services can also grow and shrink according to need. Cloud computing is particularly valuable to small and medium businesses, where effective and affordable IT tools are critical to helping them become more productive without spending lots of money on in-house resources and technical equipment. Also it is a new emerging architecture needed to expand the Internet to become the computing platform of the future.

42

Blended Learning Approach of Students

Introduction

Blended learning can be thought of as a pedagogical approach that combines the effectiveness and socialization opportunities of classroom with, the technologically advanced, active learning possibilities of the online environment. Research has shown that high level of student and instructor satisfaction can be produced the fully online environment. But both faculty and students lament the loss of face-to-face interaction. But blended learning proves to be an effective step whereby allows a faculty to begin with a course that is mostly face-to-face, and then switch it over to the online component as soon as the students' expertise in the field increases.

Blended-learning, the combination of traditional face-to-face teaching methods with authentic online learning activities has the potential to transform student learning experiences and outcome.

What is Blended Learning?

Blended Learning is a combination of face-to-face instruction and online instruction. Using the provincial Learning Management System (LMS), students and teachers in regular classrooms can access high-quality course content and use secure online tools such as the Calendar, Drop box, News, Discussion, Blogs, Journal and Surveys. Blended Learning combines the support of a classroom teacher while allowing students the opportunity to develop skills essential for success in the 21st century.

A few of the many definitions of blended learning include

1. The integration of face-to-face and online learning to help enhance the classroom experience and extend learning through the innovative use of information and communications technology. Blended strategies enhance student engagement and learning through online activities to the course curriculum, and improve effectiveness and efficiencies by reducing lecture time.
2. A course that blends online and face-to-face delivery. Substantial proportion of the content is delivered online, typically uses online discussions, and typically has some face-to-face meetings. The Sloan Consortium defines blended courses as having between 30 percent and 79 percent of their content delivered online, with the remaining portion of the course content delivered by face-to-face instruction or other non-web-based methods, such as paper textbooks.

In other words, blended learning should be approached not merely as a temporal construct, but rather as a fundamental redesign of the instructional model with the following characteristics:

1. A shift from lecture to student centered instruction in which students become active and interactive learners.
2. Increases in interaction between student-instructor, student-student, student-content, and student-outside resources;
3. Integrated formative and summative assessment mechanisms for students and instructor.

Most universities today recognize that there are particular learning needs for the students. Students entering university courses often need to develop a number of skills and capabilities to achieve success. The students come from a range of previous positions including school, the workplace and often unemployment. Students quickly need to be able to assume responsibility for their own learning, to undertake independent research and inquiry, and to communicate and argue their ideas in a succinct fashion.

Blended-Learning Approach

Blended-learning describes an approach to learning where teachers use technology, usually in the form of Web-based instruction, in concert with and as a supplement to live instruction, or perhaps utilize components of a learner-centered Web course with components that require significant instructor presence and guidance. The strength of a blended-learning approach is that it provides a means to ensure learners are supported and guided as they undertake independent learning tasks.

Use of the Web in such settings provides many affordances for the teacher and students in the form of communication channels, information sources and management tools. These aspects appear to make blended-learning particularly well suited to teacher training students, especially those in large groups where direct instructor support may be difficult to deliver Blended-learning commonly describes learning that combines traditional teaching and learning approaches with information and communication technologies. It is anticipated that blended-learning will enhance the student learning experience. A typical example of this would be blending online activities with face—to-face sessions. This can mean using the best of the best - the best use of online learning to enable classroom activities to be active and engaging learning experiences (Graham, 2006)

Blended learning consists of two features

1. It is a planned combination of online learning and Face- to- Face (F2F) instruction using a variety of learning resources.
2. It is an educational format that integrates online learning techniques including online delivery of materials through web pages, discussion boards, and e-mail with traditional teaching.
3. **Live Events:** Synchronous, teacher-led learning environment in which all learners participate at the same time. It can be in real classroom or can be virtual.
4. **Self-paced learning:** Recorded live events, Internet based or CD ROM based, which helps the learner to learn at his own pace.
5. **Collaboration:** It implies a more dynamic communication and interaction among many learners that brings about knowledge sharing.
6. **Assessment:** It is both live and online measure of learner's knowledge to determine prior knowledge as well as to measure learning transfer
7. **Performance Support:** These are reference materials that enhance learning, retention and transfer. It may be printable references, downloaded multimedia learning objects, documentations etc.

More effective pedagogy

While there is no formula that will guarantee learning for every student in every context, there is extensive, well-documented evidence about the kinds of teaching approaches that consistently have a positive impact on student learning. This evidence tells us that students learn best when teachers: create a supportive learning environment Thus blended-learning provide opportunities for:

1. More increase in active learning strategies
2. More learner-centered focus
3. A greater emphasis on peer to-peer learning.
4. A change in the way faculty allocates time for increased mentoring of individual student's innovative instruction.
5. The possibility for interaction with remote expert or peer review of projects
6. Enhance the relevance of new learning
7. Facilitate shared learning of mathematics
8. Make connections to prior learning and experience allows for more creative and interactive course assignments.

Access to knowledge

1. Assist the making of connections by enabling students to enter and explore new learning environments, overcoming barriers of distance and time.
2. Facilitate shared learning by enabling students to join or create communities of learners that extend well beyond the classroom.
3. Assist in the creation of supportive learning environments by offering resources that take account of individual, cultural, or developmental differences.
4. Enhance opportunities to learn by offering students virtual experiences and tools that save them time, allowing them to take their learning further.

Smart Classrooms

Smart Classrooms are technology enhanced classrooms that foster opportunities for teaching and learning by integrating learning technology, such as computers, specialized software, audience response technology, networking, and audio/visual capabilities. The smart classrooms demand learning initiative that assists educators to make ICT integral to learning. The strategy is about engaging the digital generation, improving individualized learning opportunities, sparking innovation in learning, enhancing teachers' digital pedagogy and getting the best from schools' ICT investment. The challenge lies in shifting from teaching and learning about ICT to teaching and learning with and through ICT. This means rather than using technology to do old things in new Ways, we want to do new things in new ways and use technology to enable and transform teaching, learning and the curriculum.

Smart Classrooms vis-a-vis

Blended Learning

Smart classroom uses following elements, mixed in varied proportions according to an organization's requirements of blended learning:

Learning through information

Material based information is the first coherent step towards starting a learning program. Web based material can now be handed to the learners, thanks to e-learning techniques, which can render the learning program easy to deliver and faster to implement. Making the information accessible all the time will give learners the liberty of scrolling through the content at their own convenience, which, in turn, will enhance understanding and enthusiasm.

Learning through interaction

The learner- instructor, learner-content, learner-learner, and Learner-infrastructure interactions become all the more important in a blended-learning environment. Web can assist all the above mentioned forms of interaction, which, together, help retain the knowledge that is acquired through information .Web simulations of real life situations allow learners to apply their knowledge practically, without the possibility of them affecting your business directly.

Learning through collaboration

Collaborative learning includes peer-to-peer discussions, conference calls, chat, team rooms and instant messaging. Technology has enhanced the concept of collaboration manifold, where learners, even though geographically remote, can communicate in real time. The collaborative environment also heightens the chances of collaboration between e-learners and subject matter experts (SMEs).

Learning through classroom interactions

Conventional, tested and, by far, one of the most effective approaches to learning, classrooms are the best places to personally connect to peers and instructors. No technology can replace the advantages of this approach, whichis exactly why no e-learning or blended-learning model will skip this element for any reason. But, as one would like to believe, blended learning has never attempted to replace classroom based learning. On the contrary, technology-based learning takes care of the basic, mechanical and mundane aspects of learning to allow classroom-based training centre around discussions on already learnt subject matter and behavioral and psychological modifications.

E-learning technology can be put to good use while learning through information, interaction and collaboration. This not only reduces cost attributed to enlarged periods of non-productive activity on the part of the employees, commuting and employing instructors, but also creates reusable content, and reiterates core messages and concepts to ingrain them in the minds of the learners. At the same time, the classroom sessions develop interpersonal skills and the ability to communicate face-to-face.

Potential constituents of a blended learning approach: The notion of blending is nothing new. Good classroom teachers have always blended their methods -reading, writing, lecture, discussion, practice and projects, to name just a few, are all part of an effective blend. As has already been discussed, blended-learning arrangements tend to combine an electronic learning component with some form of human intervention; the constituents may vary in different settings. As is clear, the medium is not limited to technology and can include: Stand-alone, Asynchronous, or Synchronous online learning / training ; Performance support tools (knowledge management tools); Traditional classroom, labs, or other 'hands-on' experiences; Reading assignments, CD-ROM or other self- paced learning; Teletraining , Telelearning, or Other media. Here is a table that categorizes the type of learning that may be used:

Video/DVD

Blended learning can include technology as common place today as using a video/DVD clip, segment, or movie. Videos used in classroom settings, regardless who produced them, can be educational, promotional, training, event, and evaluative.

Virtual Fieldtrips

Blended learning Virtual Fieldtrips can be used in any number of ways to serve a variety of educational goals. Using blended learning through the virtual field trip is a wonderful opportunity. The virtual field trip experience is an excellent model of a teaching strategy that was not possible before the advent of computers in the classroom.

Interactive Websites

Blended learning often includes the use of interactive websites. The use of interactive websites requires computer and Internet access in the learning situation. These sites provide another opportunity for teachers to use technology in their classroom, thus promoting blended learning. Interactive websites can be utilized within the class for those students who do not have Internet access and can give other students the opportunity to expand knowledge if access is available privately.

Websites for Teachers

Classroom websites help facilitate the creation of a blended-learning environment. Teachers use classroom websites to post assignments, receive homework submissions, administer tests, and post grades and classroom policies. Teachers also use classroom websites as the medium to link to blended- learning sites such as external websites, videos, software, graphics, audio feeds, and virtual field trips.

Course Management Systems

The use of a Course Management System (CMS) can assist a teacher when he or she is creating a blended learning environment in the classroom. In addition to using a classroom website to communicate and administer classroom activities (as described in the previous section), a CMS can better assess student work, share course content and help develop a community among the teachers, students, and parents. A CMS allows for the administration of blended activities into the classroom through various tools included with the software.

The success of a blend largely depends on the right mix of the elements. A good blend would provide optimum rôle of live interaction. It is essential to provide a good support and training model and should keep the cultural components in mind. A successful blend would strike the right balance between innovations and mass utility. Some of the basic factors which should be considered in identifying the blend are:

1. Course instructional goals
2. Student profile
3. Hours of learning/training

4. Teacher experience and teaching style
5. Cultural dimensions
6. Resource availability
7. Budgetary requirement for training implementation

What Kind of Learners we Require?

1. Demonstrate creativity and intellectual curiosity resulting in enjoyment, fun and resilience.
2. Exhibit a sense of self-confidence and enjoyment.
3. Are self-directed and can work independently, collaboratively and cooperatively to learn and to develop products of use with themselves and others.
4. Display innovation and entrepreneurship.
5. Continually develop communication and collaboration skills.
6. Communicate globally through e-learning spaces.
7. Are able to research effectively and have information ûuency.
8. Have developed digital literacy and understand technology operations and concepts.
9. Have developed digital proficiency to work effectively in 21st Century environments.
10. Understand digital citizenship and work on issues and challenges that are real and relevant, that make a difference to them and to others.
11. Demonstrate accountability and adaptability.
12. Have developed skills to design, create, share and publish.
13. Build critical and systems thinking enabling problem identification, formulation and solution, and decision making.
14. Use ICT purposefully to engage in real research.
15. Explore new ideas and tools in authentic contexts.

What Kind of Teachers we Require?

1. Demonstrate an ongoing commitment to professional knowledge, professional practice, professional relationships and professional values.
2. Have understanding of the transformative role of ICT for 21st Century curriculum design/interpretation, pedagogy and student learning.
3. Make conscious decisions about student learning based on an understanding of digital learners.
4. Are lifelong learners who are willing to take risks, fail and explore areas outside his or her expertise?

5. Employ a variety of methodologies, current learning theories and practices.
6. Constantly collaborate with colleagues and practicing professionals in order to consolidate understanding and to share and reflect on their learning, wonderings and discoveries.

Challenges

The challenges in a blended-learning environment can be looked in two different perspectives –learner perspective and teacher perspective. In focusing on the learner perspective, there is a need to consider the learning style and perceptual skills and abilities of students while designing blended-learning strategy. Learner's proûciency in using ICT is also important in a blended-learning environment. Therefore determining the skills and the ways students acquire and construct knowledge online is very important while designing blended-learning strategy. From the perspective of pedagogy, teaching and learning in a blended-learning environment can be highly unstable and fluctuating. One of the major challenges the teacher faces while designing a blended-learning strategy is to determine the balance between online and face-to-face instruction. There is a need of great expertise on the part of the teacher to design the strategy by considering both the educational provisions of the institute and the learner's needs in a blended-learning environment. But the issue arises in deciding the balance between online and face-to-face components. There is no unique model and the difficulty resides in identification of the balance point. Therefore it demands high attention on the part of a teacher to design learning environment with appropriate ingredients in correct proportions. It is the responsibility of authorities to provide necessary learning support in providing access to online learning so that our students become 'blended learners' with self-regulatory authentic learning experience.

Conclusion

It is inevitable that campus-based college of educational institutions will adopt blended learning approaches in a significant way. As has been demonstrated by several institutions, once there is clear policy and strong leadership, the evolution will be quick. In a matter of a few short years, college of educational institutions can be transformed in a manner consistent with their values and mitigating the fiscal and pedagogical challenges and deficiencies currently challenging the quality of the classroom experience. The academic benefit, evidence, and competitive advantages are clear; only the will and commitment remains. Blended learning can begin the necessary process of redefining college of educational institutions as being learning centered and facilitating a higher learning experience.

References

1. Allison Rossett, Felicia Dnuglis, and Rebecca V. Frazee. Strategies for Building Blended Learning, http://wwwleamingcircuits.org/2003/jul2003/rossett.htm.
2. Dutta, Subrat. (2003) “Impact of Information Communication Technology on Society.” Yojna. 47, no. 7: 24. Ibid. (2003) Yojna. 47, no. 7: 30.
3. Garrison, D.R. & Vaughan, N.D. (2008) Blended learning in higher education: Framework, principles and guidelines, John Wiley and Sons: USA.
4. Lever-Duffy, Judy, McDonald, Jean B.and Mizell, Al P. (2003). Teaching and learning with technology: Allyn and Bacon.
5. NCERT (2005) National curriculum framework 2005, New Delhi: NCERT.
6. Sonkambl, C. & Pagare, P. (2010). Use of blended learning approach in teacher education. In Z. Abasetal. (Eds.), Proceedings of Global Learn Asia Paciûc 2010 (pp. 3978-3981). AAC-E.
7. Takwale, Ram: “Challenges and opportunities of globalization for higher education in India” Alternative through e-education.
8. UNESCO (2005).ICT in schools-A handbook foteachers.Bangkok: UNESCO. 10
9. Cameron, B. (2003). The effectiveness of simulation in a hybrid and onlinenetworking course. TechTrends, 4 7(5), 18-21
10. Cottrell, D.M. & Robinson, R.A. (2003). Blended-learning in an accountingcourse. The Quarterly Review of Distance Education, 4(3), 261-269.

43

Blended Learning

Introduction

Blended learning is a student-centered approach that integrates learning experiences in online and face-to-face environments. The term 'blended learning' has gained considerable currency in recent years as a description of particular forms of teaching with technology. Teachers havebeen blendingor integratingdifferent types of learning activities and resources in classroom, laboratory, practicum, studio contexts for a very long time. Today, the term 'blended learning' has evolved to mean the integration of classroom learning with online or e-learning. Blended learning comes in many guises, although each application or method may have similar such as face-to-face delivery, flexible options, online components. In essence, there is a blending of flexible learning and teaching experiences may involve assessment, teacher/student communication, student activities, teaching activities and students resources. These articles defines blended learning, discusses its history, blended learning tools, compare various mode of learning, advantages, disadvantages and provides suggestions for creating an effective blended learning experience.

Blended Learning is an approach to learning and teaching which combines and aligns learning undertaken in face-to-face sessions with learning opportunities created online. New types of learning activities challenge our thinking as to how learning might be facilitated, creating new etiquettes of learning and teaching, and shifting the locus of control from the teacher to the learner. (Littlejohn and Pegler, 2006, p4)

History of blended learning

Technology-based training emerged as an alternative to instructor-led training in the 1960s on mainframes and mini-computers. The major advantage that blended learning offers is scale, whereas one instructor can only teach so many people. One example is PLATO (Programmed Logic for Automatic Teaching Operations), a system developed by the University of Illinois and Control Data. PLATO in particular had a long history of innovations and offered coursework from elementary to the college level. Mainframe-based training had a number of interface limitations that gave way to satellite-based live video in the 1970s. The advantage here was serving people who were not as PC-literate, the major challenge was the expense required to make this work. In the early 1980s, CD-ROMs emerged as a dominant form of providing technology-based learning as bandwidth through 56k modems weren't able to support very high quality sound and video. The limitation to CD-ROMs was tracking completion of coursework, so learning management systems emerged as a way to facilitate progress tracking. The aviation industry used this heavily to track how well one did on courses, how much time was spent, and where someone left off. AICC, Aviation Industry Computer-Based Training Committee, was formed in 1988 and companies such as Boeing used CD-ROMs to provide training for personnel. Modern blended learning is delivered online, although CD-ROMs could feasibly still be used if a learning management system meets an institution's standards. Some examples of channels through which online blending learning can be delivered include webcasting (synchronous and asynchronous) and online video (live and recorded).

The concept of blended learning has been around for a long time, but its terminology was not firmly established until around the beginning of the 21st century, in which multiple learning environments and activities are combined, has existed for quite some time. When the first Handbook of Blended Learning by Bonk and Graham was published. In this publication Graham challenged the breadth and ambiguity of the term's definition, and defined 'blended learning systems' as learning systems that "combine face-to-face instruction with computer mediated instruction." Currently, use of the term blended learning mostly involves "combining Internet and digital media with established classroom forms that require the physical co-presence of teacher and students." Long before the advent of computers and social networks, teachers created blended learning experiences using simple technologies like paper and pencil. Educators have always crafted learning experiences that incorporate a variety of activities in different environments for the purpose of reinforcing learning material. For example, consider the concept of the apprenticeship. Prior to the hands-on experience, the apprentice studied the work of the master through observation, conversation, and possibly through reading.

Contemporary definitions of blended learning take into account the role that technology can play. Technologies like CD-ROM and later the internet made it possible to create new environments for learning, new opportunities for synchronous and asynchronous collaboration, and new modes of delivery for learning materials, self-directed guides, and tutorials. More recently, blended learning figures prominently in conversations about online learning. In this context, blended learning represents a convergence of online and face-to-face experiences. Interactions across both environments are mitigated by space, time, fidelity, and personal interaction.

Word usage and context

The terms "blended," "hybrid," "technology-mediated instruction," "web-enhanced instruction," and "mixed-mode instruction" are often used interchangeably in current research literature. However, recent researchers in the United States tend to use the term "blended learning" with more regularity.

What is blended learning?

A blended learning approach to instruction combines face-to-face classroom methods with computer-based/mediated activities, resulting in an integrated learning experience for students. Blended courses combine face-to-face and online methods to varying degrees, depending on the discipline, the size of the class, student demographics, and the preferences of the instructor. There are no rules in place to prescribe what the ideal blend is.

For example, a blended approach to a traditional, face-to-face course might mean that the class meets once per week instead of the usual three-session format. Learning activities that otherwise would have taken place during classroom time such as lectures, an in-class debate, and a quiz on audio and visual material can be moved online with the help of different tools.

Note that the terms "blended" and "hybrid," tend to be used interchangeably but in current research literature, blended appears more frequently.

Why try a blended approach?

The goal of a blended approach is to leverage the best aspects of both face-to-face and online instruction for the students' benefit. The advantage of using a blended approach is that instead of using classroom time for presentation of material, for example, you can use that time to engage students by handling and clarifying their questions, to help them apply what they view/listen to in lecture, and to work with each other in face-to-face or team problem-solving. As well, online activities and assessments can usually be completed at any time of day, anywhere the student has internet access.

The Definition of Blended Learning

1. "The thoughtful integration of classroom face-to- face learning experiences with online learning experiences"
2. "Blended learning combines online with face-to-face learning. The goal of blended learning is to provide the most efficient and effective instruction experience by combining delivery modalities".
3. "Blended learning - mixed mode or hybrid - learning is the integration of face-to-face (F2F) learning with online learning activities"
4. "A solution that combines several different delivery methods, such as collaboration software, Web-based courses and knowledge management practices"
5. "Learning that mixes various event-based activities, including face-to-face classrooms, live e-learning, and self-paced instruction."
6. "Blended learning is the effective combination of different modes of delivery, models of teaching and styles of learning"
7. Blended learning is the combination of multiple approaches to pedagogy or teaching. For example:- self-paced, collaborative or inquiry-based study
8. A mix of different didactic methods and delivery formats.

Blended learning refers to any time a student learns, at least in part, at a brick and mortar facility through online delivery with student control over time, place, or pace.

"Blended learning is replacing "e-learning" as the next big thing. Blended learning programs are perhaps the highest impact, lowest cost way to drive major corporate initiatives."Alternative names

a) mixed learning
b) hybrid learning
c) blended e-learning
d) melted learning

9. Blended Learning is not so much an innovation as it is a natural by-product of the digital domain creeping into physical boundaries. As digital and social media become more and more prevalent in the life of learners, it was only a matter of time before learning became "blended" by necessity.
10. That said, there's a bit more to Blended and "Hybrid" Learning than throwing in a little digital learning.

Creating a blended learning experience

In a blended learning approach, attention is given to the overall instructional design of the learning experience. While thoughtful planning is essential, blended learning is a fluid process whereby learning needs, moments of insight, and unique pathways evolve. Ideally, the learner is offered more choice in how the learning experience unfolds. This kind of flexibility makes it easier to differentiate instruction, satisfying the needs of a diverse population of learners. Technology is used as a tool for learning and to promote a discovery-based approach to online learning and is not necessary in all blended learning scenarios.

Blended learning is a student-centered approach to creating a learning experience whereby the learner interacts with other students, with the instructor, and with content through thoughtful integration of online and face-to-face environments. A well-designed blended learning experience thoughtfully organizes content, support materials, and activities via synchronous and asynchronous learning events, all of which are delivered in a variety of modes ranging from traditional lecture to online tutorials. Communication and collaboration are necessary functions of a blended approach. Because formative assessment is embedded throughout learning events, the learner assumes responsibility for his or her learning.

In contrast to teacher-centered, rote-learning approaches, blended learning environments provide multiple ways to access content and to demonstrate mastery. As a result, they lend themselves more readily to differentiation of content and process. A blended approach also gives the learner the opportunity to be more responsible for his or her learning, which creates a learning situation that may be more meaningful on an individual level. Because the learner comes to construct knowledge through personal effort, she or he is more likely to demonstrate understanding beyond rote memorization, and to transfer what she or he has learned to new settings.

1. To personalize learning, and enhance the motivation for each student.
2. To increase the reading level.
3. To help each student master the content and skills they need.

Types of Blended Learning

a) Face-to-face Driver
b) Rotation
c) Flex
d) Online Lab
e) Self-Blend
f) Online Driver

Opportunities

1. Common Core implementation that leads to deeper learning
2. Online assessment starting in most states in 2014-15
3. Competency based systems that make it easier to manage individual progress
4. Learning environments and adaptive systems that get better as students learn
5. De-risking the shift to blended learning
6. Big data: real time dynamic information for teachers and students
7. Scaled proof points to drive policy change
8. Public engagement and elevating the debate

Blended Learning Tools

Blended learning uses the tools of the provincial Learning Management System (LMS) to teach and support learning in a face-to-face class. Through blended learning, K-12 students can access high-quality course materials, course calendars, and assignments during and outside school hours.

Students can also take part in face-to-face lessons and communicate with their teacher and classmates using a suite of secure online tools inside the password-protected LMS. These tools help students learn or review key concepts, stay organized, show what they have learned, submit assignments, track their achievement, and communicate with others. This suite of online secure tools includes:

Blog	Calendar	Checklist	Content
Discussions	Dropbox	Email	ePortfolio
Grades	Journal	Locker	News
Pager	Progress	Quizzes	Survey

Blended learning can look different in different situations. For example, when blended learning occurs in a school computer lab, students may flexibly access and complete course content online and consult with their teachers on specific projects or topics. When blended learning occurs in classrooms where technology is limited, students may learn mostly through face-to-face lessons, but use computers or other devices to complete group assignments or submit completed work to their teachers.

Comparing Blended Learning to Other Forms of Learning

Unlike e-learning classes where students are physically separate from their teacher and classmates, blended learning occurs within a face-to-face class that happens at a specific place and time. Blended learning combines the support of classroom learning with the flexibility of e-learning.

The following chart shows some examples to clarify how different types of learning and teaching might occur.

Advantages

Proponents of blended learning argue that by incorporating the "asynchronous Internet communication technology" into courses serves to "facilitate a simultaneous independent and collaborative learning experience", and this incorporation is a major contributor to student satisfaction and success in such courses. The use of information and communication technologies has been found to improve access to as well as student attitudes towards learning. By incorporating information technology into class projects, communication between lecturers and part-time students was improved, and students were able to better evaluate their understanding of course material via the use of "computer-based qualitative and quantitative assessment modules" in a study by Alexander and McKenzie (1998).

Disadvantages

Blended learning has a strong dependence on the technical resources with which the blended learning experience is delivered—these tools need to be reliable, easy to use, and up to date in order for the use of the Internet to have a meaningful impact on the learning experience. Additionally,

IT literacy can serve as a significant barrier for students attempting to get access to the course materials, making the availability of high quality technical support paramount.

It has been observed that the use of lecture recording technologies can result in students falling behind on the material-in a study performed across four different universities, it was found that only half of the students watched the lecture videos on a regular basis, and nearly 40% of students watched several weeks worth of videos in one sitting.

References

1. Garrison, R. & Kanuka, H. (2004). Blended learning: Uncovering its transformative potential in higher education. Internet and Higher Education. 7(2004). P. 95-105.
2. Levonen, J., Joutsenvirta, T. & Parikka, R. 2006. Blended Learning katsaus sulautuvaan yliopisto-opetukseen. Piirtoheitin 1/06.
3. R. Garrison & H. Kanuka, "Blended Learning: Uncovering its Transformative Potential in Higher Education," *Internet and Higher Education* 7 (2004): 95–105.
4. E. Massie, "Blended Learning: The Magic is in the Mix," in *The ASTD E-Learning Handbook*, edited by A. Rossett (New York: McGraw-Hill, 2002), 59.
5. C. Graham, "Blended Learning Systems: Definitions, Current Trends, and Future Directions," in *The Handbook of Blended Learning: Global Perspectives, Local Designs*, edited by C. Bonk & C. Graham (San Francisco, CA: John Wiley & Sons, Inc. 2006).
6. I. Allen, J. Seaman, & R. Garrett, *Blended Learning: The Extent and Promise of Blended Learning in the United States* (Needham, MA: The Sloan Consortium, 2007.)

Web Site Reference

7. http://www.teachthought.com/trends/elearning/4-benefits-of-blended-learning/
8. http://www.teachthought.com/learning/8-trends-8-opportunities-and-8-concerns-about-blended-learning/
9. http://www-07.ibm.com/services/pdf/blended_learning.pdf

44

Effectiveness of Blended Learning Programme in Teaching Biology

Introduction

The technology is an integral part in the lives of young people who are direct beneficiaries of the educational process. This was often made argument for the need to develop learning methods that use modern technology in the formative and educational. By such methods students are responsible for their own learning, on which they themselves have control and manage it according to their interests and needs. The specialists' researches reveal that the methods which combine the traditional education with the modern technologies (*blended learning*) have increased the effectiveness. Blended Learning is a strategy which integrates the teaching learning process with different learning environments like face-to-face, online, social networking etc. Its rapid growth has been facilitated by theInternet and other emerging technologies like cloud computing, social networking etc.This paper provides a view about the effectiveness of blended learning programme in teaching biology at higher secondary school students

The recent research in science education has focused on instruction that is specific science content, specific instructional strategies and how they are related to biology learning contexts and instructional outcomes.

In the present scientific and technological age, the conventional teaching methods are not sufficient to arouse interest among the students and do not meet up to the intellectual, psychological and emotional needs of the students in the new millennium. The methods of teaching biology need to be changed.

In a vast country like India, enormous work is now being done in the field of education but it is still not possible to equip each and every higher and higher secondary school with all the facilities for teaching biology in the near future. Most of the higher secondary schools, both in rural and urban area are suffering from lack of modern science laboratories. They need equally advanced gadgets to support their education. Technology enables students get a live vision of life's aspects and scientific factors. Any diagram can be explained in detail with 3d effect, it helps the student to understand the lesson clearly. Keeping in mind the investigator felt it appropriate to use blended learning for the teaching of the concepts in biology topics included in the XI standard biology syllabus (Tamil Medium).

Blended Learning

Blended learning provides platform to attract the senses of the learner for easy and happy learning. Blended learning is a programme which integrates teaching learning process with different leaning environment. Its rapid growth facilitated by the internet and other emerging technology cloud computing and social networking.

"Blended learning is the thoughtful fusion of face-to-face and online learning experiences. The basic principle is that face-to-face oral communication and online written communication are optimally integrated such that the strengths of each are blended into a unique learning experience congruent with the context and intended educational purpose."

Blended learning – an instructional practice that combines teaching methods from both face-to-face instruction and online learning, gives to educational institutions new approaches and strategies for addressing the challenges they face and for taking advantage of the exciting new learning opportunities that are now available.

Blended learning does not exclude the traditional learning methods, but adds new and modern methods as: IT tools (email, web, chat, online conferences, e-learning platforms), workshops, individual project groups, practical demonstrations, etc.

Objectives of the Study

The objectives of the study as follows

1. To find out the effectiveness of blended learning programme for the teaching of biology at higher secondary level.
2. To compare the effectiveness of blended learning programme in the teaching of biology with conventional method of teaching biology.

Hypotheses of the Study

The following null hypotheses have been formulated

1. There is no significant difference between the experimental group and control group in the achievement of biology at pre-test level.
2. There is no significant difference between the experimental group and control group in the achievement of biology at post-test level.
3. There is no significant difference between the pre-test and post-test in the achievement of biology for the experimental group.
4. There is no significant difference between the pre-test and post-test in the achievement of biology for the control group.

Sample

The sample of the study consists of 100 students studying in XI standard under State Board syllabus at perambalur district. The sample includes both boys and girls.

Tools Used

The following tools had been used for the present study: An achievement test in biology constructed and validated by the investigators Blended learning programme was developed by the investigator for the teaching of the concepts in biology topics included in the XI standard biology syllabus.

The progrmme was arranged logically based on the psychological principles of learning. Experimental design was adopted. For the experimentation pretest was conducted and sample was divided into two groups. The students of the experimental group were taught with the blended learning progrmme and the control group through the conventional method. After the treatment period the posttest was administered. The collected data were subjected to statistical analysis and the results obtained were interpreted.

Testing of Hypotheses

Hypothesis 1: There is no significant difference between the experimental group and control group in the achievement of biology at pre test level.

The't' test applied to test the significance of difference between the mean achievement test scores of the experimental group and control group of pretest level.

Table -1

Mean Achievement Test Scores of the Experimental Group Compared with that of the Control Group at Pretest level

Groups	N	Mean	S.D	't' value	Level of Significance at 0.05 level
Experimental	30	20.43	2.09	0.46	Not significant
Control	30	19.63	1.87		

The table indicates that the 't' value is not significant at 0.05 level. The students of the experimental group do not differ significantly from the students of the control group in the mean achievement test scores at pre test level.

Hypothesis 2: There is no significant difference between the experimental group and control group in the achievement of biology at posttest level

Th 't' test applied to test the significance of difference between the mean achievement test scores of the experimental group and control group of posttest level.

Table -2

Mean Achievement Test Scores of the Experimental Group Compared with that of the Control Group at Posttest level

Groups	N	Mean	S.D	't' value	Level of Significance at 0.01 level
Experimental	30	36.40	3.96	15.08	significant
Control	30	20.10	5.14		

The table indicates that the 't' value is significant at 0.01 level. Hence there is there is a significant difference between the two groups. As indicated by the mean value, it can be concluded that the students of the experimental group fared better in the achievement test than the students of the control group. This shows that learning with the help of blended learning programme will increase the achievement of the students better than learning through the conventional method.

Hypothesis 3: There is no significant difference between the pretest and posttest in the achievement of biology for the experimental group.

The 't' test applied to test the significance of difference between test scores of the pretest with that of the posttest for the experimental group.

Table -3

Mean Achievement Test Scores of Pretest Compared with that of the Posttest for the Experimental Group

Groups	N	Mean	S.D	't' value	Level of Significance at 0.01 level
Experimental	30	20.43	2.07	20.52	Significant
Control	30	37.40	3.96		

Table 3 indicates that the't' value is significant at 0.01 level. Hence, it could be concluded that there is a significant difference between the mean achievement test scores of the pretest and posttest for the experimental group. The higher mean value in the posttest shows that the students fared better in the posttest than in the pretest. This shows that the blended learning programme has helped the students to score more in the posttest.

Hypothesis 4: There is no significant difference between the pretest and posttest in the achievement of biology for the control group.

The 't' test applied to test the significance of difference between the mean achievement test scores of the pretest with that of the posttest for the control group.

Table -4

Mean Achievement Test Scores of Pretest Compared with that of the Posttest for the Control Group

Groups	N	Mean	S.D	't' value	Level of Significance at 0.05 level
Experimental	30	19.76	1.87	0.034	Not significant
Control	30	20.00	5.06		

Table 4 indicates that the 't' value is not significant at 0.05 level. Hence, it could be concluded that there is no significant difference between the mean achievement test scores of the pretest and posttest for the control group.

Findings of the Study

1. There is no significant difference between the experimental group and control group in the achievement of biology at pre-test level.
2. There is a significant difference between the experimental group and control group in the achievement of biology at post-test level. The students leaning with the help of blended learning programme fared better in biology than in students learning through the conventional method.
3. There is a significant difference between the mean achievement test scores of the pre-test and post-test for the experimental group. This shows that the blended learning programme has helped the students to score more marks in the post-test.
4. There is a significant difference between the mean achievement test scores of the pre-test and post-test for the control group. This shows that the conventional method of teaching will not help the students to score more marks in the post-test.

Conclusion

In the field of education is not possible to equip the teaching leaning in higher and higher secondary level because most of the higher secondary schools suffering from lack of modern methods of teaching, they still follow the conventional method of teaching in higher secondary level. This should be change in the modern era; they should follow the blended learning methods in their teaching learning methods because it supports the education department well in advance.

Reference

1. Barbour Michael, et al, (2012), *Online and Blended Learning: A Survey of Policy and Practice of K-12 Schools Around the World*, available at http://www.inacol.org/cms/wpcontent/uploads/2012/11/iNACOL_IntnlReport2011.pdf
2. Rogers Carl (1983), *The Interpersonal Relationship in the Facilitation of Learning*, London: Rutledge
3. The Oxford Group (2013), *Blended Learning—Current Use, Challenges and Best Practices*, report 2013, available at http://www.kineo.com/m/0/blended-learning-report-202013.pdf (accessed July 2013)

45

Blended Learning for Future Generation

Introduction

Learning is a continuous process which exists from birth to death. An individual learns various facts things, concepts, events through various medium. Blended learning combines online with face-to-face learning. The goal of blended learning is to provide the most efficient and effective instruction experience by combining delivery modalities.

Blended learning opportunities incorporate both face-to-face and online learning opportunities.

"The term blended learning is used to describe a solution that combines several different delivery methods, such as collaboration software, Web-based courses, EPSS(Electronic Performance Support System) , and knowledge management practices. Blended learning also is used to describe learning that mixes various event-based activities, including face-to-face classrooms, live e-learning and self-paced instruction"- By Purnima Valiathan.

In this paper I discussed the meaning of Blended Learning and its advantages and disadvantages. Blended Education, Hybrid learning, flipping the classroom, whatever one chooses to call it, this method of learning–which combines classroom and online education–is going places and making headlines along the way. While education experts continue to debate the efficacy of hybrid learning, its very existence has challenged them to re-evaluate not just technology's place in (and out of) the classroom, but also how to reach and teach students more effectively.

Defining hybrid or blended education is a trickier task than one might think–opinions vary wildly on the matter. In a report on the merits and potential of blended education, the Sloan Consortium defined hybrid courses as those that "integrate online with traditional face-to-face class activities in a planned, pedagogically valuable manner." Educators probably disagree on what qualifies as "pedagogically valuable," but the essence is clear: Hybrid education uses online technology to not just supplement, but transform and improve the learning process.

That does not mean a professor can simply start a chat room or upload lecture videos and say he is leading a hybrid classroom. According to Education Elements, which develops hybrid learning technologies, successful blended learning occurs when technology and teaching inform each other: material becomes dynamic when it reaches students of varying learning styles. In other words, hybrid classrooms on the Internet can reach and engage students in a truly customizable way. In this scenario, online education is a game changer, not just a supplement for status quo. But what does this theoretical model actually look like in practice?

The strategy of blending online learning with school-based instruction is often utilized to accommodate students' diverse learning styles and to enable them to work before or after school in ways that are not possible with full-time conventional classroom instruction. Online learning has the potential to improve educational productivity by accelerating the rate of learning, taking advantage of learning time outside of school hours, reducing the cost of instructional materials, and better utilizing teacher time. These strategies can be particularly useful in rural areas where blended or online learning can help teachers and students in remote areas overcome distance.

Blended learning is a formal education program in which a student learns at least in part through online delivery of content and instruction with some element of student control over time, place, path or pace. While still attending a "brick-and-mortar" school structure, face-to-face classroom methods are combined with computer-mediated activities. Proponents of blending learning cite the opportunity for data collection and customization of instruction and assessment as two major benefits of this approach. Schools with blended learning models may also choose to reallocate resources to boost student achievement outcomes.

History of the Term

The concept of blended learning has been around for a long time, but its terminology was not firmly established until around the beginning of the 21st century. One of the earliest references to the term appears in a press release in 1999, when the Interactive Learning Centers, an Atlanta-based education business, announced its change of name to EPIC learning. The article mentions that "The Company currently operates 220 on-line courses, but will begin offering its Internet courseware using the company's Blended Learning methodology." The meaning of blended learning widely diverged to encompass a wide variety of synthesis in learning methods until 2006, when the first *Handbook of Blended Learning* by Bonk and Graham was published. In this publication Graham challenged the breadth and ambiguity of the term's definition, and defined 'blended learning systems' as learning systems that "combine face-to-face instruction with computer mediated instruction." Currently, use of the term *blended learning* mostly involves "combining Internet and digital media with established classroom forms that require the physical co-presence of teacher and students."

The terms "blended," "hybrid," "technology-mediated instruction," "web-enhanced instruction," and "mixed-mode instruction" are often used interchangeably in current research literature. However, recent researchers in the United States tend to use the term "blended learning" with more regularity.

Advantages

Blended learning is a formal education program in which a student learns – at least in part– through online delivery of instruction and content, with some element of student control over time, place, path and pace. Proponents of blended learning argue that by incorporating the "asynchronous Internet communication technology" into courses serves to "facilitate a simultaneous independent and collaborative learning experience", and this incorporation is a major contributor to student satisfaction and success in such courses. The use of information and communication technologies has been found to improve access to as well as student attitudes towards learning. By incorporating information technology into class projects, communication between lecturers and part-time students was improved, and students were able to better evaluate their understanding of course material via the use of "computer-based qualitative and quantitative assessment modules" in a study by Alexander and McKenzie (1998).

Why Blended?

Time: Defined opportunities and spaces for teachers to work with small groups of students to address learning goals (individualization), enhance or extend the curriculum (rigor), or spend time analyzing student data (monitoring).

Differentiated Experiences (Rotation Model): Face-to-Face Instruction, Independent & Collaborative Practice, and Online Curricula.

Personalized Learning for Students: Adaptive and assignable, online curricula individualize instructional pathways aligned with academic goals.

Digital Literacy: Reinforcement and application of National Educational Technology Standards.

Data to Inform Practice: Small Group Learning Stations provide multiple data points to measure student growth.

How Hybrid Classrooms Are Redefining Education

In a traditional classroom, instructors use class time to lecture and disseminate support materials. Students then review these materials and complete any assignments at home, on their own time. With some luck, teachers will review those assignments in class the following day, or at least host office hours so that they can field questions and offer support. "Flipping" defies these conventions. In this method, teachers and professors use online media to deliver notes, lectures and related course materials. Students review these materials at home and at their own pace. Classroom periods are then transformed into hands-on work periods where the teacher–who will have already delivered his or her lecture digitally–is free to field questions, engage class-wide discussions or offer other means of support. According to Mary Beth Hertz of the George Lucas Educational Foundation, "flipping" reinforces student-centered learning, allowing students to master content in an individual way. But is it effective?

Disadvantages

Blended learning has a strong dependence on the technical resources with which the blended learning experience is delivered—these tools need to be reliable, easy to use, and up to date in order for the use of the Internet to have a meaningful impact on the learning experience. Additionally, IT literacy can serve as a significant barrier for students attempting to get access to the course materials, making the availability of high quality technical support paramount.

It has been observed that the use of lecture recording technologies can result in students falling behind on the material in a study performed across four different universities; it was found that only half of the students watched the lecture videos on a regular basis, and nearly 40% of students watched several weeks' worth of videos in one sitting. So we have to be very careful while implementing Blended Learning for our students.

Conclusion

"...Blended learning environments can create more and better opportunities for teacher collaboration, enable differentiated staffing and boost meaningful professional development opportunities...With sophisticated data systems, teachers have a flood of expanded and enhanced student data at their fingertips — improving efficiency and cutting down on time spent with routine tasks and record-keeping. Time saved from the thoughtful implementation of technology can be reinvested working with students, collaborating with other teachers and developing new roles...Truly understanding the potential of blended learning leads to the realization that teachers become even more important in a personalized learning environment."

Of course, no educational model is one-size-fits-all, and some hybrid classrooms are probably more effective than others. According to a scientific literature review published by the Australasian Society for Computers in Learning in Tertiary Education, a number of factors impact the success of hybrid learning. Teachers must be committed to and well trained in blended and hybrid education and its technologies, and students must have a clear understanding of what is expected of them in this new environment. As blended learning becomes more common, schools and professors will likely understand and implement it better. Yet even now, early in the game, blended education shows promise, making this an exciting time to be a student. Not all students learn the same way. This is not a particularly novel concept, but it is an important one. This is blended learning's real strength: it transforms a largely Tran's missive method of teaching–say, a professor lecturing for what feels like an eternity–into a truly interactive one. It sounds ideal on paper, but does it work? A 2010 meta-analysis published by the U.S. Department of Education suggests it does. According to the report, students exposed to both face-to-face and online education were more successful than students entirely in one camp or the other. Blended Learning is useful if we implement properly for the future generation.

Reference

1. http://www.grayharriman.com/blended_learning_articles.htm
2. http://www.grayharriman.com/blended_learning.htm
3. http://www.teachthought.com/blended-learning-2/the-definition-of-blended-learning/

46

Designing Learning Environment of Tomorrow

Introduction

For today's children, technology is the part of their world. Technology is used to live, learn, work and play. Students have more access to technology than ever before including computers, smart phones, portable media players, e-reader and so on. As children are involved in using technology, we being their teachers have to implement innovative teaching strategies in the classroom. The content produced here is designing learning environment of tomorrow by making use of sophisticated technological instruments. The purpose of this paper is to know some of the innovations done in the field of education and also to know some of the learning environment such as web based learning, active learning classroom, m-learning, network learning, game based learning etc.

Change in education is the mother of all changes' because every component of life is influenced by education. Modern world has witnessed a change in its every sphere by the way of various revolutions like green revolution, industrial revolution and today the world is the spectator of another kind of revolution, the revolution in the field of information and communication in education. It is in the need that education has to address itself to this revolution which is fast taking place and engulfing every sphere of life. The learning environment aided by learning technologies is rich in evocative images and objects which trigger active learning by allowing students to engage with what appeals to them. The learner centered environment and visual situation provided by the display of students work in this digital era is important and display space is high priority for the learning environment for today and tomorrow.

Objectives for Designing Learning Environment of Tomorrow

1. Providing stress free learning environment.
2. Providing situation as per need and choice of the learner.
3. Providing freedom of pace, place and time for learning.
4. Giving less emphasis on exam oriented learning.
5. Providing child centered and activity oriented classroom.
6. Exploring children to the new learning theories which emphasis on creative and critical thinking skills.
7. Enriching and enhancing child's mental development.
8. Providing an opportunity for the learner with more flexibility in thinking.

Web- Based Learning

As a new delivering system, web based learning is a unique hypermedia instructional program which utilizes the World Wide Web (www) resources to create meaningful learning. One of the main features of wed based learning is that it allows learners flexibility to interact with each other at anytime and anywhere.

Web 2.0

'WEB 2.0 'is commonly associated with web development and web design that facilitates interactive information sharing, on the World Wide Web. Examples of web 2.0 include web based communities, hosted services, web applications, social networking sites, video sharing sites, Wikies, blogs, mashups and folksomies. Web 2.0 site allows its users to interact with other users or to change web site contents, in contrast to non-interactive web sites where users are limited to the passive viewing of information that is provided to them. Web 2.0 web site allows users to do more than just retrieve information. They can build on the interactive facilities of web 1.0 to provide network as platform, allowing users to run software applications entirely through the browsers. Users can own the data on a web 2.0 sites and exercise control over the data.

Web Conferencing

It is used to conduct live meetings, training or presentation via the Internet. In a web conferencing, each participant sits at his or her own computer and is connected to other participants via the Internet. This can be either downloaded applications on each of the attendee's computers or a web-based application where the attendee's access the meeting by clicking on a link distributed by e-mail (meeting invitation) to enter the conference.

Video Conferencing

Video conference might be regarded as the easiest and most effective web based collaboration tool in any instructional portfolio as they provide students with direct access to content, which is crucial in other collaborative project activities. Video conference provides students with the opportunity to learn by participating in two way communication forums. Furthermore, teachers and lecturers worldwide can be brought to remote or otherwise isolated educational facilities. Students from diverse communities and backgrounds can come together to learn about one another.

Active Learning Classrooms (ALC):

Active learning classrooms are spaces that are designed to support teaching and learning in an atmosphere conducive to engage students actively in their own learning environment. Active learning classrooms are mainly meant to engage students and promote active and collaborative learning. Active learning classrooms are designed to foster interactive flexible student centered learning experience and operate using central teaching stations and students provided laptops.

Blended Learning

It is the convergence of online and face to face education. Blended learning is replacing e- learning as the next big thing. Blended learning program are perhaps the highest impact, lowest cost way to drive major corporate initiatives. Blended Learning or mixed mode of learning or hybrid learning is the integration of face to face learning with online learning activities. It will be emerged as the predominant teaching model of future. Blended learning is many things to many people, even within our relatively small online learning community. In general Blended learning combines online delivery of educational content with the best features of the classroom interaction and online instruction to personalize learning, allow thoughtful reflection and differentiate instruction from student to student.

Cloud Computing

It is the provision of dynamically scalable and often virtualized resource service over the Internet. Users need not have knowledge of expertise in or control over the technology infrastructure in the "cloud" that supports them. Cloud computing services often provide common business applications online that are accessed from a web browser, while the software and data are stored on the servers. The technical definition of cloud computing is that " cloud computing is a model for enabling convenient, on demand network access to a shared pool of configurable computing resources (eg, networks , services, storage, application, and services) that can be rapidly provisioned and realized with minimal management effort or service provider interaction". This definition states that clouds have five essential characteristics: on-demand self-service, broad network access, resource pooling, rapid elasticity and measured services.

Network Learning

Is a process of developing and maintaining connections with people with people and information, and communicating in such a way so as to support one anothers learning?Network learning can be practiced in both formal and informal settings .In formal settings the learning achieved through networked communications is formally facilitated, assessed and/ or recognized by an educational organization. In an informal setting, individuals maintain a learning network for their own interests for learning "on-the –job" , or for research purpose

Virtual Learning Environment (VLE)

It is a software system designed to support teaching and learning in an educational settings , as distinct from the Managed Learning Environment.VLE will work over the internet and provide a collection of tools such as for assessment (particularly of types that can be marked automatically, such as the multiple choice), communication uploading of content, return of students work , peer Assessments , administration of student groups , collecting and organizing student grades, questionnaires, tracking tools etc. New features of these systems include wikis, blogs, and 3D virtual learning spaces. While originally created for distance education, VLE are now most often used to supplement traditional face to face classroom activities. These systems generally run on servers, to serve the course to students Multimedia and/or web pages.

List of virtual learning environment

1. WecCT – (Now a part of black board) software applications designed to enhance teaching and learning.
2. Desire2learn- Desire2learn eLearning solutions.
3. LAMS- the Learning Activity Management System.
4. E-Front- an Open-source web based Learning management system.
5. Webtrain- Virtual live classes, enrollment, attendance, attention monitoring.
6. First class –messaging and communications solutions.

Pod Casting

Pod cast is the series of audio and video on the web that can be catalogue and automatically download. Pod casting is the method of publishing audio files to the web, which are then made available through subscription and automatically downloaded to our personal computer. One obvious use of pod casting in an educational contest is to create an archive of class lectures that students can listen to at their convenience. As pod casting is relatively new educators everywhere are still exploring the possibilities.

M-Learning

Mobile learning has different meanings for different communities. All though related E-learning and distance education, it is distinct in its focus on learning across context and learning with mobile devices. M-learning is convenient in the sense that it is accessible from virtually anywhere, which provides access to all the different learning materials available.

M-learning also brings strong portability by replacing books and notes with the small RAMs, filled with tailored learning content. Examples of M-learning are:

1. In living
2. Mobile Bristol Toolkit
3. Savannah
4. Amicitias
5. My learning Author

Game Based Learning (GBL)

It's a branch of serious games that deals with applications that have defined learning outcomes. Generally they are designed in order to balance the subject matter with the game play and the ability of the player to retain and apply said subject matter to the real world. Children are allowed to express themselves as individual while learning and engaging in social issues. The success of the game based learning strategies owes to achieve active participation and interaction being at the center of the experience, and signals that current educational methods. Experience with and affinity for games as learning tools in an increasingly universal characteristic among those entering higher education and work force.

Examples of game based learning:

1. Global challenge Award
2. The New Media Consortium
3. EDUCAUSE learning initiative.

CONCLUSION

Thus we can conclude that the use of technology or the internet increases learner motivation and engagement enhances the change in learning style. It promotes the shift to a learner centered environment. Already wide spread in the school and colleges of developed countries. The new trends in education is also seen in India, which is slowly emerging, at the same time, there is some skepticism towards using technology in education because, impact on students achievements and cost effectiveness of what are often expensive applications are unclear. What is certain is that the mere presence of computer and internet facility in the class room is not sufficient. It needs to be designed and implemented strategically in order to be effective and line up to their full potential.

REFERENCE

1. Khajaper. M (2001). The teacher education in 21st Century in India challenges ahead, Vol 39, No8, University of New Baroda, India.
2. Agarwal, A (2000) Web based learning and teaching technologies: Opportunities and challenges. Hesbay PA, Idea group publishing.
3. Pradeep Kumar T (2013) web based technology in education, First edition, APM Publication Corporation, New Delhi.
4. Patil Priyaj Murtuj,(2012) Internet in education. Edutrack Vol 11, No 5.

47

Proactive Nature of Teachers Towards use of Technology

Introduction

Education is undergoing constant changes under the effects of globalization. The effects of globalization on education bring rapid developments in technology and Communication. These developments are bringing changes in learning systems and the roles performed by teachers. Unless the teachers, perceptions of their roles match with their role expectations, then only role performance matches the expectations. This study is to find the if perceptions of teachers regarding their roles and competencies are changing with that of changing scenario and whether the teachers from SSC,CBSE,IGCSE and ICSE are trying to be proactive to develop ICT competencies that are expected of them in a globalized world.

Teacher Education system is an important vehicle to improve the quality of school education. The revitalization and strengthening of a Teacher Education is a powerful means for the up-liftment of educational standards in the country. It inculcates the skills and competencies among the teachers and makes them professionally competent to meet the demands of the society.

An educational institution performs a significant function of providing learning experiences to lead their students from the darkness of ignorance to the light of knowledge. The key personnel in the institutions who play an important role to bring about this transformation are teachers. As stated by NCTE (1998) in Quality Concerns in Secondary Teacher Education, ¯The teacher is the most important element in any educational program. It is the teacher who is mainly responsible for implementation of the educational process at any stage.

This shows that it is imperative to invest in the preparation of teachers, so that the future of a nation is secure. The importance of competent teachers to the nation's school system can in no way be overemphasized. The National Curriculum Framework 2005 places demands and expectations on the teacher, which need to be addressed by both initial and continuing teacher education. Teacher education generally includes four elements: improving the general educational background of the trainee teachers; increasing their knowledge and understanding of the subjects they are to teach; pedagogy and understanding of children and learning; and the development of practical skills and competences.

Need of the Study

1. networking of educational efforts in secondary education will be a boon, especially to developing countries.
2. pressure on the secondary education system for greater access and space for participation in Information and Communication Technology (ICT).
3. The challenge is to provide the young adults with the proper global competencies as well as appropriate environment and education management system that would foster networking among global educational institutions.
4. There is every reason to be proud of dreaming for better tomorrow and translating it into a reality.

Objectives of the Study

1. To study the reactiveness of teachers to meet the challenges of globalization in State Board secondary schools.
2. To study the reactiveness of teachers to meet the challenges of globalization in CBSE/ICSE secondary schools.
3. To study the reactiveness of teachers to meet the challenges of globalization in IGCSE/IB secondary schools.
4. To compare the reactiveness of teachers in State Board, CBSE/ ICSE and IGCSE/IB Secondary Schools located in Mumbai to cope with the challenges posed to teaching profession as a result of globalization.

Design of the Study

The comparative part of the study seeks to find out reactiveness of the teachers of the State Board, CBSE/ ICSE and IGCSE/IB Secondary Schools in using the Technology in effective teaching - learning process.

Sample of the Study

The sample of this study consists of 80 teachers (20 each) from International, National and State educational institutions in Mumbai. Stratified Random Sampling technique is used for selecting teachers from the schools.

Tools for Data Collection

Secondary School Teachers' Reactiveness Scale (an open ended questionnaire) is prepared by the researcher to assess the reactiveness of the teachers in the institutions of secondary schools.

Findings and Conclusions

The proactiveness of teachers towards purposes for which they are using computers is higher (90%) at the IGCSE board level schools as compared to SSC board (61.67%) where it is the least.

The proactive nature of teachers towards knowledge of popular websites and purposes of visiting those websites is higher (80%) at the IGCSE and CBSE boards level schools as compared to SSC board (53.33%) where it is the least.

The proactiveness of teachers towards Networking with other institutions is higher (38.33%) at the IGCSE and ICSE Boards level schools as compared to CBSE board (16.67%) where it is the least. Overall, all the boards have given less importance in technological networking with each other institutions as revealed in the percentage terms which is below 50%. The proactiveness of teachers towards using ICT to make teaching and learning effective is higher (65%) at the CBSE board level schools as compared to ICSE board (53.33%) where it is the least. The variance among the boards in percentage terms is minimum revealing that all boards are using ICT to certain extent. Combining all the 4 parameters referred above, the effective proactive-ness towards technology follows the order as under:IGCSE,ICSE,CBSEandSSC .**Suggestions**

Regarding the use of computers, websites, networking and ICT integrated class rooms, 1. SSC teachers require more practical experience and learning.

2. Teacher educators should concentrate in developing ICT skills

3. Still more student populations are in SSC boards than IGCSE boards. More attention need to be given to SSC board teachers in developing ICT skills.
4. SSC board schools need better infra structural facilities for ICT
5. Proper training and evaluation is need of the hour for SSC teachers

Conclusion

Everyone wants teachers to use technology in the classroom. But you're busy—meeting standards, preparing students for tests — and maybe you're not too fond of computers, anyway. Never fear – there are easy ways to bring your classroom up-to-date, technologically. Now, as teacher educators, this is our dream and duty to make our student-teachers to prepare for global teachers.

References

1. Aggarwal, J.C. (2001). *Teacher and Education in a Developing Society.* New Delhi: Vikas Publishing House Pvt. Ltd.
2. Aggarwal, J.C. (2008). *Education in the Emerging Indian Society.* New Delhi: Shipra Publications.
3. Agrawal, Mamta, Jain, V.K. and Chandrasekhar, K. (2004). *Factors Influencing Effectiveness of Secondary Schools of Delhi.* Independent Study (DEME) NCERT. retrieved ttp://www.ncert.nic.in/publication/journals/pdffiles/indianeducationreview/January 2011.pdf
4. Bates, Richard. (2008). *Teacher Education in a Global Context: Towards a Defensible Theory of Teacher Education.Journal of Education for Teaching, Volume 34, Issue 4, pages 277 - 293* retreived from http://hdl.handle.net/10536/DRO/DU:30017494
5. Best, J.W., and Kahn, J.V. (2005). *Research in Education.* New Delhi: Pearson education, Inc. Pearson Prentice Hall.
6. Eric, B. (2003). *Globalizationand Higher Education Research.* DOI: 10.1177/1028315303007002002, Journal of Studies in International Education, vol. 7 no. 2 **128-148** retrieved from ttp://www.beerkens.info/files/Beerkens Globalisation%20and%20HE JSIE 2003.pdf
7. Experiment-Resources.com (2008). Statistics Tutorial. Retrieved 16 Jul. 2011 from Experiment Resources: http://www.experiment-resources.com/statistics-tutorial.html
8. ICSE School Boards retrieved from http://www.cisce.org/ICSE%20SYLLABUSES%202012%20FINAL%20CRC/1.Syllabus%20Regulations.pdf

9. ICFAI Center for Management Research (2005). *Business Research Methods.* Hyderabad.
10. IGCSE school Boards retrieved fromhttp://www.cie.org.uk/
11. *Karaman, K. (2010). Globalization and Education.* Journal: Zeitschrift für die Welt der Türken, Vol: 2 Issue: 3 Pages/record No.: 131- 144 http://www.doaj.org/doaj?func=abstract&id=664796
12. Kelly, A. (2009).*Globalization and Education: A Review of Conflicting Perspectives and their Effect on Policy and Professional Practice in the UK."* #EJ827822, *Globalization*Societies and Education, v7 n1 p51-68 retrieved from http://www.tandfonline.com/doi/abs/10.1080/14767720802677333
13. Kothari. C. R. (2006). *Research Methodology, Methods & Techniques.* Delhi: New Age International Publishers.
14. Koul,L.(2007). *Methodology of Educational Research.* Delhi: Vikas Publishing House Pvt Ltd.
15. NIEPA, (2003) *Globalization and Challenges for Education.* New Delhi: Shipra Publications.
16. One-way ANOVA. (2012) Retrieved from http://www. gs. washington.edu/academics/courses/akey/.../lecture7.pdf
17. Pandey V.C (2004) *Digital Technologies and Teaching Strategies.* New Delhi: Isha Books.
18. Taylor and Francis Group (2007).*Globalization, Societies and Education.*ISSN 1476-7724, Online ISSN: 1476-7732 Published By: Routledge, Volume Number: 9
19. T-TEST. Retrieved from http://stattrek.com/hypothesis-test/difference-in-means.aspx
20. T-TEST. Retrieved from http://www.indiana.edu/~educy520/sec6342/week_10/ttest_exp.pdf
21. Von Hippel, Paul T. (2005), *Mean, Median, and Skew: Correcting a Textbook Rule :* Journal of Statistics Education 13 (2). Volume 13, Number 2 (2005), www.amstat.org/publications/jse/v13n2/vonhippel.html
22. Walia J.S (2005). *Principles and Methods of Education.* Punjab: Paul Publishers.
23. Wakefield, Peter, Pumfrey, D.(2009). *Illuminating and Improving National curriculum Development: Students' Perceptions and Suggestions. A Pilot Study in a State Secondary school*; EJ833063 Educational Review, v61 n1 p63-83